12.50EM

W9-BZG-641

T-groups: A survey of research

T-groups
A survey of research

Edited by

C. L. Cooper
Department of Psychology,
The University, Southampton

I. L. Mangham
Department of Management Studies,
The University, Leeds

WILEY–INTERSCIENCE
a division of John Wiley & Sons Ltd.
LONDON   NEW YORK   SYDNEY   TORONTO

Copyright © 1971 by John Wiley & Sons Ltd.
All Rights Reserved. No part of this publication
may be reproduced, stored in a retrieval system, or
transmitted, in any form or by any means, electronic,
mechanical, photo-copying, recording or otherwise,
without the prior written permission of the
Copyright owner.

Library of Congress catalog card number 79-146549

ISBN 0 471 17122 0

Printed in Great Britain
By Unwin Brothers Limited
The Gresham Press, Old Woking Surrey England
A member of Staples Printing Group

301.1832
C776t

Preface

What is a T-group?

The training or T-group is an approach to human relation training which, broadly speaking, provides participants with an opportunity to learn more about themselves and their impact on others and, in particular, to learn how to function more effectively in face-to-face situations. It attempts to facilitate this learning by bringing together a small group of people for the express purpose of studying their own behaviour as it occurs when they interact within a small group. There are certain features that distinguish this type of group from a conventional group discussion. Tannenbaum, Weschler and Massarik (1961) have outlined the main distinctions. First, the training is primarily 'process-oriented' rather than 'content-oriented'. That is, the primary stress is on the feeling level of communications rather than on the informational or conceptual level. This emphasis is accomplished by focusing on the here-and-now behaviour and themes in the group. Second, the training is not structured in a conventional manner. Opportunities are provided for the individuals to decide what they want to talk about, what kinds of problems they wish to deal with, and what means they want to use in reaching their goals. No one tells them what they ought to talk about. As they concern themselves with the problems caused by this lack of direction, they begin to act in characteristic ways: some people remain silent, some are aggressive, some tend consistently to initiate discussions, and some attempt to structure the proceedings. With the aid of the staff member, these approaches or developments become the focal points for discussion and analysis. The staff member, or trainer, draws attention to events and behaviour in the group by occasional interventions in the form of tentative interpretations which he considers will provide useful data for study. Third, the heart of a T-group laboratory is found in small groups, allowing a high level of participation, involvement and free communication. Intense involvement with the group is an essential feature of T-group programmes, in contrast to other methods. On the face of it this involvement should be of advantage in producing lasting changes in the attitudes and behaviour of participants. It is certainly true that most studies report few attitudinal changes for participants who show *low* involvement in training activities.

It is exceedingly difficult to arrive at an exact figure, but it is probably no

v

105722

exaggeration to claim that thousands of managers, administrators, social workers, teachers and university students in North America, Western Europe, and the Far East now have direct experience of T-group training. As this technique of human relations training grows in popularity so it tends to attract more and more suspicion and some outright hostility. One significant factor is that the detractors rarely include ex-participants; indeed some of the ex-participants become, in Massarik's (1965) phrase, the 'overly zealous proponents' of the method. As Greening (1964) has pointed out, it is inevitable and appropriate that people should have emotions and values about this kind of training, but these feelings—for or against—are not in themselves an adequate basis for an evaluation of the method. Whilst not denying the importance of the long-overdue consideration of the ethical aspects (Lakin, 1969) of this type of training, this book proceeds from the position that human relations laboratory training exists, that managers volunteer or are sent on such courses, and that the experience has measurable consequences. It is this aspect, and not the propriety of T-groups, that we wish to review and evaluate.

C. L. COOPER

I. L. MANGHAM

References

Greening, T. C. (1964) 'Sensitivity training: cult or contribution.' *Personnel*, **41** (3), 18–25.

Lakin, M. (1969) 'Some ethical issues in sensitivity training.' *American Psychologist*, **24**, 923–928.

Massarik, F. (1965) 'Some first (and second) thoughts on the evaluation of sensitivity training: A sensitivity training impact model.' Washington, D.C.: National Training Laboratory.

Tannenbaum, R., I. R. Weschler and R. Massarik (1961) *Leadership and Organization*. New York: McGraw-Hill.

Acknowledgements

The value of this book was greatly enhanced by the advice and comments of Dorothy Stock Whitaker, Peter B. Smith, Fred Massarik, Stephen Fink, Vernon L. Allen and Galfrid Congreve.

We would also like to thank our indexer, Diana Marshallsay, and our secretary and typist, Margaret Freeman.

Acknowledgements are also due to the following authors and publishers for permission to reprint articles in this book:

Culbert, S. A. (1968) 'Trainer Self-Disclosure and Member Growth in Two T-groups'. *Journal of Applied Behavioral Science*, **4**, 47–73.

Friedlander, F. (1967) 'The Impact of Organisational Training Laboratories upon the Effectiveness and Interaction of Ongoing Work Groups'. *Personnel Psychology*, **20**, 289–309.

Friedlander, F. 'The Primary of Trust as a Facilitator of Further Group Accomplishment'. To appear in the *Journal of Applied Behavioral Science*.

Gassner, S., J. Gold and A. M. Snadowsky (1964) 'Changes in the Phenomenal Field as a Result of Human Relations Training'. *Journal of Psychology*, **58**, 33–41.

Harrison, R. and B. Lubin (1965) 'Personal Style, Group Composition and Learning'. *Journal of Applied Behavioral Science*, **1**, 286–301.

Lubin, B. and M. Zuckerman (1967) 'Affective and Perceptual Cognitive Patterns in Sensitivity Training Groups'. *Psychological Reports*, **21**, 365–376.

Lubin, B. and M. Zuckerman (1969) 'Level of Emotional Arousal in Laboratory Training'. *Journal of Applied Behavioral Science*, **5**, 483–490.

Mann, R. D. (1968) 'The Development of the Member-Trainer Relationship in Self-analytic Groups'. *Human Relations*, **19**, 84–117.

Rubin, I. (1967) 'The Reduction of Prejudice through Laboratory Training'. *Journal of Applied Behavioral Science*, **3**, 29–50.

Smith, P. B. (1964) 'Attitude Changes Associated with Training in Human Relations'. *British Journal of Social and Clinical Psychology*, **3**, 104–113.

Steele, F. I. (1968) 'Personality and the "Laboratory Style"'. *Journal of Applied Behavioral Science*, **4**, 25–46.

Valiquet, M. I. (1968) 'Individual Change in a Management Development Programme'. *Journal of Applied Behavioral Science*, **4**, 313–325.

The authors would also like to extend their appreciation to the editors and publishers of the *Journal of Management Studies* and the *Training and Development Journal* for providing them with permission to reprint articles previously published in their journals.

Contents

Introduction

The problems of research

Questions asked about the consequences of T-group training have been numerous and few have been answered clearly and unequivocally. They range from the philosophical and ethical—is it right to interfere with people's psyches (essentially incapable of an empiric response)—to the pragmatic but highly important, is training transferable. There are also the questions about the dynamics of the process itself. How does the group develop? What relationships are critical to this development? How important are factors such as trainer behaviour, length of training, composition of the group, trust, feedback?

The questions, other than the ethical ones, can be placed in two categories (Lakin, 1969); those concerned with basic or pure research and those concerned with applied research. This distinction, we submit, applies not so much to the *manner* of the research as to its *purpose* (Suchman, 1967). There can be little doubt as the following chapters will testify, that the more one can satisfy the rules of scientific method in designing and carrying out a piece of applied or evaluative research, the more confidence that can be placed on the objectivity of the findings. The manner, therefore, is, hopefully, similar but the desired outcomes are often different. The primary objective of basic research, in answering a question such as 'what is the nature of sub-group formation in sensitivity training groups', is the discovery of knowledge, the proof or disproof of a hypothesis. It is essentially hypothesis-oriented, no action *need* follow. Therefore, the major criterion of the 'success' of research into questions at the basic end of the research continuum is, as Campbell and Dunnette (1968) suggest, whether or not the findings are *scientifically* valid.

Where they are on less sure ground is when they argue that the research into questions at the applied end of the continuum should reach the disarmingly simple standards 'necessary for scientifically evaluating training'. The primary objective of research into applied questions—does the training transfer, what are the outcomes—is to determine the effectiveness of certain procedures. Here the 'success' of the research is judged by its usefulness to the trainer in improving his techniques or to the manager in implementing his organizational development programme. No doubt in these circumstances scientific criteria will still determine the degree of confidence one

may place in the findings of a piece of research, but administrative considerations—will the research affect the training programme, can we
arrange control groups, do we have the time and facilities for pre and post-
measures—will play a very large role in the way the study is conducted.

Obviously, the distinction is not one of black and white. Much research
is a mixture of basic and applied types but it is a distinction which can be
useful in looking at research in T-group training since it does help to
illuminate some of the difficulties encountered by researchers.

Basic research, for example, in order to satisfy scientific procedures may
make excessive demands on participants and trainers and, in so far as it
makes these demands, can be detrimental to the overall impact of the
training. Occasionally basic researchers adopt a manipulative, exploitative
approach which runs counter to the philosophy of T-group training.
Frequently the design of the basic research requires that information be
withheld from the training staff and the participants to prevent 'contamination of the results'. This approach is unlikely to receive much support or
encouragement. Basic research also can be seen as adopting a neutral, high-
distance stance *vis-à-vis* the 'subject' and this too runs counter to the values
intrinsic to T-group training.

Ideally, as we have mentioned earlier, the manner of research into
T-groups should meet the conditions necessary for the establishment of
scientific confidence. Depending upon the specific nature of the investigation this would mean: (1) measures taken before, during and after the
training; (2) measures and observations to include not only attitudes and
perceptions but also *behaviour* of subjects; (3) matching of experimental
with control groups and (4) control of the interactional effects of measures
and behaviour (Campbell and Dunnette, 1968).

The ideal flow chart for a piece of research into T-groups would be
similar to that appropriate for any experimental design. Since at this stage
the problems of basic and applied research are similar we can illustrate by
reference to the latter alone. The flow chart for evaluating a T-group
training programme would look as below.*

Such a flow chart would illustrate optimum principles and sequences to
be followed in conducting a valid experimental design to evaluate a training programme.

In T-groups the ideal has rarely been achieved. Virtually each and every
step outlined in the flow diagram brings problems. Let us walk a piece of
research through in order to understand the problems better.

---

* Adapted with permission from Greenberg, B. G. and B. F. Mattison (1965) The
Ways and Wherefores of Programme Evaluation, *Canadian Journal of Public Health*
46, p. 298.

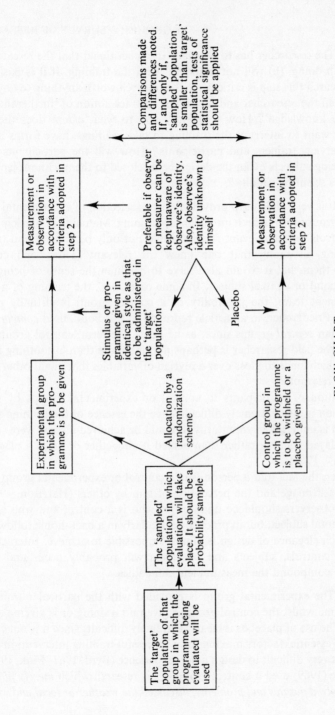

FLOW CHART

The 'target' population of that group in which the programme being evaluated will be used

The 'sampled' population in which evaluation will take place. It should be a probability sample

Allocation by a randomization scheme

Experimental group in which the programme is to be given

Control group in which the programme is to be withheld or a placebo given

Stimulus or programme given in identical style as that to be administered in the 'target' population

Placebo

Preferable if observer or measurer can be kept unaware of observee's identity. Also, observee's identity unknown to himself

Measurement or observation in accordance with criteria adopted in step 2

Measurement or observation in accordance with criteria adopted in step 2

Comparisons made and differences noted. If, and only if, 'sampled' population is smaller than 'target' population, tests of statistical significance should be applied

Step 1: The researcher has to persuade the practitioner that the research is (a) worth doing, (b) will not 'interfere' with the training. If it is basic or pure research this step is critical—is the research worth anything to anyone other than the researcher and the rather abstract notion of 'furtherance of scientific knowledge'? How frequently and to what extent does the researcher want to interrupt the training to take readings, have forms filled out, interview trainers and participants? How will the participants feel about being subjects? Can the design be disclosed to them without jeopardizing its scientific validity?

Step 2: It is very difficult to provide rigorous selection of experimental and control groups for research into T-group training. Matching of participants and controls on the relevant factors would not only be difficult and time-consuming, assuming that one knew the relevant factors and could measure them, but it would also serve to heighten the sense of being an experimental or control subject. In some cases, e.g., the training of a top management team, the possibility of a control group is virtually non-existent. Friedlander, in an article reprinted in this book, used *comparison* rather than *control* groups since, as he notes, the term 'control group' as used by the field researcher is perhaps nothing more than 'a soothing misnomer which tends to gloss over a myriad of variables that might otherwise be quite relevant'.

Allocation of participants to control or experimental groups by randomization is also extremely difficult since the essence of the training may be that it is undertaken voluntarily. It could be achieved if some were to be given delayed training rather than denied it altogether or given a placebo (Massarik, 1965).

Further, the fact that a person is in a control or experimental group can bias his self-image and the perception of him by others (Harrison, 1967). Ideally, observers should be unaware of who is a control and who is an experimental subject, but in practice particularly in a back-home follow-up study such elegance of design is almost impossible to achieve. Interaction between controls, subjects and observers will probably occur and will certainly compound the measurement difficulties.

Step 3: The experimental group is provided with the particular training programme whilst the control group is given no training or is given a substitute. The use of placebos is clearly extremely difficult; since it is not clear what the essential factors making for a successful training intervention are. Thus it is very difficult to design a non-experience (Byrd, 1967; Fink, 1969). Dunnette (1969) used a control group in his research which *merely played games, solved puzzles and problems, discussed the weather or local and world affairs, and 'diligently' avoided any discussion related to interpersonal factors.* In terms of basic research no doubt such a design was practicable, in terms of applied or evaluative research the payoff may not be worth the costs of enforced estrangement over a period of days.

Step 4: The measurement or observation stages also give rise to problems. If participants are asked to respond to questions about their behaviour in groups, they may be alerted to work towards the 'correct answers' and to complete the later measures not on the basis of actual changes but on the basis of what they perceive to be desirable changes. To combat this the researcher seeks to reduce response set, to phase out normative questions, and, possibly, to be obscure about his intentions. Both researcher and participant can end up playing mutually inauthentic roles and, in so far as this happens, the 'scientific' results are sceptical. Research in other fields (i.e. experimental psychology), whereby the subjects seek to guess and then to satisfy the intuitions of the researcher, are not uncommon.

The way around such a problem is to be authentic in the researcher–subject relationship and to explain intentions and research design. Such directness, of course, raises the spectre of 'contamination of results' and one is back to square one: what is the purpose of the research and for whom is it intended? If it is to further scientific knowledge and essentially for the consumption of fellow-researchers, then our measures must be stringent and rigorous and must not influence the training outcomes. If it is to help design better programmes and is for general consumption then we might even design the instruments so that they can influence the training even whilst we are evaluating it. In fact, this may be the only course open to researchers in T-groups since there is a potential conflict in using measures that can be perceived as mechanistic in a situation which is designed to provide an organic and spontaneous experience.

Measures taken well after the experience create further problems. In following-up transfer of training, for example, we cannot realistically link training and outcomes in a simple causal chain. Administrative changes, promotion, salary overhead, new responsibilities, delegation, may have brought about much greater changes even on such factors as 'use of conflict', 'relational facility', 'listening' than has T-group training (Mangham and Cooper, 1969).

Purpose and organization of the book

The research presented in the following chapters is both basic and applied. Wherever possible we have sought to include work which has adopted a scientific manner even where it has not been primarily undertaken for a scientific purpose. Much of the work presented falls into the grey area between basic and applied research; we hope, however, that it will not be summarily dismissed as unsound and unscientific. We had two purposes in mind in writing this book; (1) to provide the practitioner with a compendium of the empirical literature into the effects and dynamics of T-groups in order that he may be in possession of information necessary in making practical decisions associated with organizing and the conduct of T-group training; and (2) to provide the researcher with an up-to-date account of T-group research, which we hope will clarify the present state of such research and enable him to decide on what should constitute the research focus in the future. This latter objective stems from the fact that there are so many instruments, criteria, and approaches used in T-group research (of all kinds) that it appears that there must be a lack of agreement about what constitutes the research focus.

In an effort to meet these objectives the book has been organized in the following manner. First, in terms of format, each chapter contains a brief review of all the empirical literature in a particular area and is then followed by one or two research articles printed in their entirety. The articles have been selected, wherever possible, on the basis of the following criteria: the use of adequate control groups; when assessing change, measures taken before and after training; minimum variability in the training experience between groups; adequate sample size—all in all, research judged by the authors and fellow-colleagues to be a major contribution to the development of a particular area of T-group research. By including the research article in full, we hope to provide the researcher with the latest and most methodologically sound models of research design in each of the mainline areas of T-group research as well as providing the practitioner a 'look-in' at the kind of methodology employed in these areas.

Second, in terms of chronology, we start by reviewing the literature, in Chapters 1 to 3, which evaluate the effectiveness of the T-group. For if, as Bunker (1965) has pointed out, lasting and effective attitude and behaviour change cannot be demonstrated, the remaining issues such as the impact of the trainer or the effect of different group compositions on learning, would be superfluous. Then, in Chapters 4 to 6, we attempt to review the studies concerned with the *process* or dynamics of the group, concentrating on the trainer behaviour, group composition, and intra-group dynamics (i.e. trust, feedback, etc.). In Chapter 7, we attempt to follow the fate of the group by reviewing the studies concerned with assessing the course of development of the T-group.

References

Bunker, D. R. (1965) 'Individual applications of laboratory training.' *Journal of Applied Behavioral Science*, **1**, 131–148.

Byrd, R. E. (1967) 'Training in a non-group.' *Journal of Humanistic Psychology*, **7**, 18–27.

Dunnette, M. D. (1969) 'People feeling: joy, more joy, and the "slough of despond".' *Journal of Applied Behavioral Science*, **5**, 25–44.

Campbell, J. P. and M. D. Dunnette (1968) 'Effectiveness of T-group experiences in managerial training and development.' *Psychological Bulletin*, **70**, 73–104.

Fink, S. (1969) 'The non-design of a laboratory.' *Human Relations Training News*, 13.

Harrison, R. (1967) 'Problems in the design and interpretation of research on human relations training.' In *Explorations in Human Relations Training and Research*. National Training Laboratories, Number 1.

Lakin, M. (1969) 'Some ethical issues in sensitivity training.' *American Psychologist*, **24**, 923–928.

Mangham, I. L. and C. L. Cooper (1969) 'The impact of T-groups on managerial behaviour.' *Journal of Management Studies*, **6**, 53–72.

Massarik, F. (1965) 'Some first (and second) thoughts on the evaluation of sensitivity training: A sensitivity training impact model.' Washington, D.C.: National Training Laboratory.

Stock, D. (1964) 'A survey of research on T-groups.' In L. P., Bradford, J. R. Gibb, and K. D. Benne, (Eds), *T-Group Theory and Laboratory Method*. New York: John Wiley.

Suchman, E. A. (1967) *Evaluative Research Principles and Practice in Public Service and Social Action Programmes*. Russell Sage Foundation.

CHAPTER 1

The Effectiveness of T-groups in Producing On-the-Job Change*

The crucial problem in assessing the after-effects of T-group training is in the selection of the measures of change. The kinds of behavioural change that the method is designed to produce—increased job effectiveness, inter-personal competence—are not simple, unidimensional changes, and there are no easy criteria for their measurement. The investigator is usually forced to rely on evaluations made by observers—the trainee himself, his work associates or someone brought in specifically for the purpose. Since each of the categories of observers is open to bias, many of the better studies have used procedures for checking the amount of agreement between different observers (Smith, 1969).

The earliest follow-up study was conducted by Miles (1965) and involved 34 American elementary school principals who had participated in a two-week T-group laboratory in 1958. He used two control groups of untrained principals for comparison, one randomly chosen and the other nominated by the trained principals. All were asked to describe, via an open-ended change-description questionnaire, the ways in which they had changed their job-centered behaviour over an eight to ten month period following the T-group. These self-reports were compared with similar descriptions completed by 6 to 8 of their work associates. 73 per cent of the T-group trained participants, in comparison to 29 and 17 per cent of the nominated and random control groups respectively, were reported to have changed ($p < 0.01$). Most of the changes reported referred to increases in sensitivity to others, egalitarian attitudes, skills of communication and leadership, and group task and maintenance skills. Miles' data show not only a statistically significant difference in change between the trained and the control groups,

---

* A condensed and revised version of a paper which was published by the authors in the *Journal of Management Studies*, 6, 1969, 53–72.

which might be expected, but also a consistency in the kind and direction of change reported by work associates of the trained group.

In addition to the open-ended instrument which revealed the changes enumerated above, Miles employed two other measures; the Ohio State Leader Description Questionnaire (Stogdill and Coons, 1957) and the Group Participation Scale (Pepinsky, Siegal and Van Alta, 1952). In the case of these measures no significant behavioural changes which could be attributed to the laboratory experience were found. Miles notes in retrospect that the O.S.L.D. questionnaire in particular seems unsuitable for use as a change-measuring instrument, since each participant's score is derived by summating a number of his associates scores thus potentially distorting the total score through averaging effects. Nonetheless, the O.S.L.D. questionnaire has been demonstrated to be useful in measuring change in non T-group training situations (Fleishman, Harris and Burtt, 1955).

Miles also considered the organizational factors that could influence on-the-job changes. He collected organizational measures in the following areas:

(1) Security—as measured by length of tenure in present job.

(2) Power—as measured by the number of teachers in the participant's school.

(3) Autonomy—as measured by the length of time between required reports to immediate superiors.

(4) Perceived Adequacy of the Organization's Functioning—as measured by a Likert-type rating scale.

The results of these measures indicate that the majority of high changers during training who have high or moderate power and security at work also derive the most lasting benefit from the experience. Those who are seen to change little during the training and also are seen to have little power and little security derive less benefit on their return to work. The middle group— high short-run changers with low organizational power and security and low short-run changers with high power and security—show about a 50 per cent chance of net change on the job.

To further test the generality of Miles' findings, Bunker (1965) studied a sample of participants from six different training laboratories conducted by the National Training Laboratories during 1960 and 1961. His basic methodology followed Miles in that a matched-pair control group was obtained by participant nomination and open-ended behaviour-change descriptions were obtained from 6 to 8 coworkers and 'self' for each subject. Bunker used a total of 346 subjects, trained and controls. In addition, he developed and utilized an objective coding system, which was designed 'to increase scoring reliability in assessing the descriptive statements returned by the various raters and which also sought to provide an assessment of the components in each subject's total change score'.

Bunker found that 66·7 per cent of the T-group trained participants as compared with 33·3 per cent of the matched-pair control group were reported by their work associates to have changed. As with the Miles' study, non-trained subjects were also perceived to have changed, in Bunker's case one-third of them were so reported. This is possibly attributable (1) to real change occasioned by events other than T-groups, which have no monopoly of the change market, or (2) to the fact that when respondents are asked to accommodate a researcher by providing change descriptions they hate to disappoint him and so tend to look for something to put down. As Bunker notes, vague and global descriptions occur with about equal frequency for both experimental and control describers and such 'please-the-researcher' responses are likely to be an important component of the base rate of change. Nonetheless, the agreements in the detailed descriptions of behaviour changes for the experimental subjects are significantly higher than for the control subjects and make it more credible that training effects are in fact being measured. The changes which were reported more often for the experimental subjects as compared with the matched controls were:

Receiving Communications: more effort to understand, attentive listening.

Relational Facility: cooperative, easier to deal with.

Awareness of Human Behaviour: more analytic of other's actions, clearer perception of people.

Sensitivity to Group Behaviour: more conscious of feelings of others, more sensitive to the reactions of others.

Sensitivity to Other's Feelings: sensitivity to the needs and feelings of others.

Acceptance of Other People: more tolerant, considerate, patient.

Tolerant of New Information: willing to accept suggestions, less dogmatic.

In addition, he found that 74 per cent of those in the upper-third of the distribution of total change scores were in the upper-third of the distribution of laboratory learning scores. Bunker concludes from this that back-home application of laboratory learning appears to be much less probable for those who do not become actively involved in the training process.

The only British study (Moscow, 1969) to use the verified change procedure, has shown that T-group participants drawn from management show changes very similar in type and frequency to those reported by Bunker.

Schutz and Allen (1966) report the results of a study of 71 participants in the 1959 Western Training Laboratory in Human Relations. The participants completed the FIRO-B questionnaire before and after the two-week laboratory and six months later. This questionnaire is composed of six Guttman scales of nine items each, which purports to measure an individual's 'expressed' behaviour and behaviour 'wanted from others' in the interpersonal areas of inclusion, control and affection. These participants also completed a series of open-ended questions asking for their perception of both positive and negative effects of the laboratory. FIRO-B was also given to a group of 30 college students at approximately equal intervals to serve as a control group for the effects of passage of time and the normal test re-test fluctuations. Schutz and Allen's hypothesis that the laboratory experience would change people selectively, depending upon their initial personality was supported. For example, they claimed that the overly dominant would become less dominant; the overly submissive would become more assertive; the overly affectionate tend to become more discriminating; and the reserved become more friendly. They note that if this ideal were to be achieved it would mean, quantitatively, that before and after scores would differ in an *unsystematic* fashion. Therefore, correlations between before and after scores for the laboratory participants and between after and follow-up scores should be significantly lower than corresponding correlations for control group subjects. This turned out to be the case, the overall correlations between administrations for all scales combined were much lower for the experimental group than for the control.

The qualitative material (gathered by the open-ended questionnaire), was subjected to an extensive content analysis using a technique of dichotomous decisions, developed by Schutz (1952). Overall, 83 per cent of all responses indicated favourable effects of the laboratory experience; 4 per cent indicated an unfavourable change and 13 per cent indicated no change at all. The primary effects are reported by the participants as follows (1) increased intellectual understanding of interpersonal, individual and group behaviour; and (2) increased personal effectiveness and competence as a person. A great many of the respondents felt that their insight and awareness about people had increased and many found specific applications to their back-home jobs. Participants also reported a decrease in personal feelings of tension, an increase in flexibility, honesty, confidence and acceptance in their relations with other people. Some reported no change and still others reported worsening of relations with others. However, the latter, in almost every case reported, felt the overall effect was positive even though the initial results were not rewarding.

Schutz and Allen note that the effects of the laboratory took time—some two to four months—to be evidenced. They also note that the majority of positive effects remain constant or increased with time though one-fifth of the effects faded. Participants attributed the changes primarily to the T-group itself. Virtually not one mentioned activities which they considered peripheral to the T-group, such as films and seminars of on-the-job application.

It is to be noted that this study is based entirely on self-report methods and that the control group which only numbered 30 was in no sense a matched-pair group. Participants were obviously older and differed occupationally from the control subjects and the initial FIRO-B scores differed between the groups, which may indicate the inappropriateness of a student control group. That the participants in the WTL laboratory apparently did not consider the seminars of on-the-job applications to be important is a strange finding and one which is not supported by the work of Bunker and Knowles (1967) who have made a comparison of behavioural changes resulting from laboratories of different lengths and containing different emphases.

They report a comparative study of enduring behaviour changes following human relations training laboratories of three weeks and two weeks duration. A behaviour change description questionnaire, similar to that described in the previous paragraph was used to elicit descriptions of a subject's post-laboratory behaviour changes as seen by the subject himself and seven of his coworkers. (This follows on the work of Lippitt (1949).) A matched control sample was obtained and assessed in the same manner.

Two inter-related measures of change were derived from the questionnaires: the 'total change score' composed of the total number of different changes mentioned by a subject and his coworkers; and the 'verified change score' composed of those behaviour changes which are mentioned by two or more persons in a set of descriptions. A set of seventeen inductively derived content categories were also used to make a qualitative analysis of the changes. The results show that while both laboratory trained samples differed from the control sample on both measures, they also differed significantly from each other. Both the perceived change score and the verified change score reveal more changes made by the three-week sample. The content analysis suggests that the three-week laboratory participants made more overt behavioural changes as opposed to the more passive attitudinal changes made by the two-week sample. Bunker and Knowles note however, that duration of training was not the only independent variable involved. From an analysis of the training activities they note that the three-week laboratory spent some twelve hours of programme time dealing with the application of training to the on-the-job situation, often with direct attention to an individual's specific problems whilst the two-week laboratory entirely excluded this activity. Therefore, the two-week programme was qualitatively different including a greatly reduced emphasis on the application of laboratory learnings to the participants ongoing organizational situations. The specific programme activities, therefore, concerned with the transfer of training appear to have fulfilled a particularly important training function, since the three-week trained participants not only showed more changes but also more active changes. The data presented in this study suggests that participation in specific back-home planning activities may help the trainees to cope with the organizational requisites for behaviour consistency. Bunker and Knowles conclude that if learning is to be transferred and integrated into the participants organizational relationships, a programme activity separate from the T-group and aimed directly at facilitating the application of learning to the on-the-job situation should be included in the overall design of the laboratory.

Valiquet (1968) randomly selected some sixty participants from T-group type programmes run within a company. Final results were available for 34 participants and 15 matched-pair control group subjects, each subject, control and experimental, nominating some five observers. Using Bunker's categories Valiquet discovered statistically significant differences between experimentals and controls on the total number of changes, both those reported by more than two independent observers and those reported by the subjects themselves. Furthermore Valiquet's study adds to Bunker's in that 'risk-taking' and 'function flexibility'—the ability to be an effective group member and to accept change—were shown to be higher for ex T-group participants. Valiquet concludes that these differences occurred because the programme reaped the rewards of in-company training, higher risk but greater pay-off in terms of on-the-job application.

The studies of Miles, Bunker and Schutz provides substantive evidence that changes do take place in perceived and rated behaviour on the job as a result of sensitivity training, but they provide no evidence of the difference between this kind of training and other training programmes. Boyd and Ellis (1962) have made an important contribution in this area by comparing the effects of T-group training with the effects of a more conventional programme of human relations training built around case discussion and lectures. Both forms of training lasted for two weeks and were part of an in-company training programme for a Canadian Utility company. There were 42 subjects, in three different groups, participating in the T-group training programme; 10 subjects in the lecture/case discussion programme (matched in terms of age, length of service, education and kind of position as nearly as possible to the participants in the T-group programme), and

12 untrained matched-control group subjects. The evaluation was made six weeks and six months after the completion of the courses and was assessed by interviews with the subject's supervisor, 2 peers and 2 subordinates. Observed behavioural changes were obtained for each participant attending either training programme and also for the non-trained matched-control group, assessed in terms of the number of observers reporting change in subjects.

The observers of the non-trained managers reported least positive change —some 36 per cent; observers of the participants in the lecture/case discussion programme were in the middle—some 52 per cent observed change; and 70 per cent of observers of the T-group trained personnel reported a change. The difference between the various groups is statistically significant; differences in the number of observed positive changes on the part of the laboratory trained group, as compared with the non-trained group and the lecture/case group, were significant beyond the 5 per cent level. It is also notable that the T-group participants were observed to have made *undesirable* changes more often than members of either the non-trained group or the lecture/case discussion group.

In analysing what the participants said they had learned from each programme, Boyd and Ellis report: 'Learning about group behaviour was distinctive of the Laboratories. This included such things as the loss of contributions to the group through failure to listen, the effect of pressure in creating resistance, and how unstated purposes often impede group work. Learning about other people occurred in both groups . . . . However, the laboratory resulted in more direct learning by experience as against conventional training which tends to a more intellectual learning about a subject.' It is noteworthy that not only do observers report more positive changes for the T-group subjects but also a greater variety of change. Boyd and Ellis summarize this as follows: 'One of the most frequently reported changes in behaviour for the laboratory group was an increase in listening which accounts for about 12 per cent of the reports. By listening is meant paying more attention to what other people are saying, being easier to communicate views to and so on. Equally frequent is better understanding and better contribution in group situations such as meetings. Third, but still accounting for 10 per cent of the comments was an increase in tolerance and flexibility. To a lesser extent the laboratory participants were said to have more self-confidence and to express themselves more effectively.'

Chris Argyris (1965) also reports an evaluation of the relative effectiveness of lecture *versus* laboratory education in the subject areas of interpersonal relationships and group dynamics. Using a very complicated design and applying a set of categories previously discussed, he concludes that the processes generated in the lecture approach are very similar to those which create difficulties in back-home groups. The lecture groups did not increase in interpersonal competence whereas the experimental groups in nearly every case showed significant overall changes in the direction of increasing interpersonal competence. He concludes that a relatively 'poor' laboratory produced more behavioural change than the lecture approach.

On the negative side

Unfortunately, the critics of the T-group approach do not appear to base their criticisms on very thorough research (McNair, 1957). Nonetheless, there are one or two studies other than the impressionistic which document the less effective groups. Harrison (1962), conducting an evaluation of a programme instigated by Argyris, found that participants in a T-group activity showed significant changes in concept usage when describing other participants. However, when describing associates who had not participated in the training the findings of change were equivocal. What is more these participants reported great difficulty and some frustration in responding to others who did not or who had not participated in the training with them. In effect, Harrison's findings reveal that few positive effects of T-group training were carried beyond the training situation itself except in situations where ex-participants interacted with other ex-participants.

Harrison (1966) followed up these findings by a further study investigating conceptual change which used a larger number of subjects, a longer period of training, and a design which measured change at more than one point in the post-training period. Harrison's major point was that participants in training would become more oriented to interpersonal process. They were expected to change in their description of others towards the use of more concepts dealing with feelings, attitudes, emotions and perceptions. His second hypothesis was that changes in concept usage would be related to ratings of participants' behaviour in the laboratory. The data support the hypotheses in most respects. There is a significant change in concept usage following the training experience, and this change appears to be progressive shortly after the experience, reaching significant proportions when measured three or four months later. The second hypothesis is also supported: those who are seen as seeking, facilitating, and using the feedback of other's feelings and perceptions towards themselves tend to change towards the use of more expressive concepts. In short, he claims that interpersonal concept systems are amenable to change through group experiences and these changes appear to be associated with the extent to which the individual participates in the training process itself, a point which we had stressed earlier.

Somewhat less encouraging, Wolfe (1965) reports a study of the use of T-group type exercise in an in-service development programme designed specifically for school administrators and supervisors. He notes that an analysis of time utilization failed to reveal significant changes in patterns of behaviour. Likewise he claims that there was no significant change perceived in the behaviour of participants by those with whom they worked closely.

Argyris (1964) reports a study of twenty top executives in a large corporate division where he found a significant shift on the part of an experimental group towards a set of values that encouraged the executives to handle feelings and emotions, to deal with problems of group maintenance, and to develop greater feelings of responsibility on the part of their subordinates for the overall effectiveness of the organization. His study shows, however, that the impact of laboratory education only continued at a high level for just over six months. During the tenth month there was a fade out of training. A further study was undertaken and data was obtained to suggest that the executives had not in fact lost their capacity to behave in a more open manner, but they had had to suppress some of this because of organizational factors which were not conducive to openness. Again one cannot help but notice the effect of the organization upon the trainee.

Conclusion

We can conclude with some general points about the quality of the research to date. Nearly all of it suffers from methodological weakness of some form or other: in most of the studies where participants and controls are rated by peers, subordinates and superiors it is the participants who nominate the raters. This could give rise to distortion in that raters obviously are aware that the subject has or has not been on a T-group, and, if they are reasonably close to the subject, they are likely to have discussed its intended effects with him. The experience of the authors has been that on more than one occasion when research forms have been sent out prior to the T-group programme, the respondent has discussed the items with his colleagues or boss. It is conceivable that the immediate feedback given in such a pre-laboratory experience may be far more effective than the T-group itself. There is, therefore, some danger of contamination of findings by the method of participant nomination of raters and rater knowledge of T-groups and their aims. A further problem is that most of the studies available to date have not used pre and post-measures but have relied heavily on post-only questions such as 'in what ways if any has X changed his behaviour in the past year?'. One of the difficulties of a pre–post measurement design, however, is that one has to decide before the training what effect is expected. If one does this one cannot be certain, as Smith (1969) suggests, of having measured the requisite variable before training.

Still another drawback is contained in the very nature of the question asked above. X may have changed his behaviour, but this does not necessarily make him more effective at his job, as Underwood's (1965) findings, though based on small numbers, indicate. There is little evidence to support or discount the notion that greater openness, better listening, toleration, etc., contribute to effective company performance, though Willits (1967) provides some evidence that the degree to which managers communicate 'openly' with their company presidents is found to correlate significantly with overall company performance.

With these reservations, it is reasonable to conclude that there is moderately strong evidence of lasting and effective change in individuals participating in T-group training. In particular the studies we have cited provide confirmation that:

(1) Significantly more changes are reported for T-group trained participants than either matched-pair control group subjects or participants of other training programmes comparable in length and in objectives.

(2) There is a high agreement among observers in the kind and direction of change reported: improved skills in diagnosing individual and group behaviour, clearer communication, greater tolerance and consideration, and greater action skill and flexibility. (The latter is less well demonstrated than any of the former.)

(3) Finally, the changes noted in these studies were found to last for some time after training, though there are conflicting reports of fade-out after 10–12 months.

References

Argyris, C. (1964) 'T-groups for organizational effectiveness.' *Harvard Business Review*, **42**, 71.

Argyris, C. (1965) 'Explorations in interpersonal competence—I.' *Journal of Applied Behavioral Science*, **1** (1), 58–84.

Boyd, J. B. and J. D. Ellis (1962) *Findings of Research into Senior Management Seminars*, Toronto: The Hydro-Electric Power Commission of Ontario.

Bunker, D. R. (1965) 'Individual applications of laboratory training.' *Journal of Applied Behavioral Science*, **1**, 131–148.

Bunker, D. R. and E. S. Knowles (1967) 'Comparison of behavioural changes resulting from human relations training laboratories of different lengths.' *Journal of Applied Behavioral Science*, **3** (4), 505–523.

Fleishman, E. A., E. F. Harris and H. Burtt (1965) *Leadership and Supervision in Industry*. Columbus: Personnel Research Board, Ohio State University.

Harrison, R. (1962) 'Impact of the laboratory on perception of others by the experimental group.' In Argyris, C., *Interpersonal Competence and Organizational Behavior*. Homewood, Illinois: Richard D. Urwin, 261–271.

Harrison, R. (1966) 'Cognitive change in participation in a Sensitivity Training laboratory.' *Journal of Consulting Psychology*, 3 (6), 517–520.

Lippitt, R. (1949) *Training in Community Relations; Research Exploration Towards New Groups*. New York: Harper.

McNair, M. P. (1957) 'Thinking ahead: What price human relations.' *Harvard Business Review*, 15–39.

Moscow, D. (1969) 'The influence of interpersonal variables on the transfer of learning from T-groups to the job situation.' *Proceedings of International Congress of Applied Psychology*. Amsterdam, 380–386.

Miles, M. B. (1965) 'Changes during and following laboratory training: A clinical–experimental study.' *Journal of Applied Behavioral Science*, 1 (3), 215–243.

Pepinsky, H. B., L. Siegel and E. L. Van Alta (1952) 'The criterion in counselling a group participation scale.' *Journal of Abnormal and Social Psychology*, 47, 415–419.

Schutz, W. C. (1952) 'Reliability, ambiguity and content analysis.' *Psychological Review*, 59 (2), 119–129.

Schutz, W. C. and V. L. Allen (1966) 'The effects of a T-group laboratory on interpersonal behaviour.' *Journal of Applied Behavioral Science*, 1 (3), 265–286.

Smith, P. B. (1969) *Improving Skills in Working with People: the T-group*. London: Department of Employment and Productivity.

Stogdill, R. M. and A. E. Coons (1957) *Leader Behavior: Its Description and Measurement*. Ohio: Bureau of Business Research.

Underwood, W. J. (1965) 'Evaluation of a laboratory method of training.' *Journal of the American Society of Training Directors*, 14, 34–40.

Valiquet, M. I. (1968) 'Individual change in a management development program.' *Journal of Applied Behavioral Science*, 4, 313–325.

Willits, R. D. (1967) 'Company performance and interpersonal relations.' *Industrial Management Review*, 91–109.

Wolfe, W. W. (1965) 'A study of a laboratory approach to in-service development programmes for school administrators and supervisors.' Unpublished Ph.D. Dissertation, University of Texas.

Individual Change in a Management Development Program[*]

Michael I. Valiquet

Development Associates Ltd, Ottawa, Canada

Research into laboratory processes and outcomes has suffered from a lack of precise methods and continuity of effort essential to the construction of empirically grounded theoretical models of learning and behavior change. Data are presented here from a study of perceived behavior changes in employees of a large industrial concern one year after their participation in training. Participants are seen by co-workers as increasing significantly more than controls in effective initiation and assertiveness, in capacity for collaboration and operational skill in interpersonal relations, and in diagnostic awareness of self and the ability to fulfill perceived needs.

Further systematic inquiry into the determinants of laboratory education is needed to complete the spectrum of alternative designs and outcomes.

The primary purpose of this study was to assess one aspect of an organizational development program conducted on an experimental basis by a large industrial concern in several of its operating units. This facet was the degree in which the stated values underlying the program had been translated by participants into actual changed behavior and attitudes on the job. Since the basic hypothesis of training is that of 'transfer' (the transmissibility of what is learned in the training situation to the customary work situation), verification of the direction and extent of such transfer becomes an important link to any overall program evaluation.

As understood by the evaluator, the primary goal of the program was to achieve increased utilization of the unit's human resources and improved collaboration in working toward common goals. To this end, the participants were assisted in analyzing the consequences of their own actions and encouraged to consider and experiment with alternative managerial assumptions, attitudes, and behavioral patterns.

Operationally, the program comprised three phases: identification of the basic causes of ineffectiveness; the determination of the changes necessary

* Published in *Journal of Applied Behavioral Science*, **4**, 1968, 313–325. The author is greatly indebted to Warren Bennis for his enduring interest and encouragement throughout the research, and to Roger Harrison for his many helpful suggestions in the writing of this paper.

to correct this ineffectiveness and development of the requisite competencies to make the changes; and, finally, the actual implementation of the changes on a controlled schedule for specific positions and teams in such a way as to build employee understanding, commitment, and collaboration in the changes.*

Given this conceptual framework, the evaluator chose to develop a research design and methodology which would provide valid data for assisting the impact of the program on the attitudes and behavior of participants in terms of the stated training objectives. In brief, this aim involved the selection of criteria which were at once measurable and operationally meaningful, the development of adequate measuring devices, and, finally, the application of these instruments to data gathered with respect to the individual's on-the-job behaviour and attitudes.

A secondary purpose of this study—but of no less significance to the applied behavioral scientist than the evaluation itself might be to the organizational practitioner—concerns the area of methodology. Evaluative research on the application of laboratory training has tended to suffer from a lack of precise methods and a lack of replication. This tendency is probably part of the syndrome of any new science, reminiscent of the Gilbreths' quest for the 'one best way', and representing both cause and effect of the paucity of normative data. Researchers have somehow avoided building upon the methods and instruments of others. The painstaking work necessary for improvement and refinement has not been done, and instrumentation has therefore remained crude.

Research design and methods

The present study, on the other hand, uses an instrument which has been developed through two previous studies (Miles, 1960; Bunker, 1965). The intention here was twofold: first, to further test the reliability of the instrument used by Miles and Bunker; and second, to add to their work in providing the beginning of a body of normative data on differential learning outcomes of laboratory training. As Bunker (1965) remarks, 'There is strong evidence that groups, individuals, and entire training programs have differential learning outcomes' (p. 147). Miles' research treated of a single occupational group; Bunker's work increased the generality of the findings by dealing with a large heterogeneous population of strangers. The

---

* One facet of the strategy for change which distinguished this program from similar efforts was the use of change agents drawn from within the company, well-versed in the technical skills and organizational milieus in which they were to operate and uniformly trained in behavioral science theory and methodology.

present study, for its part, examines managers in an in-company training setting.

A random sample of 60 experimental subjects was chosen from lists of participants in the program at four different company locations. These departments were chosen because in each of them the training had begun at least a year previously, giving the participants an opportunity to test and internalize the new values, attitudes, and behavioral skills in their working environment, and allowing the researcher to tap whatever residual effects had survived the state of early posttraining euphoria and erosive constraints in the working environment.

A 'matched-pair' control group was obtained by asking each experimental subject to nominate another manager who held an identical or almost similar functional role to that of the participant but who had not participated in the training. This method of choosing controls permitted the researcher to negate the effects of large discrepancies in ability or opportunity on the potential for change.

The primary data source was an 'open-ended perceived change' questionnaire completed by five 'describers' for each subject. These describers were chosen at random from a listing submitted by each subject of seven to ten names of persons with whom he had worked closely for at least a year. Subjects were asked to select a variety of peers, superiors, and subordinates deemed qualified to assess the subject's on-the-job behavior and any perceived change in that behavior 'over the last year'.

The open-ended question to describers was posed thus: 'Over a period of time people may change in the ways they work with one another. Do you believe that the person you are describing has changed his/her behavior in working with people over the last year as compared with the previous year in any specific ways?' A similar question was put to the subjects themselves to elicit descriptions of their own behavior.

The major strategy then was one of classifying the types of changes comprising each subject's 'total-change score' (the total change perceived by the describers) and of determining whether any significant difference existed between the experimental and control groups. The method of assessing the change and arriving at a 'total-change score' is described below.

Criterion selection. The large volume of verbal material contained in the responses to the open-ended question required an objective method for classifying and counting the responses to permit statistical comparison. The content categories chosen for classifying the data involved 21 constructs which had been inductively derived by Bunker and which had been found to be both organizationally relevant and personally meaningful to a large

2

number of respondents from diverse organizational settings.* These constructs or variables seemed intuitively to encompass the attitudinal and behavioral change-goals of the program—openness, consensus, management of conflict, self-control, distribution of influence, and so on. Moreover, since these constructs had been inductively derived and tested over a sufficiently long period in a broad spectrum of organizational cultures, it was felt that they could be confidently imposed on the cultural mix very likely to be represented in our sample of four widely decentralized divisions.

The scoring task thus involved assigning each mention of a specific change to one of the 21 content categories. The latter fall into three comprehensive sets: overt changes in behavior (A), inferred changes in insight and attitude (B), and global or nonspecific changes (C). The descriptions scored in the 'A' categories tend to refer to overt operational changes—the subject is seen as doing more or less of something or acts more often in a particular way. Set 'B', on the other hand, includes responses based on first-order inferences by the describer as to the internal state of the subject based on behavioral cues (e.g., attributions of insight or sensitivity to group processes). The 'C' category set is used as an empirical dustbin for the many nonspecific and marginally scorable descriptions of vague behavioral changes and gross changes in character which may be received from describers. In addition, it is likely that these global descriptions incorporate a large part of the 'normal' or base rate of change and growth evident in most people.

It should be noted that while precise category fit, according to the scoring conventions to be described below, was demanded for category sets 'A' and 'B', less rigid requirements were imposed on set 'C', on the grounds that it comprised changes which were either doubtful or irrelevant to the research task. With this lone qualification, the scoring in each category depended upon an explicit statement of qualitative or quantitative difference in the subject's on-the-job behavior or attitudes. Changes could be positive or negative, reflecting increases or decreases in quantity and greater or lesser utility.

Scoring. For each describer response a score of one was assigned for each category in which there was one (or more) mention. The total-change score for each subject was then obtained by adding up the individual scores on each of the five describers' responses. Next, by combining all cell values

---

* The author is indebted to Professor Bunker for permission to use the scoring system that he and his colleagues at the National Training Laboratories developed and tested. To save space, his inductively derived categories for content analysis have not been repeated here. (See Bunker, 1965, p. 139.)

(0 or 1) in the matrix of categories and describers for all subjects, a variety of change scores can be obtained: the total-change score for experimental subjects *vis-à-vis* controls, separate scores for category sets 'A', 'B', and 'C'; for self-ratings as opposed to describer ratings; for different experimental groups by location; and a 'verified' change score developed by counting the number of observations on a particular subject where two or more describers concur.

The completed questionnaires were stripped of group identification to ensure a blind-process and were independently recorded to check drift in the use of the categories.

Results and conclusions

While the rate of return on mailed questionnaires is notoriously low, and the resultant problem of subject 'self-selection' can be extremely destructive to otherwise well-conceived research strategies, the simplicity of this questionnaire and the accompanying explanatory letter combined to give decent response statistics. Of the random sample of 60 experimental subjects originally canvassed, 39, or 65 per cent, replied; and of the 31 control subjects provided by these, 18, or 58 per cent, returned questionnaires. After others were eliminated because of recent transfers or lack of describer response, 49, or 54 per cent of both the original experiment and control group, were included in the study. Of approximately 450 describers who received questionnaires, over 50 per cent returned usable responses.

The initial comparison of experimental and control subjects is made on the basis of total-change scores. This analysis, presented in Table 1, with the distribution of the total research population divided into thirds,* indicates that a significantly greater proportion of participants than nonparticipants were in the middle and top thirds of the distribution of change scores.

The probability of obtaining a value of chi-square as large as 11·37 if the two groups were not different is less than 0·001. While the value of chi-square is substantially smaller than that obtained by Bunker, the results are comparable at his stated level of significance.

When this same type of analysis is executed solely on the basis of the changes recorded by describers in category set 'A', the results are (coincidentally) identical (see Table 2), indicating that participants in the training

* This procedure has been followed for the purposes of comparison with Professor Bunker's experiment. Cell values have been combined to permit use of the chi-square test. To provide a more stringent check of such a small research population ($N = 49$) and cell values, the 'exact' procedure for calculating chi-square was employed where necessary and found not to reverse any decisions concerning the null hypothesis. (See Croxton and Cowden, 1955, p. 686.)

Table 1—*The distribution of total-change score*

Total-change score	Experimental subjects	Control subjects	Total
Upper two-thirds (Scores of 4 to 17)	28	5	33
Lower one-third (Scores of −1 to 3)	6	10	16
N	34	15	49

$\chi^2 = 11 \cdot 37$
$(\text{d.f.} = 1)$
$p(\chi^2 = 11 \cdot 37) < 0 \cdot 001$

Table 2—*Distribution of experimental and control subjects with respect to change scores in category 'A'*

	Experimental subjects	Control subjects	Total
Upper two-thirds (Scores of 2 to 10)	28	5	33
Lower one-third (Scores of 0 and 1)	6	10	16
N	34	15	49

$\chi^2 = 11 \cdot 37$
$(\text{d.f.} = 1)$
$p(\chi^2 = 11 \cdot 37) < 0 \cdot 001$

program (experimental subjects) demonstrated significantly greater behavioral change toward program goals than did nonparticipants (control subjects).

Repeating the same procedure independently for the attitudinal category set 'B' (see Table 3), a similar pattern occurs, although this time only to the 0·01 level of significance. A somewhat *post hoc* interpretation of this result is that the participants, while not necessarily embracing the managerial alternatives advanced during their training sessions, nevertheless felt free to experiment with the new modes of behavior. This would account for the higher frequency of actional as opposed to attitudinal change, and such a supposition would be supported by the significantly higher level of 'Risk Taking' observed in experimental subjects (see Table 5). Whatever the symbolic effects of the training may have been, a professed goal of the program was 'freedom of choice' of individual managerial behavior, a goal which, from the indications outlined above, appears to have been largely met. Only when the experimental control comparison is extended to the

Table 3—*Distribution of experimental and control subjects with respect to change scores in category 'B'*

	Experimentals	Controls	Total
Upper two-thirds	22	4	26
Lower one-third	12	11	23
N	34	15	49

$\chi^2 = 7.07$
(d.f. = 1)
$p(\chi^2 = 7.07) < 0.01$

'global' change data (i.e., category set 'C') does no significant difference between the two groups occur.*

This empirical result lends credence to the hypothesis advanced earlier that the 'C' category changes constitute an important component of the 'normal' or 'base' rate of change observable in nearly all human beings, and emphasizes the discriminating power of the other change categories.

Lest the indications at this juncture of the analysis be deemed more artifactual than substantive, the raw data are now subjected to a more demanding test. Table 4 presents the difference between experimental and control groups on the basis of 'verified' change scores, i.e., where a subject had one or more specific observations of change confirmed by concurrence among the responses of two or more describers.

The questions well might arise as to whether describer bias induced by awareness of the subject's participation or nonparticipation in the program

Table 4—*The number of subjects with one or more verified changes*

	Experimentals	Controls	Total
One or more changes verified by describer concurrence	25 (73%)	2 (20%)	27
No verification	9 (27%)	13 (80%)	22
N	34	15	49

$\chi^2 = 15.22$
(d.f. = 1)
$p(\chi^2 = 15.22) < 0.001$

* Of the total research population, five experimental and nine control subjects were described as having changed along these lines. The two-cell table yields a nonsignificant chi-square value of 1.14.

would affect the results, whether the describers could easily contrive a set of situationally relevant behavioral changes, and whether indeed they would be motivated to do so. The high number of 'no change' as well as positive change responses received from describers, the random process of describer selection, the discriminating power of the many change categories, as well as the Table 4 results, make such an occurrence seem highly unlikely. More than two-thirds of the experimentals, as compared with fewer than one-third of the controls, had one or more specific changes confirmed by the reports of two or more describers. This difference in the proportion of verifications adds substance to the interpretations made of Tables 1, 2 and 3, and compares closely with the findings of Bunker.

Finally, Table 5 presents an analysis by scoring category of the differences in proportions of subjects reported as changed in each of the two groups. Some notable similarities and differences with respect to Professor Bunker's results are brought to light. First, we must concur with his findings that laboratory training outcomes tend to be individual and varied, even where the program is conducted in a single industrial organization. In only one of the scoring categories does the proportion of subjects reported as having changed exceed 50 per cent.

Table 5—*Differences between experimental and control groups proportion of subjects reported to have changed*

	Scoring category	Proportion perceived to have changed		Differences
		Experimentals	Controls	
A–1	Sending	0·29	0·07	0·23[a]
A–1	Receiving	0·18	0·07	0·11
A–2	Relational Facility	0·35	0·13	0·22[a]
A–3	Risk Taking	0·32	0·07	0·26[b]
A–4	Increased Interdependence	0·56	0·13	0·43[b]
A–5	Functional Flexibility	0·35	0·07	0·29[b]
A–6	Self-Control	0·35	0·13	0·22[a]
B–1	Awareness of Behavior	0·18	0·07	0·11
B–2	Sensitivity to Group Process	0·12	0·07	0·05
B–3	Sensitivity to Others' Feelings	0·32	0·13	0·19
B–4	Acceptance of Others	0·32	0·07	0·26[a]
B–5	Tolerance of New Information	0·32	0·13	0·19
B–6	Confidence	0·12	0·07	0·05
B–7	Comfort	0·21	0·07	0·14
B–8	Insight into Self and Role	0·44	0·13	0·31[b]

[a] $p < 0.05$.
[b] $p < 0.01$.

However, whereas Bunker found that 11 of the 15 categories discriminated between experimental and control subjects beyond the 0·05 level of significance, here only 8 of the 15 so discriminate.

The simplest explanation of this result would appear to lie in the differences between the two programs studied, particularly in terms of the stated goals of each and the environments in which the programs took place. Bunker studied heterogeneous groups of strangers who after training dispersed to a wide variety of occupational roles in a broad range of organizational types and sizes. The goals of the NTL program he studied are probably best described in terms of *all* of the criterion variables used in this research. The present study, on the other hand, while not treating of a single occupational group, is concerned with a relatively lesser number of occupational roles in a particular organization. Moreover, the operational goals of this program were couched strongly, and specifically, in terms of *adapting the changes with which students were experimenting to the organizational setting*. What is implied here is that the participants of this program tended to focus on the *application* of a narrower range of program values.

This line of reasoning is reinforced by a further difference between the two studies. Bunker found that seven of the eight categories in set 'B' discriminated at the 0·05 level or better while only four of the seven categories in set 'A' had comparable power. In the present study the situation is somewhat reversed, with some interesting qualitative differences. Six of the eight behavioral categories discriminate at the 0·05 level or better, while only two attitudinal categories demonstrate similar power. The reasoning advanced earlier seems relevant here. Participants perhaps felt free to experiment with new modes of behavior on the job while not necessarily fully convinced of their effectiveness. As some behavioralists argue, attitude change may not be a necessary antecedent to behavioral change. A further divergence between the two studies which supports this argument is that where Bunker found no significant difference in his experimental and control groups with respect to 'Risk Taking' (A-3), it is here found to be significant at the 0·01 level. This, perhaps, may be explained by the fact that Bunker's experimental group was exposed to a stimulus situation of shorter duration and remote from its operational environment, whereas the subject program was relatively continuous and carried out for the most part within the operational environment. What is implied here is that gradual and protracted training within a generally supportive atmosphere may better lend itself to experimentation and the exposing of one's self and one's ideas, than returning from a 'cultural island' to the perhaps erosive effects of an environment which has not necessarily been conditioned to change. Additionally, there is the fact that the training here was accompanied by other forms of change—organizational, structural, et cetera—which may have reinforced a spirit of experimentation.

Another significant divergence from Bunker's results lies in the discriminating power of Category A-5, 'Functional Flexibility'. Whereas Bunker discovered this factor also to be relatively nonsignificant, here it is found to be of major importance. Reasoning similar to that advanced for the high incidence of 'Risk Taking' appears relevant. Given that a score for 'Functional Flexibility' requires evidence of *both* diagnosis and the ability to act to fulfill perceived needs, it seems reasonable to expect higher incidence of the second criterion in an organizational climate which has been carefully nurtured at all management levels to accept the reality of change and the necessity of adapting to it.

The findings with respect to 'Increased Interdependence' (A-4) and 'Insight into Self and Role' (B-8) are also somewhat dissimilar to those of Bunker. Here they are found to be of greater significance, which, in the case of 'Increased Interdependence', may merely reflect the relevance of the variable to this particular program and organization. It is interesting to note, however, that the same common theme of increased operational skill in interpersonal relations, together with increased capacity for collaboration observed by Bunker, also exists here, albeit with different emphasis.

The increase in diagnostic awareness of self and role observed here distinguished program participants from controls at a higher level of significance than in the case of a heterogeneous group of NTL participants. It may be that an improved perception of one's own attributes and limitations, particularly with respect to the job, is more readily acquired through social interaction with one's actual 'family' group, rather than in the comparative psychological safety of a 'stranger' group.

One further qualitative difference between the two programs lies in the cluster of categories which Bunker describes as 'increased and more effective initiation and assertiveness' (A-5, A-3, B-6). While the NTL programs seem not to have had their major impact in this area, the two actional variables are found here to be quite significant. 'Confidence' (B-6) is not; but perhaps the significant increase in 'Self-Control' (A-6) as a sort of tempering or 'braking' effect, together with improved 'Functional Flexibility' (A-5), may reflect the participants' diagnosis that their major needs did not lie in this direction.

Implications for laboratory education

When the results are compared with Bunker's study of a large, heterogeneous population of strangers, his general findings are supported, but with some interesting qualitative differences. In particular, the greater number of significant changes observed in this study occurred in the overt, operational categories rather than in the inferred, attitudinal categories, as was more often the case in Bunker's study. A variety of factors may have been at play in producing this differential result, the most important of which appear to have been the composition of the groups (family *versus* strangers), the apparent program goals, and the environment of change in each case.

Tentatively, it is suggested that actional, as opposed to attitudinal, change may be better supported in a program specifically designed for such a purpose and buttressed by concomitant changes of other kinds in the organization. The program studied here seems to have been able to thwart the psychological resistances—particularly the waning of the training 'honeymoon'—which have plagued so much development effort in the past. This is not to say that *all* participants learned to accelerate their adaptive processes and to obtain better control over them. To hope for so much would be quixotic. The data do indicate, however, that a majority of the laboratory participants were able to integrate their newly acquired attitudes and behavioral skills into their personalities and ongoing work relationships.

But as Bunker and others have stressed, now that improved criterion measures of long-range behavioral change are available, there is an urgent requirement for further systematic investigation and comparative analysis of alternative training designs, processes, and outcomes to enrich the soil of substantive knowledge concerning laboratory education and to enhance the range and validity of alternative programs. Until this is done, the processes of choice remain slightly more scientific than augury.

References

Bunker, D. R. (1965) 'Individual applications of laboratory training. *J. appl. Behav. Sci.*, **1** (2), 131–148.

Croxton,F. E. and D. J. Cowden (1955) *Applied General Statistics.* 2nd ed. New York: Prentice-Hall.

Miles, M. B. (1960) 'Human relations training: Processes and outcomes. *J. counsel. Psychol.*, **7** (4), 301–306.

CHAPTER 2

Before and After the T-group*

In this chapter we shall review the evidence that has accumulated around what Martin (1957) terms *internal criteria*. Internal criteria are measures linked directly to the content and processes of the training programme but which do not necessarily have implications for behaviour away from the programme. External criteria are those linked directly with job behaviour, and research studies bearing on this area are reviewed below. The areas we shall be considering are: studies concerned with attitude change, perceptual change, personality change, and growth in diagnostic ability.

Attitude Change

In designing evaluation research to assess the impact of T-group training during the training period a number of approaches are possible. One may design measures related to the outcomes one expects, such as measures of self-awareness or attitude flexibility or diagnostic ability. Or one may design a wide variety of measures for the purpose of detecting whatever changes do in fact occur, expected or not. Most of these studies initially undertaken used the second strategy, since there were few measures available for assessing the kinds of social skill attributes associated with T-group training (Smith, 1969). As a result of these studies and the development of more sophisticated techniques of attitude and behaviour measurement, more measures of the first type have been devised. It is with studies utilizing the more sophisticated techniques that we shall be concerned.

It is common in a T-group for the participants to analyse the staff member's behaviour and to discuss their feelings and beliefs about authority, power and leadership. A large number of the attitude change studies have in one form or another examined participants' attitudes toward authority. Kernan (1964) attempted to see if attitudes toward authority as measured

* A slightly modified version of a paper published by the authors in the *Journal of Management Studies*, 7 (1970), 224–239.

25

by Adorno's F-scale were affected by T-group training. 40 T-group participants and 20 control subjects were tested before and after a three-day T-group for engineering supervisors. He found no significant change in participants' F-scale score as a result of the training. In addition, he found no changes in responses to measures of attitudes toward the use of different leadership types, or changes in Thematic Apperception Tests of 'tolerance, toughness, friendliness, interpersonal problems, dominance or nurturance'. The pre and post-tests, however, were carried out under different conditions (some participants completed the questionnaires under actual job conditions while others off the job), which makes the results less satisfying.

Carron (1964) used Adorno's F-scale and the Leadership Opinion Questionnaire in evaluating T-group training in terms of changed attitudes (with a group of Research and Development Managers). He obtained attitude measurements on both T-group participants and control group subjects at four different points in time: before training, immediately after training, six months later, and at a follow-up 17 months after the end of the training. The LOQ is concerned with two kinds of leader behaviour, consideration and initiating structure. The consideration dimension measures the degree to which a leader shows concern for the well being of his subordinates, helps the groups, uses participative decision-making and is generally supportive of his subordinates. The initiating structure dimension measures the degree to which the leader plans, organizes and controls, defines procedures and responsibilities and generally the degree to which he establishes a structure to guide his subordinates in their work. Carron found, analysing the data across groups, that the training programme did change authoritarian and leadership attitudes but that they were not permanent (not noted some 17 months later). He felt, however, that the 'across group analysis' was not an adequate method of analysing attitude change since it measured only magnitude and not direction of change and 'statistical averages for a group simply do not tell what is happening to the individual members'. The changes measured by the F-scale and the LOQ became clearer when he employed a vector analysis of the data showing both magnitude and direction. He found that the training had the effect of decreasing authoritarian attitudes and of causing participants to place higher value on consideration and less value on structure, which he interprets as desirable change. This opinion is contrary to substantial evidence (Fleishman and Harris, 1962; Halpin, 1957) to suggest that attitudes and behaviour characterized by high consideration *and* high structure are associated with effective and successful leadership for widely different organizations (House, 1967). In other words, the study indicates that the participants believed more in the need for one kind of desirable leader behaviour, namely consideration, and less in a second, namely structure.

Asquith and Hedlund (1967) administered the LOQ and the SI (Supervisory Index) to evaluate the changes in attitude toward supervisory practices during a management development training programme involving a one-week T-group. No change in participants' attitudes on either of these instruments was found. The T-group, however, was only one part of the training programme and it could be that the management lectures which made up the bulk of the programme may have interfered with the results of the T-group. In addition, no attempt was made to use a control group as a basis of comparison.

Nonetheless, results of studies utilizing the LOQ yield far from satisfactory evidence that the T-group has lasting effects on attitudes.

A different measure of attitude has been used in a number of studies on participant attitude change, the FIRO-B (Schutz, 1958). This questionnaire assesses the respondents' attitudes toward two salient areas in the behaviour of any T-group, control or power and affection or close personal relations. It is composed of six Guttman scales of nine items each. The scales measure an individual's *expressed* behaviour and the behaviour *wanted from others* in the interpersonal areas of inclusion,* control, and affection. Smith (1964) used the FIRO to compare 108 T-group participants with 44 control group subjects on other management training courses. Subjects completed the FIRO questionnaire near the beginning and again near the end of their course. Before an assessment was made of participant change, measures were obtained during the T-groups which indicated that the FIRO scales were indeed correlated with participant behaviour in the group. Smith argued that changes to be expected in this questionnaire would not be increases or decreases but movements toward the median position on the scale, since extreme scores, as Schutz (1958) points out, are consistent with a more rigid, inflexible attitudinal style. It was found that T-group-trained participants showed a marked tendency for their scores on the control and affection scales to move toward the median. It may be, however, that this movement is a function of initial score bias such that the high initial scorers moved downward and the low initial scorers moved upward, and in addition, that there may be more high and low initial scorers among the T-group trained than the control group subjects.

Controlling for initial scores, Cureton (1968) replicated Smith's study in a group of students in a college of education. 50 students participated in a T-group and 48 in a more conventional course on human relations. Pre and

---

* The inclusion scales have been frequently omitted since they were found by Smith (1964) to be highly correlated with the affection scales.

post-training FIRO scores were obtained and the T-group trained participants showed a movement toward the median on the FIRO sub-scales
while the 48 controls showed significantly less movement.

Changes in the FIRO scores were also obtained by Schutz and Allen
(1966) for 71 participants in the Western Training Laboratory in Human
Relations. The participants completed the questionnaire before and after
the two-week laboratory and six months later. FIRO was also given to a
group of 30 college students at approximately equal intervals to serve as a
control. Overall correlations between administrations were much lower for
the T-group trained participants than for the control group. That is, the
former showed significantly more change on the FIRO sub-scales than the
latter. Directionality was not considered. They also found that the T-group
changed people selectively on the basis of their initial personality attributes
such that overly dominant became less dominant while overly affectionate
more discriminating.

Changes on the FIRO were not found by Meigniez (1961) using a French
translation of FIRO in 3 French T-groups (no control group). The lack of
any significant change in this case may be attributed to cultural differences
in attitudes toward control and affection.

Baumgartel and Goldstein (1967) used the FIRO and the Allport–
Vernon 'Study of Values' to test the prediction that participants would
become more like the highly valued members of the group in their attitudes
over the course of the group. The participants' ranked their fellow-students
to determine which were the 'most-valued' members of the T-group. The
various scores for each of the sub-scales of the FIRO and the Study of
Values questionnaires, administered at the start of the course, were correlated with the sociometric ranking of the most-valued members obtained
at the end of the course. There were two significant correlations with sociometric position: highly-valued members had high expressed control scores
on the FIRO and lower religious value scores on the Study of Values. The
FIRO and the Study of Values were re-administered at the end of the
course to test the above hypothesis. Only the reduction in religious value is
supported by the data, there was no significant change in the expressed
control scores. However, two other FIRO scores did show significant
changes: participants increased in their wanted control scores and decreased
in their wanted affection scores. The conclusion is drawn that some support
for the expectation was found that the 'uses of internal criterion of poor
ratings would seem to be promising for assessing effects of training'. Very
little supporting evidence was found, however, to justify such a claim. In
addition, one must question the assumption made that 'if we can learn the
characteristics or attributes of those persons who are esteemed as group

members in the natural course of events, presumably people with high interpersonal competence, then we can use a measure of the *amount of change toward the characteristics* as an indicator of a positive training outcome'.

Several attitude change studies have been conducted which utilize questionnaires directly relevant to the group being studied. Elliott (1958) for instance, compared 16 employees of an engineering company who participated in T-group training with 15 employees (matched for age, intelligence, and organization function) who were not trained. Two measures of change were used; the Supervisory Attitude Scale developed by Castle (1952), and a second one, developed by the investigator, entitled 'How Groups Work'. On both scales changes toward a greater emphasis on human relations in supervision were found for the trained employees which was significantly greater than for the untrained men. While the sample is small the results are interesting in view of the fact that the Castle scale has not been shown to change in response to other human relations training courses.

Bowers and Soar (1961) conducted a study into the effects on teacher's attitude and behaviour of a T-group training programme. They used an untrained control group of teachers, similar to the trained ones. A comparison of pre and post-training results indicated that T-group trained teachers showed significant positive change in their attitudes toward pupils and democratic leadership, but the control group also showed a change so that the difference between them was not significant. Further analysis of the data shows that teachers who were well-adjusted, as measured by the personality inventory, and those who emphasized verbal presentation in their classroom behaviour, were more likely to change their attitudes toward student participation than the equivalent group of teachers without training. The authors conclude, therefore, that the effect of the training was to help teachers realize their potential, that is, to increase the degree of difference between greater and lesser skill.

The studies reviewed in this section examined change in the attitudes toward social behaviour of those trained, behaviour which is regarded as the most important in the case of non-directive training groups. The main attitudes considered were those toward power or leadership and affection behaviour. Overall the studies seem to indicate that changes in these attitudes did occur as a result of training, and in some cases, that they moved in the direction of a more flexible position. One must take note, however, of the ambiguity of the findings. Like so many areas of T-group research, there remains a great deal to be done, both in terms of replication and original research which seeks to link attitude changes, if any, with specific dynamics of the groups.

Perceptual change

One of the questions often asked of the T-group is whether this type of training will in some way affect the personality of the participants involved. One aspect of this question is whether the group members increase the 'clarity and accuracy of their perception of their own behaviour'. Most of the measures used in studies of this sort have focused on the change in the discrepancies between a person's description of 'actual self', 'ideal self', and 'average-other perceptions of self'.

An early study designed to assess the discrepancy between 'actual self' and 'ideal self' was carried out by Bennis, Burke, Cutter, Harrington and Hoffman (1957) with 12 students who participated in a semester-long T-group. They assessed changes in perception of actual and ideal self using a 34-item inventory of possible role behaviours (for example, 'tries to understand the contributions of others'). The students rated each of the possible role behaviours on a 7-point scale on the basis of how descriptive the items were of them and how descriptive they were of ideal role behaviour. No significant increase in similarity between actual and ideal was found.

In a study with a larger sample, Burke and Bennis (1961) obtained ratings of 'actual self', 'ideal self', and 'self as rated by others' from 84 participants of six different NTL* groups. They used a Group Semantic Differential questionnaire of 19 bipolar, adjectival rating scales with instructions to participants to respond in three ways: (1) 'The way I actually am in this T-group', (2) 'The way I would like to be in this T-group', and (3) 'Each of the other people in this group'. The ratings of others were averaged to provide a pooled or average description of each participant on each of the 19 scales. They found that the discrepancy between actual self and ideal self was much less at the end of the training than at the beginning. They also found that the participants showed more change in actual self than in perceived ideal self, which they suggest is the result of an emphasis in the T-group of here-and-now behaviour in the group rather than of the ideal group member. In addition, a participant's perceived actual self and the perception of him by others in his T-group were more similar at the end of the training than at the beginning. But in this case the group members changed much more in the ways in which they perceived other individuals in the group than these individuals changed in their perception of self, which, they suggest, indicates an increase in the consensual validation of behaviour by members of a T-group. Since no control group was used it is difficult to assess whether the changes are a function of the T-group or simply the passage of time or some other extraneous factor.

* NTL—National Training Laboratory, currently the central focus of T-group training in the United States.

Grater (1959) used the Bills' Index of Adjustment and Values to obtain descriptions of 'actual self', 'ideal self', and 'others' before and after an 11-week leadership training course for 30 university students. The course was not entirely a T-group in that it focused mainly on leadership problems experienced by the participants and minimized interpersonal behaviour and feedback in the group situation. Even though the training course lacked some of the elements of a T-group, results similar to those of Burke and Bennis were obtained. The discrepancies between 'actual self' and 'ideal self' were significantly reduced over the course of training (once again due mainly to changes in perception of actual self); and the expected decrease in the discrepancy between descriptions of actual self and the average group member was found, but not at a statistically significant level.

Carson and Lakin (1963) replicated the Burke and Bennis study with only two groups of subjects but improved upon the original design by providing a control condition. Participants filled out a 16-item rating scale questionnaire in respect to themselves and every other participant in their group two-weeks before and two-weeks after training. One group was used as its own control by completing the questionnaire six weeks prior to training. The results were less than satisfactory, one group supported most of the results in the original study while the other showed little change following training (incidentally, this was the group which acted as its own control).

Unlike the aforementioned studies, Gassner, Gold and Snadowsky (1964) conducted a comprehensive, well-controlled study of phenomenal-self changes. In the first part of the study they administered Bills' Index to 46 students one day prior to and two days after the completion of the T-group. 21 students who submitted applications for a forthcoming T-group were used as a control, responding to the above questionnaire over an equivalent time interval. They found a significant decrease in the discrepancy between perceptions of actual self and ideal self in both the T-group trained and control group subjects. In addition, both groups showed a significant decrease in discrepancy between perceptions of actual self and average-other perceptions. This aspect of the results was similar to the Grater and the Burke and Bennis findings. However, when the degree of change between the T-group and the control group on both of the above discrepancy measures was examined, it was found that the T-group changes did not differ significantly from the control group.

In the second part of the study, 45 T-group trained students were compared with 27 students enrolled in psychology courses at the same university. In this study a modified form of the Burke and Bennis graphic-rating scale series was administered to the participants at the introductory session of the T-group. Control group subjects completed the rating scales over a comparable time interval. In this study they found no significant decrease in discrepancy between perceptions of actual self and ideal self in either the T-group or the control group subjects. They did find, however, a significant decrease in the discrepancy between the perceptions of actual self and average-other perceptions. However, when the groups were compared the difference between them was not statistically significant. The two control conditions in this study add an important dimension to this line of research since it provides us with a basis of comparison. A better control group, however, might have been one in which the subjects were participating in a more conventional course of instruction in human relations, such as a lecture or group seminar, and one covering the same time interval as the T-group.

While all of the above studies have assessed in one form or another training induced changes in clarity of self-perceptions, none of them has forged the link between the changes and the means employed to produce them. Research of this sort has only recently been undertaken. The best example of this is a study conducted by French, Sherwood and Bradford (1966) to test whether changes in self-identity are influenced by the amount of personal feedback received. Data was collected from two two-week T-groups (ten members each) at a number of points in time: beginning of the first week, end of the first week, end of the second week, and ten months after the T-group (to test whether changes in self-identity were permanent or whether there was regression to the pre T-group level). Each subject filled out a questionnaire containing 19 bipolar scales measuring different dimensions of self-identity. The amount of personal feedback was experimentally manipulated: on the one extreme, high feedback condition, the participant was rated on one of the bipolar scales by the nine other T-group members in terms of his present behaviour, those ratings were fed back to him in written form, and his behaviour on this scale was discussed in detail with two members of his T-group. On the other extreme, low feedback condition, he was not rated by the other members of the group, no information was fed back to him, and there was no scheduled discussions.

Five conditions with different amounts of feedback were produced and it was expected that changes in self-identity would be greater for the condition with the greatest amount of feedback. They found no consistent change in self-identity during the first week of training, most change during the second week, and less change (though still statistically significant) for the follow-up period. With respect to the systematic amount of feedback on different amounts of change in self-identity they found that Condition E, which contained no feedback, showed less change than the other conditions (all of whom contained some personal feedback) for the total time period. However, they found little statistical difference between A, B and C conditions of feedback, although they contend that there was no measure to determine how much feedback was actually produced in each condition. In addition, they tested two other hypotheses: (1) the greater the importance or centrality of a dimension of self-perception to the participant, the greater the change in his self-identity, and (2) the lower a person's self-evaluation or the higher his dissatisfaction on a dimension of self-perception, the greater the change on his self-identity. Some support for the second hypothesis was found, while there was no support for the first hypothesis. They conclude by saying that their 'results give some support to the proposition that a person's self-identity is influenced by the opinions that others have of him which they communicate to him and that the more that is communicated the more change there is in self-identity'.

There are, of course, pitfalls in this research: (1) the number of subjects used in the study was small, (2) no control was employed, and more importantly (3) there is no evidence that experimental manipulation was successful. This should not, however, detract from the importance of the study, which is the first of its kind to assess phenomenal self changes in terms of the means employed to produce them.

In summary, while it may be reasonable to expect changes in the way in which an individual sees himself as a result of T-group training, the only well-controlled study (Gassner and coworkers, 1964) to assess this leads to the suggestion that the T-group does not produce these changes any more than the simple passage of time or the mere act of re-taking a self-description questionnaire after a period of thinking about one's previous responses. This seems to suggest either that the self-perception questionnaires are empirically inadequate and thus interfere with attempts to measure self-percept change or that T-group training does not have a measurable effect on the self-concept of the participant.

Personality change

Turning to another criterion measure during the training period, we were surprised to find less than a handful of studies relating T-group experiences to personality change itself. It may be that interest in this area is slight because changes in such fundamental personality traits may be just too much to expect in such a short-lived experience.

Most of the criterion measures used in these studies are obtained by means of standardized personality questionnaires or projective tests. In an early study, Zimet and Fine (1955) assessed the consequences of a T-group

105722

on 15 New York chief school administrators in the public schools. In order to evaluate the personality changes a picture story technique was used. This Picture Story Test (PST) consisted of 18 pictures; 6 from the TAT, 6 from the School Apperception Test, and 6 from a previous research study. Each subject was asked to make up a story to fit each of the pictures. The PST was administered during the initial and final sessions of the 16-weekly sessions in the laboratory. The pre and post-test protocols were recorded, transcribed and coded. The stories were then analysed for attitudes expressed by each subject and were represented by scores on each of a number of scales. There were 6 scales in each of 3 major areas of attitudes toward self, attitudes toward other adults, and attitudes toward children. In addition, the Combs Desires list which is made up of 36 items was used to measure change in motivation.

On balance, the school administrators' conception of self, others, and children as recorded in the PST indicated movement in the direction of *increased* adequacy, liking, acceptance and equality. When the Combs Desires' items were analysed for pre and post-tests differences, a change in a positive direction was found on a number of items. Increases were found in their 'desire to believe best about another'; 'desire to help, aid, assist someone of a group in a social or humanitarian sense'; 'desire not to hurt, punish, or kill, not to attack, destroy, avenge, inflict pain to self or society'. As the authors suggest, 'on the whole the changes that were recorded in this instrument indicate movement in the "democratic" direction'.

While these results are in the direction one might expect in terms of T-group goals, the danger of making inferences from studies without adequate control groups has been demonstrated innumerable times (for example, Gassner and coworkers, 1964).

Using a larger sample but again lacking a control group, Massarik and Carlson (Dunnette, 1962) designed a study to assess changes in personality variables similar to the previous study. Based on a before and after administration of the California Personality Inventory, they found that 48 hours of T-group interaction among 70 students brought about only minor changes in the expected direction of increased spontaneity and slightly lowered overall control.

In addition to the variables of adequacy and spontaneity, David Reisman's theory of social character based on the concepts of inner and other-directedness has been linked to the goals of the T-group. As Kassarjian (1965) suggests:

'Sensitivity training as it is offered in many training laboratories through the country has often been labeled as being an ideal training experience for organization men, for teaching the techniques of other-direction. On the other hand, some supporters of sensitivity training claim quite the opposite, that sensitivity training opens the communication channels within the person . . .. Hence it is training for inner-direction.'

With this difference of opinion in mind Kassarjian (1965) sought to investigate whether there was a shift toward inner or other-direction after an extensive T-group experience. He undertook this investigation into four student and six adult T-groups, using control groups of similar composition. The T-group subjects were administered the I–O Social Preference Scale (Kassarjian, 1962), a measure of inner and other-direction, at the beginning and end of the training period. Control group subjects were given the instrument during the same week, at the beginning and the end of the week. The I–O Social Preference Scale consists of 36 forced-choice items, which yielded predicted relationships with other variables in previous research, notably with the Strong Vocational Interest Blank and Allport–Vernon–Lindzey Scale of Values.

The t tests tabulated between the means of the control and the experimental groups for the student and adult groups yielded no significant differences in shifts. Thus, the short-term effects of the T-group do not seem to be related to a shift toward either inner or other-direction. Since previous research has had predictable success with the I–O scale it is unlikely that the scale does not measure inner and other-direction. It is more likely, as Kassarjian suggests, that 'to expect that a single training experience over a 10 to 15-week period would create a measurable change in the basic underlying social character of a person that has taken 20 to 40 years to instill, may well be too much to expect . . .'.

It has frequently been suggested (Miles, 1965; Smith, 1964) that T-groups should increase one's sensitivity to the needs of others and insight into one's own motives and behaviour as it affects others. Rubin (1967) has set out to test this prediction. He has hypothesized that as a result of T-group training: (1) an individual's level of self-acceptance should increase; (2) an individual's level of acceptance of others should increase; and (3) those who increase in self-acceptance should increase more in acceptance of others than those who do not change or decrease in self-acceptance. The Dorris, Levinson, Hanfmann Sentence Completion Test (SCT) (1954) was used to measure the effect of T-groups upon an individual's level of self-acceptance. The SCT includes 50 sentence stems. Half of the stems use first-person pronouns, and half, a third-person pronoun or pronoun or proper name. The first and third-person items are matched in context, for example, when he gets angry he . . .; when I get angry I . . .. The individual stem completions were coded in such a way that the more willing a person was to admit 'ego-threatening' material the greater his level of self-acceptance. In addition to self-acceptance a 15-item scale was developed to measure human-heartedness (HH) or acceptance of others.

Fifty participants who were involved in a two-week residential T-group programme were used in the study. The subjects were randomly split into two groups of unequal size. The smaller group ($N = 14$) was tested via mailed questionnaire two weeks prior to their participation, which provided subjects to serve as their own control. The entire group was then tested upon their arrival but before the first group session. The final measures were obtained the morning of the next-to-last day of the laboratory.

Analysis of the data by partial correlation found substantial support for the hypotheses. The first two hypotheses were upheld but the one suggesting that those who increase in self-acceptance will increase more in HH than those who decrease or do not change in self-acceptance was too broad. As Rubin states 'it appears instead that some minimum increases in self-acceptance (20 per cent in this study) is necessary in order for any significant change in HH to be immediately observable.' While these results are encouraging, there is still the strong possibility that any one of a number of other human relations training methods would produce similar results. Further research using comparison groups, that is, groups trained by some other method, should be encouraged to discount the above possibility.

In conclusion, it seems that personality change, as measured by standardized personality questionnaires and projective techniques, has not been demonstrated. While some of the studies are encouraging, a number of problems remain. First, the multiplicity of research instruments and criteria used makes any comparison or integration of the findings impossible. This state of affairs reflects the lack of agreement and clarity about the T-group goals relevant to personality change and, consequently, about the research focus in this area. Second, few control or comparison groups are used. And lastly, as Campbell and Dunnette (1968) emphasize 'changes in such basic personality variables may be just too much to expect from such a relatively short experience, even if the T-group is a good one'.

Diagnostic ability

This section covers changes in the ability to diagnose interpersonal phenomena and the related field of changes in the use of interpersonal concepts.

One of the earliest studies in this area was conducted by Bass (1962) in which he assessed the effects of T-groups on sensitivity to interpersonal behaviour. He showed parts of the film *Twelve Angry Men* to 34 managers before and after a two-week T-group. To measure sensitivity, he queried each participant about the film by use of an incomplete sentence test. Each participant was asked to respond to such questions as: 'The reason that the architect (Henry Fonda) went to the drinking fountain was that . . .' or 'The old man changed his vote because . . .'. From the results, Bass concluded that the T-group resulted in participants becoming more sensitive to the interpersonal relationships in the film.

It could be argued, however, that merely taking the test or seeing the film twice enhances scores. Under the circumstances control groups, both of trained (by some other method) and untrained subjects, should have been used to discount the above possibilities. Bass did, however, show the film to two other groups of trainees after training only, in order to assess possible effects of seeing the film twice. Since all the groups responded similarly on the post-test questionnaire, it was suggested that the increased sensitivity must be due to the training and not to seeing the film on two occasions.

In addition, he found that the sensitivity scores obtained by the sentence completion technique matched opinions of peers and staff psychologists', which he concludes '. . . the inference being that management training laboratories do increase participant's sensitivity'. It must be pointed out, however, that this ability to understand interpersonal relationships though demonstrated in response to the film *Twelve Angry Men* was not assessed in this study in relation to the T-group or the participants within it.

Harrison (1966) built upon the work of a number of cognitive theorists in attempting to measure changes in concept preference in interpersonal perception. His major hypothesis was that T-group trained participants should become more oriented to intrapersonal process, that is, they should change in their descriptions of others toward the use of more concepts dealing with feelings, attitudes, emotions, and perceptions. In addition, they should use more descriptions oriented to interpersonal process: the dominant or submissive relationships a person establishes, his warmth or coldness, his comfort or discomfort with others. Further, Harrison argued that if conceptual changes are caused by the training, then the extent of the change should be related to effective participation in the training activities.

115 participants took a modified form of Kelly's Role Repertory Test before, three weeks after, and three months after training. The results were processed by a coding scheme developed by Harrison (1962) and, in addition, each participant was rated by his group in terms of how he responded to feedback on his own behaviour.

As predicted, there was a change toward the use of more inferential-expressive concepts but this only became significant during the 12th to 24th week following the laboratory. In addition, Harrison found that the feedback ratings were correlated with inferential-expressive change scores.

Harrison notes, somewhat cautiously, that in studies of this kind it is often impractical to obtain an adequate control group. He argues that experimental manipulation lessens the possibility of the results being simply an artifact of the measurement process and the relationships found in his study between ratings of active learning and changes in concept usage provide strength to his argument.

Argyris (1965) used a set of categories designed by himself to measure interpersonal competence as a basis to evaluate the relative effectiveness of lecture *versus* T-group training in the areas of interpersonal relationships and group dynamics. Though this is primarily an evaluation study Argyris does succeed in demonstrating that T-group trained participants do change behaviourally in the way they tackle case studies. They tend, on the whole, to be much more trusting and open in discussing and diagnosing case studies than do control groups of lecture trained course members.

Finally, Oshry and Harrison (1966) report a study in which data was collected from 46 participants in a two-week T-group for middle managers. They used the Problem Analysis Questionnaire, which is designed to measure diagnostic style in individual patterns of analysing interpersonal work problems. They hypothesized that participants with regard to the 'focus of work-related problems' should (1) increase in perceived impor- tance of self as a cause, (2) decrease in perceived importance of others as cause(s) and (3) decrease in perceived importance of environmental factors as causes. As predicted there were statistically significant increases in the perceived importance of self as a cause of work-related problems and statisti- cally significant decreases in the perceived importance of other(s) and environmental factors.

The authors also found that although the T-group tends to orient participants away from the back-home environment, the diagnostic orienta- tions learned about self in relation to the T-group appears to generalize to learnings about self in relation to work. Specifically, the analysis of the questionnaire suggested that at the end of the T-group but before re- entering his work environment the participant perceives:

(1) His work would seem to him to be more human and less impersonal.

(2) He sees clearer connections between how well interpersonal needs are met and how well the work gets done.

(3) He sees himself clearly as the most significant part of his work problems.

(4) He sees no clear connection between his new perceptions and how he translates these into action.

The authors themselves are well aware of the serious limitations of a single research design without controls but they believe that the results from a pilot project are of sufficient interest to warrant publication.

Conclusion

In concluding this chapter we can only point to the essentially mixed results. Very few of the studies reviewed yield unequivocal results, possibly because of inadequate measures or poor research design. Perhaps it is unwise to expect basic perceptual or personality changes to be manifested; perhaps critical changes do occur, but these are not measured by the available instruments. For example, a participant may learn how to manage his feelings of hostility better, to use his aggression more appropriately and a relatively crude measure will not necessarily pick this up. It is noticeable that none of the measures utilized take into account the nature of the eliciting situation—hostility or aggression in one set of circumstances may be critically different from its use in another. For example, a participant could score highly on hostility in an early session and highly in a late session but his hostility may be functional and appropriate in the later session. Unless we take into account the nature of the eliciting situation, we simply record no change in hostility.

In view of the measurement difficulties, therefore, it would be less than fair to conclude that T-group training has no lasting effect on perceptual or personality variables.

References

Argyris, C. (1965) 'Explorations in interpersonal competence—II.' *Journal of Applied Behavioral Science*, **1**, 255–269.

Asquith, R. H. and D. E. Hedlund (1967) 'Laboratory training and supervisory attitudes.' *Psychological Reports*, **20**, 618.

Bass, B. M. (1962) 'Reactions to "12 Angry Men" as a measure of sensitivity training.' *Journal of Applied Psychology*, **46**, 120–124.

Baumgartel, H. and J. W. Goldstein (1967) 'Need and value shifts in college training groups.' *Journal of Applied Behavioral Science*, **3**, 87–101.

Bennis, W., R. Burke, H. Cutter, H. Harrington and J. Hoffman (1957) 'A note on some problems of measurement and prediction in a training group.' *Group Psychotherapy*, **10**, 328–341.

Bowers, N. D. and R. S. Soar (1961) 'Evaluation of laboratory human relations training for classroom teachers.' Unpublished manuscript, University of South Carolina.

Burke, H. L. and W. G. Bennis (1961) 'Changes in perception of self and others during human relations training.' *Human Relations*, **14**, 165–182.

Campbell, J. P. and M. D. Dunnette (1968) 'Effectiveness of T-group experiences in managerial training and development.' *Psychological Bulletin*, **70**, 73–104.

Carron, T. J. (1964) 'Human relations training and attitude change: a vector analysis.' *Personnel Psychology*, **17**, 403–424.

Carson, R. C. and M. Lakin (1963) 'Some effects of group sensitivity experience.' Paper read at Southeastern Psychological Association meeting, Miami Beach, Florida, April 1963.

Castle, P. F. C. (1952) 'The evaluation of human relations training for supervisors.' *Occupational Psychology*, 25, 191–205.

Cureton, L. (1968) Unpublished M.Ed. thesis, University of Sussex.

Dorris, R. J., D. Levinson and E. Hanfmann (1954) 'Authoritarian personality studied by a new variation of the sentence completion technique.' *Journal of Abnormal and Social Psychology*, 49, 99–108.

Dunnette, M. D. (1962) 'Personnel management.' *Annual Review of Psychology*, 13, 285–314.

Elliott, A. G. P. (1958) 'An experiment in group dynamics.' Unpublished manuscript. Simon Engineering Ltd.

Fleishman, E. A. and E. F. Harris (1962) 'Patterns of leadership behavior related to employee grievances and turnover.' *Personnel Psychology*, 15, 43–56.

French, J. R. P., J. J. Sherwood and D. L. Bradford (1966) 'Change in self-identity in a management training conference.' *Journal of Applied Behavioral Science*, 2, 210–218.

Gassner, S., J. Gold and A. M. Snadowsky (1964) 'Changes in the phenomenal field as a result of human relations training.' *Journal of Psychology*, 58, 33–41.

Grater, M. (1959) 'Changes in self and other attitudes in a leadership training group.' *Personnel and Guidance Journal*, 37, 493–496.

Halpin, A. W. (1957) 'The leader behavior and effectiveness of aircraft commanders.' In Stogdill, R. M. and Coons, A. E. (Eds.), *Leader Behaviour: Its Description and Measurement*. Ohio: Ohio State University, 65–68.

Harrison, R. (1962) 'The impact of the laboratory on perceptions of others by the experimental group.' In C. Argyris (Ed.), *Interpersonal Competence and Organizational Effectiveness*. Homewood, Ill.: Irwin-Dorsey.

Harrison, R. (1966) 'Cognitive change and participation in a sensitivity training laboratory.' *Journal of Consulting Psychology*, 30, 517–520.

House, R. J. (1967) 'T-group education and leadership effectiveness: a review of the empiric literature and a critical evaluation.' *Personnel Psychology*, 20, 1–32.

Kassarjian, W. M. (1962) 'A study of Riesman's theory of social character.' *Sociometry*, 25, 213–230.

Kassarjian, H. H. (1965) 'Social character and sensitivity training.' *Journal of Applied Behavioral Science*, 1, 433–440.

Kernan, J. P. (1964) 'Laboratory human relations training: its effect on the "personality" of supervisory engineers.' *Dissertation Abstracts*, 25, 665–666.

Martin, H. O. (1957) 'The assessment of training.' *Personnel Management*, 39, 88–93.

Meigniez, R. (1961) 'Evaluation des resultats de la formation.' L'Association Francaise pour l'Accroissement de la Productivite, Paris.

Miles, M. B. (1965) 'Changes during and following laboratory training: a clinical-experimental study.' *Journal of Applied Behavioral Science*, 1, 215–242.

Oshry, B. I. and R. Harrison (1966) 'Transfer from here-and-now to there-and-then: Changes in organizational problem diagnosis stemming from T-group training.' *Journal of Applied Behavioral Science*, 2, 185–198.

Rubin, I. (1967) 'The reduction of prejudice through laboratory training.' *Journal of Applied Behavioral Science*, 3, 29–50.

Schutz, W. C. (1958) *FIRO: A Three-Dimensional Theory of Interpersonal Behavior*. New York: Holt, Rinehart & Winston.

Schutz, W. C. and V. L. Allen (1966) 'The effects of a T-group laboratory on interpersonal behavior.' *Journal of Applied Behavioral Science*, 2, 265–286.

Smith, P. B. (1964) 'Attitude changes associated with training in human relations.' *British Journal of Social and Clinical Psychology*, 3, 104–113.

Zimet, C. N. and H. J. Fine (1955) 'Personality changes with a group therapeutic experience in a human relations seminar.' *Journal of Abnormal and Social Psychology*, 51, 68–73.

Attitude Changes Associated with Training in Human Relations[*]

Peter B. Smith

School of Social Studies, University of Sussex

Members of training groups in human relations change their attitudes toward social behaviour in a way that members of other groups do not. Those trained showed a convergence toward median scores on scales measuring their attitudes toward power and close personal relationships. These attitudes were found to be related to perceptions of their actual behaviour by other group members. Perceptions of the behaviour of those scoring median on the attitude scales were generally consonant with current descriptions of 'effective' behaviour.

Introduction

Training in human relations by non-directive methods has now been under way in the United States for more than 15 years. Despite the pioneering work of Bion (1961) more than 20 years ago in London, only in the last 5 years have such methods been widely used in Britain. The phrase 'training in human relations by non-directive methods' is used here to mean any method which relies primarily on the trainee achieving insights into the nature of social behaviour by discovery rather than by formal instruction. The intentions of those developing non-directive training have been to set up conditions which facilitate such learning by discovery. This has normally meant bringing together a group of people for the purpose of studying the behaviour of their own group, with the aid of a staff member, often known as the trainer. The trainer's task is to indicate by occasional interventions, in the form of questions or tentative interpretations, the areas of behaviour which he regards as providing useful data for study. Such trainer interventions often do not focus directly on the tasks which the groups may set themselves, but on the processes by which the goals of the group are achieved. The development of these methods in Britain has been surveyed by Crichton (1962).

The assessment of the insights which are achieved by those undergoing training poses methodological problems which few studies have yet over-

[*] Published in the *British Journal of Social and Clinical Psychology*, 1964, 3, 104–112.

come. Miles (1959, 1960) has provided a concise summary of contemporary training aims in terms of increases in:

'Sensitivity: the ability to perceive what is actually going on in a social situation (including both behavioural events and inferred feelings of other persons).

Diagnostic ability: the skill of assessing on-going social situations in a way that enables effective action; the employment of appropriate explanatory categories to understand reasons for presented interaction.

Action skill: the ability to intervene effectively in on-going situations in such a way as to maximize personal and group effectiveness and satisfaction . . .'.

The most direct test of increases in these three variables would be a study of the job behaviour of those trained, since a crucial component of training must be that the insights achieved are transferable by the individual into his normal life-situation. Miles (1960) showed that the job behaviour of 34 schoolteachers was perceived to change after training, both by the teachers themselves and by their associates. The teachers perceived themselves in ways which Miles classified as 'more sensitive to the needs of others' and 'showing greater action skill', while the associates most often saw the teachers as showing improved leadership skills and communicating more openly. These changes were not found among the controls. In a study by Harrison, reported in Argyris (1962), changes were examined in the ways in which those who had been trained perceived associates who had not. It was found that descriptions by at least some managers of their untrained associates showed an increased use of 'interpersonal–emotional' terms. The controls described their associates uniformly in terms of 'rational–intellective' concepts. The trained managers were thus utilizing data about their associates which the controls were discarding as unimportant. This change would be most closely related to increases in Miles' variable sensitivity. These and other studies of training outcomes are discussed more fully in Smith (1962b).

The present study examines changes in the attitudes toward social behaviour of those trained; such changes may *imply* increases in Miles' three variables. The attitudes considered were those toward control behaviour, which is concerned with power, and affection behaviour, which is concerned with close personal relationships. Control and affection behaviours are among the most important in the interaction of non-directive training groups. Issues relating to control behaviour often focus on the role of the trainer who, by refusing to lead in the expected manner, sets the group a leadership problem which it must solve. Likewise, issues relating to affection behaviour usually arise as concerns about how much each individual shall reveal of his personal feelings. The training group is a situation which arouses mild anxiety in many people. Faced with ambiguity, each person soon shows his characteristic patterns of origination of control and affection behaviours.

Attitudes toward control and affection behaviours were measured on four Guttman scales derived from Schutz's (1958) FIRO. For each behaviour one scale (the 'expected' scale) measures how often the respondent expects to show the behaviour himself, and the second scale ('wanted' scale) measures how often he wants others to show the behaviour. If the simple postulate is established that we seek to repeat those patterns of behaviour that we find rewarding, both scales can be considered as yielding data as to what the respondent finds more rather than less rewarding. A respondent with a high 'expected' score and a low 'wanted' score will be most highly rewarded when his behaviour is more active than that of others in his group. Conversely, a respondent with a low 'expected' score and a high 'wanted' score will be most highly rewarded when he can behave more passively than most members of his group. In this paper the difference between a man's 'expected' and 'wanted' scores will be referred to as his reward score. The use of the reward score will be to predict whether an individual prefers control behaviour to affection behaviour. As such it clearly measures only the *relative* rewards derivable by the individual from these two behaviours; there is not usually any reason to expect reward scores to relate to an individual's *overall* reward levels, for example whether he is satisfied or dissatisfied with his membership of a group. This distinction is a familiar one in economics, and has been discussed at length in Homans (1961) and Thibaut and Kelly (1959). Reward scores were divided as nearly as possible into equal thirds described as positive, zero and negative. A positive reward score is one for which the 'expected' score exceeds the 'wanted' score.

Schutz suggests that those with positive or negative reward scores tend to respond to anxiety-provoking situations in a fixed way, whereas those with zero reward scores are less anxious and therefore more able to respond to any situation adaptively. For example, in the case of control behaviour, the negative reward scorer tends to avoid or withdraw from situations in which he must exercise control, so as to minimize his anxieties about controlling people; the positive reward scorer exercises compulsive control wherever he can, in order to reassure anxieties that he is basically incapable of controlling others; but the zero reward scorer is able both to control and to be controlled, as the situation demands, without undue anxiety.

The changes resulting from non-directive training will vary with the personality of each individual. Those with positive reward scores may be expected to learn of some of the unintended effects of their behaviour, and to become more skilled in regulating their patterns of interventions in accord with the needs of the situation. Those with negative reward scores may learn of the greater rewards to be derived from active intervention. A convergence toward the median may therefore be predicted. This expectation may be compared with Berlew's (1960) findings relating sensitivity to motive strength. Using projective tests, he found that ability to predict other people's perceptions of their own behaviour was greatest among those who scored median on tests of need-power and need-affiliation. If projective measures of need-power and need-affiliation can be considered as equivalent to Guttman scale measures of attitudes toward control and affection, Berlew's findings indicate maximum sensitivity among median scorers.

The mechanism whereby such convergence toward the median might occur can be readily envisaged. One of the processes encouraged by trainers is the 'giving and receiving of feedback'. This is a process whereby group members tell each other what impact their behaviour has had on them. Training group members thus obtain a much fuller picture of the effects of their behaviour on others than they do in everyday life. The permissive atmosphere of a training group provides the member with an opportunity to try out and learn new roles or methods of responding to familiar situations.

The prediction of appreciable changes in attitudes after training poses the question of whether the attitudes are related to actual behaviour. Since the FIRO scales used take the form of action-oriented statements (e.g. 'I let other people decide what to do'), a positive relationship may be foreseen. Borg (1960), Sapolsky (1960) and Smith (1962a) have reported significant relationships between FIRO scores and independent measures of actual behaviour, such as amount of verbal participation.

Method

All subjects were either managers on training courses or undergraduates studying management at various universities. All but two were men. The managers were predominantly graduates of between 30 and 40. The 108 experimental subjects were members of eleven non-directive training groups, four of undergraduates and seven of managers. The 44 control subjects were members of six discussion groups, one of undergraduates and five of managers. These discussions were led by a staff member, acting in a more or less directive role, and considered aspects of social psychology relevant to management problems. Manager groups mostly met intensively for a few weeks while undergraduate groups lasted through the academic year.

The attitude measure used was Schutz's (1958) FIRO questionnaire, which consisted originally of six Guttman scales describing the respondent's perception of how often he performs certain behaviours and how often he likes others to do so. The four scales used in this study were slightly revised for British usage, and were those describing attitudes toward control and affection behaviours.

Subjects completed the FIRO questionnaire near the beginning and again near the end of their course. At the same time all but three groups made checklist nominations of the behaviours which they had perceived in other members of their group. These nominations were used to test the validity of the FIRO reward scores. The checklist comprised six control behaviours, six affection behaviours and three behaviours which were not classifiable as control or affection behaviours:

Control behaviours

   Striving for individual recognition
   Discussing usefulness of meetings
   Dividing up the task
   Making rules or laying down procedures
   Attempting to dominate or to control
   Rebelling or obstructing the group

Affection behaviours

   Laughing and showing happiness
   Attempting to preserve group unity
   Reconciling antagonisms
   Attempting to draw people in
   Showing close friendship
   Discussing close personal details

Other behaviours

   Withdrawing from group activity
   Disliking or rejecting others
   Submitting to others' wishes

Results

The coefficients of reproducibility of the four Guttman scales of FIRO are shown in Table 1. Highly significant test–retest reliability was found for both control and affection reward scores. When positive, zero and negative scores were compared, using the scores obtained early and late during each group's duration, chi-square for control was 53·3, and for affection 39·4

3

Table 1—*Coefficients of reproducibility of*
FIRO scales

FIRO scale	Coefficient
Expressed control	0·91
Wanted control	0·93
Expressed affection	0·96
Wanted affection	0·94

(Smith, 1962a). Both these values of chi-square are significant for 4 degrees of freedom at $p < 0.001$.

While the reward scores are therefore reliable within gross limits, this does not necessarily mean that no changes occurred in the attitudes of those trained. The predicted changes are:

(i) a fall in positive reward scores, and

(ii) a rise in negative reward scores.

Table 2 compares the changes in non-directive training groups and the control discussion groups.

Table 2—*Number of subjects showing rise or fall in reward scores*

	Initial reward scores								
	Positive			Zero			Negative		
Subjects	+	=	−	+	=	−	+	=	−
Experimentals									
Controls	5	6	29	11	5	11	20	6	15
Affection	4	7	12	11	5	12	30	9	8
Controls									
Controls	8	3	11	2	2	5	7	3	3
Affection	3	2	8	5	2	6	8	2	6

In the experimental groups, 91 scores changed in the predicted direction and 32 in the reverse direction. This is highly significant ($p < 0.001$: 1-tailed binomial test).

In the control groups, 36 scores changed in the direction predicted for the experimental groups and 24 in the reverse direction. This change is not significant. When the change found in the experimental group is compared with that in the control group, the difference is again significant ($p < 0.001$). The most marked changes in the experimental groups were the fall in positive control reward scores and the rise in negative affection reward scores. The method of analysis adopted can give no indication of the magnitude of the changes found, but it does show that they occurred frequently.

The division of control and affection reward scores into equal thirds means that the subjects can be subdivided into nine separate types. However it is not expected that the behaviour of each of the nine types will be differentially perceived by others. For example, subjects with negative reward scores will be predominantly inactive, making it difficult for others to perceive control or affection behaviours: it is predicted that they will be perceived as showing 'neither control nor affection' behaviours. The nine types have been combined into the five classes for which different predictions may be made. These are:

1. Control reward score positive and affection reward score negative.
2. Affection reward score positive and control reward score negative.
3. Both reward scores positive, or one positive and the other zero.
4. Both reward scores zero.
5. Both reward scores negative, or one negative and the other zero.

The general predictions were made that positive reward scores would be associated with frequently occurring perceptions of control and affection behaviours, while zero reward scores would be associated with a chance occurrence of perceptions of the behaviours, and negative reward scores with a significant lack of perceptions of the behaviours. The specific predictions derivable for each class are shown in Table 3.

The occurrence of each of the 15 behaviours on the checklist was analysed separately. The degree to which each of the five classes was characterized by the various behaviours was established by consideration of the occurrence of checklist nominations in the class, relative to their occurrence in the total sample. Ratios were computed for each behaviour and every class, as follows:

$$\text{Ratio} = \frac{\text{Actual no. of nominations in class}}{\text{Expected no. of nominations in class}}$$

where

expected nominations = total nominations for all classes × the proportion of total subjects in the class.

Table 3 tests whether the most and least characteristic behaviours of members of each class were those that had been predicted from FIRO reward scores. The ratios were rank ordered and the predictions tested by the Mann–Whitney U-test.

The predictions are significantly upheld for Classes 1, 3 and 4, and

Table 3—*Relationship between behaviour predicted from FIRO reward scores and behaviour assessments by other group members*

Class	Prediction	p
1	C will predominate	$<0\cdot02$
2	A will predominate	$<0\cdot10$
3	C and A will predominate	$<0\cdot01$
4	No predominant behaviour	C<N, A n.s.
		A<C, N n.s.
		N<C, A n.s.
5	N will predominate	n.s.

Key: C—Control behaviour
A—Affection behaviour
N—Behaviours which are neither control nor affection
The classes are defined above.

approach significance for Class 2. Class 5 contains those group members whose behaviour is least easily perceived, so that the failure of the prediction is not unexpected.

This paper has outlined some of the stated aims of those active in non-directive training. It has also given evidence as to the changes actually found in some training groups. If the training is successful, there should be a close correspondence between training aims and actual changes. The ratios calculated show which of the behaviours on the checklist were perceived as most characteristic of group members of the various personality types derived from the FIRO reward scores. Since those trained tend toward zero reward scores, those who already have zero reward scores should come closest to exemplifying Miles' three training aims—'sensitivity', 'diagnostic ability' and 'action skill', while those with positive or negative scores should be less well placed.

Table 4 shows the distribution between the five classes of the behaviours on the checklist. For each behaviour a value of chi-square was computed to test the randomness of the occurrence of the behaviours. The table includes only those behaviours which were perceived differentially among members of the different classes ($p < 0\cdot05$). The table shows marked differences between the behaviours characterizing the different classes, and also in the degree to which the classes were characterized by distinct behaviours. Members of Class 1 were characterized by self-oriented high activity control behaviours and a mimumum of affection behaviour. Members of Class 2 were characterized by the absence of control behaviours rather than a high incidence of affection behaviours. Members of Class 3 showed predominantly high activity behaviours, both control and affection, many of which

Table 4—*Behaviour of the different classes of training group members*

Behaviours	Class					Chi-square
	1	2	3	4	5	
Control						
Striving for individual recognition	1·68	0·73	1·28	0·51	0·64	36·86
Discussing usefulness of meetings	1·12	0·74	1·17	1·24	0·85	12·94
Dividing up the task	0·89	0·52	1·06	2·25	0·95	11·27
Attempting to dominate or to control	1·57	0·56	1·49	0·36	0·58	38·00
Affection						
Laughing and showing happiness	1·02	0·79	1·25	0·98	0·83	14·36
Reconciling antagonisms	0·40	1·10	1·14	1·86	0·94	10·27
Showing close friendship	0·37	0·96	1·58	0·64	0·78	17·68
Neither						
Withdrawing from group activity	0·82	0·86	0·61	0·98	1·42	22·30

The classes are defined on p. 49. Ratios are obtained by dividing actual numbers of checklist nominations by the number to be expected on the basis of nominations in the total population. The table includes only those behaviours whose distribution between the classes differed from randomness at $p < 0.05$. The values of chi-square are shown on the right.

were self-oriented. Conversely, Class 5 showed a lack of high activity control behaviours and typically withdrew from group activity. The most frequent behaviours in Classes 1, 2, 3 and 5 were thus high activity self-oriented behaviours or else withdrawal from group activity.

However, it is the behaviour of Class 4 members which is of particular interest because the class is made up of zero reward scorers, towards which other members of training groups have been shown to change their attitudes. Members of Class 4 were the most clearly characterized of any class, obtaining both the highest and lowest values of the ratio. The characteristic behaviours were those that take into account not only the needs of the individual but also those of the group. In contrast to the infrequent self-oriented behaviours, the Class 4 member was often perceived as 'dividing up the task', 'reconciling antagonisms' and 'discussing usefulness of meetings'.

Discussion

The training group in human relations is a potent agent for change of attitudes about social behaviour. The effects of the individual's learning about the ways in which others perceive his behaviours may include marked changes in his habitual behaviours and in the way others come to perceive these behaviours. The evidence cited in support of these statements in this paper gives only general indications of their probable truth. Human relations training is currently conducted with many different emphases and no evidence is yet forthcoming as to whether these different emphases affect the training outcomes. The two Leeds training groups were conducted as 'sensitivity training', which usually means that the trainer indicates a greater preference for discussing participants' feelings rather than the development of group roles. On the other hand the six Simon (Engineering) training groups had trainers who behaved in more varied ways and the groups participated also in more formal lectures and exercises in social psychology. The three Cambridge training groups showed an intermediate emphasis.

Burke and Bennis (1961) reported increases in similarity of perceptions of individuals by self and others in training groups. Such a study gives no evidence as to increases in *sensitivity*, since perceptions late in the life of a training group are based on much greater information than earlier perceptions. The present study, in contrast, shows that attitudes changed toward the median, and that median scorers were perceived in ways that have been described; but early perceptions were not separated from late ones. Thus the changes found could not be artifacts derived from the possibility that training group members may come to know each other much better than the control group members.

Early writers in the field of human relations often stressed the need to reduce or eliminate social conflict. Their critics (e.g. Whyte (1956), McNair (1957)) tended to feel that this emphasis represented an attack on individuality, a too-ready advocacy of submission to group pressures in the interests of smooth social working. Recent writers on human relations training have laid much more emphasis on the need to recognize and bring into the open substantive conflicts (e.g. Argyris, 1962). Effective group behaviour is seen as that which is based on a realistic knowledge of differences of viewpoint as well as of similarities. Parallel thinking is implicit in Miles' definition of 'action skill' cited earlier, where he states that interventions should maximize both personal and group satisfactions. Where these are not reconciled there will be conflict. This conception of effective behaviour is well illustrated by the present findings. The zero reward scorer is perceived as showing close friendship as infrequently as the self-oriented control behaviours. Indeed there is a tendency for him also to be perceived as 'rebelling or obstructing the group', but chi-square for this behaviour does not quite achieve the required significance level.

The changes in attitudes found can be seen as a response to a situation in which customary behaviours proved to be inappropriate. Whether the changes persist will depend primarily on the reactions of the trained man's associates in the weeks after his return from the course, and on the degree of continuing support which he receives from others who participated in the training.

References

Argyris, C. (1962) *Interpersonal Competence and Organizational Effectiveness.* London: Tavistock.

Berlew, D. E. (1961) 'Interpersonal sensitivity and motive strength.' *J. abnorm. soc. Psychol.*, **63**, 390–394.

Bion, W. R. (1961) *Experiences in Groups.* London: Tavistock.

Borg, W. R. (1960) 'The prediction of role behaviour in small groups from personality variables.' *J. abnorm. soc. Psychol.*, **60**, 112–117.

Burke, R. L. and W. G. Bennis (1961) 'Changes in perceptions of self and others during human relations training.' *Hum. Relat.*, **14**, 165–182.

Crichton, Anne (1962) 'Personnel Management and Working Groups.' *Institute of Personnel Management, Occasional Papers*, **18**.

Homans, G. C. (1961) *Social Behaviour: Its Elementary Forms.* New York: Harcourt–Brace.

McNair, M. (1957) 'What price human relations?' *Harvard Bus. Rev.* **35**.

Miles, M. B. (1959) *Learning to Work in Groups.* New York: Teachers' College, Bureau of Publications.

Miles, M. B. (1960) 'Human relations training: processes and outcomes.' *J. couns. Psychol.*, **7**, 301–306.

Sapolsky, A. (1960) 'Effect of interpersonal relationships upon verbal conditioning.' *J. abnorm. soc. Psychol.*, **40**, 241–246.

Schutz, W. C. (1958) *FIRO: A Three-Dimensional Theory of Interpersonal Behaviour.* New York: Rinehart.

Smith, P. B. (1962a) 'Role differentiation in small social groups.' Cambridge: Unpublished Ph.D. thesis.

Smith, P. B. (1962b) 'A survey of research into attitude and behaviour changes resulting from "human relations" training.' *Working Papers in Industrial Management*, I. Industrial Management Division, University of Leeds.

Thibaut, J. W. and H. H. Kelley (1959) *The Social Psychology of Groups.* New York: Wiley.

Whyte, W. H. (1956) *The Organisation Man.* New York: Simon & Schuster.

Changes in the Phenomenal Field as a Result of Human Relations Training*

Suzanne M. Gassner
Jerome Gold
Alvin M. Snadowsky

Department of Student Life,
The City College of the City University of New York

A. Introduction

Fundamental to the phenomenological approach to the understanding of human personality is the differentiation between the phenomenal self (including the self-concept) and the general phenomenal field (7). A relatively high degree of congruence between an individual's self-concept and his ideal self is considered to be an indication of good adjustment (6, pp. 55–75; 8; 13). Moreover, it has been found that an individual's acceptance of himself is positively and significantly correlated with his acceptance of others (2, 11, 12, 14).

Recently, a number of experiments reported that human-relations training leads to changes in the phenomenal self. Burke and Bennis (5), using an adaptation of Osgood's Semantic Differential to test the changes brought about by a three-week human-relations training program, reported a significant reduction in the discrepancy between the participants' self-image and ideal image. Grater (9) arrived at similar results using the Bills' Index of Adjustment and Values to test the effectiveness of an 11-week leadership training program for 30 college students. However, the hypothesized decrease in the discrepancy between the average other person and the ideal self was not found to be significant, though results were in the predicted direction.

The City College of New York conducts a three-day human-relations training program (HRP) based on the design pioneered by Bradford, Lippitt and Gibb (4). The aims of the program are to help the participants gain an understanding of behavior (both their own and that of others) and to provide an atmosphere conducive to change. Initial evaluation of the HRP was

* Published as a separate and in *The Journal of Psychology*, 1964, **58**, 33–41. We wish to thank the City College Fund for the grant-in-aid which supported the publication of this research.

55

based on the participants' responses to a postmeeting reaction form. Reactions to the program were overwhelmingly enthusiastic, with 99 per cent of the students reporting that they had gained new skills and insights. Staff trainers have also reported that program participants became progressively more effective group members during the course of the HRP.

Based on these preliminary observations, it appears that The City College human-relations program, though considerably shorter in duration than those programs mentioned above, might nevertheless produce similar fundamental changes in the phenomenal self. It is therefore hypothesized that participation in the HRP causes an increase in the similarity between (a) an individual's self-concept and ideal-self concept and (b) an individual's self-concept and image of the average other.

The possibility that changes occur in areas of the participant's phenomenal field other than in his phenomenal self also seemed worth investigating. Bass (1) studied the kinds of changes that occur in the general phenomenal field as a result of the training programs. He found that human-relations training leads to an increase in participants' sensitivity and understanding of interpersonal relations. Other kinds of attitude changes may be produced as a result of such programs. An integral part of the HRP is the demonstration and practice of skills required for effective democratic leadership. It is therefore expected that a significant increase in an individual's understanding of democratic leadership functions, and changes in his attitudes concerning such functions, occur as a result of participation in the HRP.

The first two experiments of this investigation, which parallel those reported in the literature, used a modified form of the Bills' Index of Adjustment and Values and a graphic rating scale to measure the changes that occurred in the divergence between the self-concept, the ideal-self concept and the image of the other, for participants in the HRP. In the third experiment, attitudes toward democratic leadership functions, and understanding of them, were measured. However, unlike several of the research efforts referred to above, the instruments used were also administered to a control group.

B. Experiment 1

1. Method

(a) Subjects. Ss were 67 City College undergraduates. Forty-six were student trainees who attended the sixth semiannual HRP, the Experimental (E1) group. Twenty-one were students who submitted applications for the forthcoming program, the Control (C1) group.

(b) *Procedure*. One day prior to the onset of the HRP and two days after the completion of the Workshop, a modified form of the Bills' Index of Adjustment and Values (3) was administered individually to each subject. Ss were told that they were participating in a study to obtain information about the beliefs and attitudes that C.C.N.Y. students have about themselves and other people. Using a series of 50 adjectives, Ss rated themselves on the following statements: (a) 'This is characteristic of me', (b) 'I would like this to be characteristic of me', and (c) 'Most C.C.N.Y. students my age would like this to be characteristic of them'. Each statement headed a separate page followed by the series of adjectives.

(c) *Scoring*. The absolute discrepancies between the various statements on each of the adjective ratings were calculated for each S. The geometric mean was computed to provide a D score for each S for both administrations. Nonparametric statistics were used in the analysis of the data, because the distribution of the D values is not known.

2. *Results*

Results of the Wilcoxon matched-pairs signed-ranks test (Table 1) show that there was a significant increase in similarity between self-perceptions and ideal-self perceptions in both the E1 and C1 groups. In addition, both groups showed a significant increase in similarity between self-perceptions and average-other perceptions.

Table 1—*Increase in similarity between self-ideal and self-other perceptions sixth HRP—modified Bills' Index of adjustment and values (Wilcoxon matched-pairs signed-ranks test with z score transformations)*

Population	T	N	z	p
Self-ideal				
Experimental	242·5	46	3·26	0·0006[a]
Control	18·0	21	3·40	0·0006[b]
Self-other				
Experimental	87·0	46	4·96	<0·0001[a]
Control	15·0	21	3·48	0·0004[b]

[a] one-tailed test
[b] two-tailed test

However, when the changes in self-ideal D scores (from the first to the second administration of the test) were examined, it was found that E1 group changes did not differ significantly from C1 group changes. Similarly, self-other D scores did not change in a significantly different fashion for the two groups (Table 2).

Table 2—*Tests of the differences between D scores for the experimental and control groups*

Test	Experiment 1 (N=67)		Experiment 2 (N=72)	
	Self-ideal	Self-other	Self-ideal	Self-other
Rank test (z)	0·04	1·57	0·44	1·59
Sign test (χ^2)	0·06	0·57	0·06	3·60

C. Experiment 2

1. *Method*

(*a*) *Subjects*. Ss were 72 City College undergraduates. Forty-five were student trainees who attended the seventh HRP (E2 group) and 27 were students enrolled in psychology courses at the college (C2 group).

(*b*) *Procedure*. In the E2 group, a modified form of the Burke and Bennis graphic-rating-scale series was administered to the trainees at both the introductory session and the closing session of the HRP.

Ss were told that they were participating in a study of word meanings and that 'the object of the study is to find out how you like to describe yourself and others'.

Three concepts were rated against a uniform series of bipolar traits that were selected for their relevance to the attitudes being measured. The concepts were (a) the way I actually am in a City College group, (b) the way I would like to be in a City College group, and (c) the way other City College students generally act in a group. Each concept headed a separate page and was followed by the series of 18 scales.

The instructions given for the second administration were 'to take into account your experiences during the past three days. You may feel free to change your original responses or to respond as you did initially. In any case your answers should be an accurate description of yourself and other people as you see them.'

Control group Ss completed the graphic rating scale twice, with a three-day time interval, during regularly scheduled classroom sessions. The instructions were identical to those used for the E2 group.

(*c*) *Scoring*. D scores were computed using the procedure described in Experiment 1.

2. Results

The results of the Wilcoxon matched-pair signed-ranks test (Table 3), indicate that in the E2 and C2 groups there was a significant increase in similarity between self-perceptions and average-other perceptions. However, unlike the findings of Experiment 1, there was no significant increase in similarity between the self-concept and the ideal-self concept in either the E2 or C2 groups.

Table 3—*Increase in similarity between self-ideal and self-other perceptions seventh HRP—graphic rating scale (Wilcoxon matched-pair signed-ranks test with z score transformations)*

Population	T	N	z	p
Self-ideal				
Experimental	405·5	45	1·26	0·10[a]
Control	156·0	27	0·79	0·43[b]
Self-other				
Experimental	232·0	45	3·21	0·0007[a]
Control	105·0	27	2·02	0·041[b]

[a] one-tailed test
[b] two-tailed test

Using both the rank test for two independent samples and the sign test (Table 2) it was found that when the changes in the E2 and C2 groups were compared, the differences were not statistically significant.

D. Experiment 3

1. Method

(a) *Subjects*. Ss were 122 City College undergraduates. Ninety-four were student trainees who attended the seventh and eighth HRPs (E3 groups) and 28 were students enrolled in psychology courses at the City College (C3 group).

(b) *Procedure*. At the introductory sessions of the seventh and eighth HRPs, a 'Democratic Leadership Attitude Scale' was administered to a group of 43 and 51 trainees respectively. The 23 items of the scale were selected from the Ideology Questionnaire* by a panel of judges (staff trainers). Only

* Adapted from an Ideology Questionnaire developed by David Jenkins and others at Bethel National Training Laboratories in Group Development.

questions that measured attitudes toward and understanding of democratic leadership were chosen. Ss were asked to rate the statements on a five-point scale (from strongly disagree to strongly agree). They were told that the statements referred to opinions regarding a number of leadership issues about which some people agreed and others disagreed. The second administration was conducted during the final evaluation session. Ss were instructed to 'feel free to change your original responses or respond as you did initially'.

Control group Ss completed the first administration of the Democratic Leadership Attitude Scale during a regularly scheduled classroom session. Two days later Ss were again asked to complete the forms.

(c) *Scoring.* Using the judges' responses as a criterion, each of the 23 items was assigned a correct answer that was either 'agree' or 'disagree'. Subjects received points as follows: (a) If the correct answer was 'agree' an answer of 'agree or strongly agree' received $+1$; an answer of 'disagree or strongly disagree' received -1; and an answer of 'undecided' equalled zero. (b) If the correct answer was 'disagree', the scoring was in reverse to the above. The maximum score was 23; the minimum, -23.

2. *Results*

Whereas both E3 and C3 groups were initially equal in their attitudes toward and understanding of democratic leadership concepts, the difference between the groups after the HRP was statistically significant (Table 4). This difference was caused by the increase in understanding of democratic leadership concepts that occurred in the experimental group.

Table 4—*Tests of the differences between means on the democratic leadership attitude test*

Group	N	Pre-test	Post-test	t
Seventh HRP				
Experimental	43	12·7	16·4	5·32[b]
Control	28	12·6	12·3	0·52
t	—	0·098	3·94[b]	—
Eighth HRP				
Experimental	51	12·5	15·8	6·75[b]
Control	28	12·6	12·3	0·52
t	—	0·096	3·27[a]	—

[a] Significant at 0·01 level
[b] Significant at 0·001 level

E. Discussion

HRP trainees shifted their perceptions of themselves and others in the predicted directions. This aspect of the results is similar to the findings that Grater, and Burke and Bennis report. However, unlike the experiments they report, when a control group was used, it was found that similar changes in the phenomenal-self attitudes could be demonstrated, and the extent of change between E and C groups was shown to be statistically insignificant. The control group adds an important dimension to this research because the information it provides forces a rejection of the initial conclusion that HRP participation causes change in the phenomenal self. If a control group had been used in previous research, the conclusions may have been modified or reversed and personality structure may have been found to be more stable than the earlier experiments have indicated.

Another possible interpretation of the results of earlier studies is that methodological inadequacies of self-rating scales counteracted attempts to measure changes in the phenomenal self. Wylie (16) suggests that a subject may try to present himself as having attitudes other than those that are actually true of himself, and that he may not be willing to reveal certain information about himself. A further consideration is the effect of familiarity on future responses to scale words. Taylor (15) found a marked increase in the similarity between the self-image and the ideal-self image on repeated tests conducted over a short time interval. Finally, Jourard and Lasakow (10) have pointed out that subjects will describe their attitudes and opinions much more openly than they otherwise will, when the things described do not relate directly to the subjects' own perception of their personality; such studies do not cause as much defensiveness on the part of the participants and thus contribute less to distortions in their responses. These interpretations suggest that conclusions pertaining to changes in the phenomenal self that occur over a short period of time should be re-examined.

Human-relations training seems to stimulate growth and understanding in areas not directly related to the phenomenal self. Because highly significant changes in the participants' understanding of an attitudes toward democratic leadership were found to occur during the training experience, while no such changes occurred for members of the control group, it was concluded that the HRP is effective in teaching certain leadership principles and in developing particular attitudes toward democratic methods. This study and the one conducted by Bass (1) point to other dimensions of the phenomenal field which have been demonstrated to change over a short time period. It might be worthwhile, therefore, to investigate further the kinds of changes in concepts, other than those pertaining to the phenomenal self, that may be the outcome of human-relations training.

F. Summary

Recently research claims to demonstrate that changes in the phenomenal self occur as a result of human-relations training. Participants in a three-day human-relations program were tested on an adjective checklist and a graphic rating scale, which were used as indices of change in the phenomenal self. In general, predictions that a reduction in the trainees' discrepancy scores between the self-concept and both the ideal self and the image of the other were confirmed. Similar changes were observed to occur in the control group, but the differences between the results for the experimental and the control groups were not significant. However, when a measure of attitudes toward and understanding of democratic leadership functions was administered to both training participants and a control group, a highly significant change was found to occur for the experimental group, while no such change was observed in the control group. This information suggests that (a) personality structure may be more stable than the reports of recent experiments indicate, (b) methodological inadequacies of self-rating scales may interfere with attempts to measure changes in the phenomenal self, and (c) the measurement of attitudes other than those relating to the self is a fruitful area for further investigation in human-relations programs.

References

1. Bass, B. (1962) 'Reactions to Twelve Angry Men as a measure of sensitivity training.' *J. Appl. Psychol.*, **46**, 120–124.
2. Berger, E. M. (1952) 'The relation between expressed acceptance of self and expressed acceptance of others.' *J. Abn. & Soc. Psychol.*, **47**, 778–782.
3. Bills, R. E. (1958) 'Manual for the Index of Adjustment and Values.' Auburn: Alabama Polytechnic Inst.
4. Bradford, L. P., G. L. Lippitt and J. R. Gibb. (1956) 'Human relations training in three days.' *Adult Leadership*, **4** (10), 11–26.
5. Burke, R. L. and W. G. Bennis (1961) 'Changes in perception of self and others during human relations training.' *Hum. Relat.*, **14**, 165–182.
6. Butler, J. M. and G. V. Haigh (1954) 'Changes in the relation between self-concepts and ideal concepts consequent upon client-centered counselling.' In C. Rogers, and R. Dymond, (Eds.), *Psychotherapy and Personality Change.* Chicago, Ill.: Univ. Chicago Press.
7. Combs, A. W. and D. Snygg (1959) *Individual Behaviour. A Perceptual Approach to Behavior.* (2nd ed.) New York: Harper.
8. Cowan, E. L., F. Heitzler and H. S. Axelrod (1955) 'Self-concept conflict indicators and learning.' *J. Abn. & Soc. Psychol.*, **51**, 242–245.
9. Grater, M. (1959) 'Changes in self and other attitudes in a leadership training group.' *Person. & Guid. J.*, **37**, 493–496.
10. Jourard, S. M. and P. Lasakow (1958) 'Some factors in self-disclosure.' *J. Abn. & Soc. Psychol.*, **56**, 91–98.

11. McIntyre, C. J. (1952) 'Acceptance by others and its relation to acceptance of self and others.' *J. Abn. & Soc. Psychol.*, **47**, 624–625.
12. Omwake, K. (1954) 'The relation between acceptance of self and acceptance of others shown by three personality inventories.' *J. Consult. Psychol.*, **18**, 443–446.
13. Rogers, C. R. (1951) *Client-Centered Therapy*. Boston: Houghton Mifflin.
14. Sheerer, E. T. (1949) 'An analysis of the relationship between acceptance of and respect for self and acceptance of and respect for others in ten counselling cases.' *J. Consult. Psychol.*, **13**, 169–175.
15. Taylor, D. M. (1955) 'Changes in the self concept without psychotherapy.' *J. Consult. Psychol.*, **19**, 205–209.
16. Wylie, R. C. (1960) *The Self Concept: Critical Survey of Pertinent Research Literature*. Lincoln, Nebr.: Univ. Nebraska Press.

The Reduction of Prejudice through Laboratory Training*

Irwin Rubin

Alfred P. Sloan School of Management,
Massachusetts Institute of Technology

An experiment was conducted to test the hypothesis that increases in self-acceptance, resulting from sensitivity training, have the theoretically predictable but indirect effect of reducing an individual's level of ethnic prejudice. The role of an individual's level of psychological anomy,† hypothesized to condition the influences of sensitivity training, was also examined. The results suggest that sensitivity training may well be a powerful technique in the reduction of ethnic prejudice, particularly among those who are low in psychological anomy.

Introduction

Robert Kahn has stated (1963, p. 14), 'The theory of T Groups implies that reduction in prejudice should be one of the results of a general increase in sensitivity to the needs of others and insight into one's own motives and behavior as it affects others. No research is available, however, to test this prediction'.

Prior research (Bunker, 1963, 1965; Gordon, 1950) has shown that one of the effects of sensitivity training is an increased level of self-acceptance among the participants. In addition, it has been demonstrated that the way a person feels about himself is positively related to the way he feels about others (e.g., Stock, 1949; Sheerer, 1949). These two factors when combined, suggest the following question: Does raising a person's level of self-acceptance have the theoretically predictable but indirect effect of raising his level of acceptance-of-others?

The crux of this experiment is not that sensitivity training *per se* can be demonstrated to increase acceptance-of-others. The salient point to be tested is that demonstrated changes in a theoretically related variable (self-acceptance) produce this effect.

* Published in *Journal of Applied Behavioral Science*, 3, 1967, 29–50. The author is grateful to Professors Edgar Schein, and William McKelvey and to David Meredith, all of M.I.T., for their many helpful comments on various drafts of this paper.
† For the definition of this term, see p. 70.

A second area of interest concerns the factors that might condition the kinds of learning an individual experiences as a result of sensitivity training. Certain personality types may be more susceptible than others to the influences of sensitivity training (Miles, 1960; Steele, 1965). The personality variable chosen for investigation in this study was psychological anomy. The rationale for this choice will be discussed in detail later.

Hypotheses

The following specific hypotheses were tested:

1. As a result of sensitivity training, an individual's level of self-acceptance will increase.

(a) An individual's focus during the T-group sessions (as determined by trainer ratings), leaning toward more personal areas, will be associated with increased self-acceptance.

2. As a result of sensitivity training, an individual's level of acceptance-of-others will increase.

3. Those low in anomy will increase more in self-acceptance and acceptance-of-others than those high in anomy.

(a) An individual's level of anomy will be unaffected by sensitivity training.

4. Those who increase in self-acceptance will increase more in acceptance-of-others than those who do not change or decrease in self-acceptance.

5. Changes in self-acceptance *will lead* to changes in acceptance-of-others.

Definition of variables

Sensitivity training

The major independent variable in this study is what has come to be known as sensitivity training or laboratory training.* In a broad sense, it can be defined as . . .

an educational strategy which is based primarily on the experiences generated in various social encounters by the learners themselves and aims to influence attitudes and develop competencies toward learning about human interactions (Schein and Bennis, 1965, p. 4).

Many phenomena occur within the T-group, and it is not within the scope of this study to examine the differential impact of each of these upon the variables of 'self-acceptance' and 'acceptance-of-others'. An attempt,

* For a complete discussion of all that is involved in a sensitivity training experience, see Schein and Bennis (1965).

however, was made to control for the effect of two specific aspects of all that occurred within the T-group. The trainers involved were asked to provide *for each individual*—at the end of the laboratory—the following information: (1) To what extent did the person explicitly discuss the topic of race relations (on a scale from 'not at all' to 'very much', i.e., 50 per cent of the time)? (2) What was the nature of the individual's focus during the T-group (on a 7-point scale from Group Process = 1 to Personal Development = 7)?

Self-acceptance

The term 'self-acceptance', as it is used in this paper, involves a willingness to confront ego-alien as well as ego-syntonic aspects of the self and to accept rather than deny their existence. Implicitly, it connotes some sense of rationality or 'realistic acceptance' as opposed to, for example a person's claim, 'I am superman, I accept myself as superman. Therefore all of you are underlings!'

The Dorris, Levinson, Hanfmann Sentence Completion Test (S.C.T.) (Dorris, R. J., Levinson, D. and Hanfmann, E., 1954) was used to measure the effect of sensitivity training upon an individual's level of self-acceptance. The S.C.T. includes 50 sentence stems. Half the stems use first-person pronouns and half, a third-person pronoun or proper name.* The first- and third-person items are matched in content;† e.g.,

When he gets angry he
_____
When I get angry I

The measure of self-acceptance used in this study was derived in the following manner: Individual stem completions were coded‡ for ego-threatening content.§ The term, 'ego-threatening', was defined as follows:

---

* First- and third-person items randomly distributed rather than appearing sequentially.

† The person instructed to complete each of the stems as quickly as he can using more than one word. After finishing all the items, he is asked to go back, reread his responses, and place a (+) sign next to those sentences that he feels refer to some personal experience or that reflect the way he might feel or act under the specified circumstances. If a sentence has no personal relevance, a (−) sign is used. In introducing the self-reference technique, the authors assumed that the denial of self-reference may be indicative of the subject's lack of awareness of the personal tendency expressed in the completion.

‡ Each pair of items was copied on separate pieces of paper. The respondent's identification number was placed on the *reverse side*. This procedure made it impossible for the coders to know whether the response was 'pre' or 'post'. It also eliminated the halo effect that might have been created by reading an individual's total record.

§ The correlation coefficient between two independently coded samples was 0·89. (See Johnson, 1949, p. 97, for the formula used to compute this coefficient.) The author gratefully acknowledges the assistance provided by his colleague, Tim Hall in this phase of the study.

'Any item which states or strongly implies any attitude, feelings, or action, which if accepted by* ———————— as *applying to oneself*, would involve confronting at least a mild degree of psychological pain'. For example, expression of fears, socially unacceptable responses, admission of inferiority or incompetence, extreme hostility or aggression, and so on were coded as threatening.

The assumption was then made that the more willing a person is to admit the personal relevance of ego-threatening material, the greater his level of self-acceptance. Therefore, the number of ego-threatening responses next to which the respondent placed a (+), divided by the total number of ego-threatening responses (# ET), yields the measure of self-acceptance (ETA)† used in this study.

It is important to note that, by this definition, self acceptance (ETA) can increase because the numerator increases or the denominator decreases. To clarify this point, it is hypothesized that the absolute number of statements coded as being ego-threatening will *not* change as a result of sensitivity training. The rationale here is that sensitivity training will not rid a person of his basic conflicts and anxieties nor does it attempt to help him make light of his times of crises. Instead, in some ideal sense, sensitivity training may help a person to find in himself the natural tools that enable him to effectively cope with these things. This will result, for example, from positive, nonevaluative feedback, the opportunity to test ideas and beliefs (increased 'reality testing' about oneself), and a high level of trust and openness resulting in greater authenticity. An environment is created within which there should be a reduction of an individual's need to use projective defense mechanisms which act to distort his perception of himself and others.

Acceptance-of-others

Harding and Schuman (1961) conceptualize prejudice as the departure from or failure to adhere to three ideal norms of behavior: the norm of rationality, the norm of justice, and the norm of human-heartedness. In this experiment it was decided to focus upon the norm of human-hearted-

* For the females, the phrase, 'the majority of women associated with the nursing profession', was inserted because virtually all the females in the experimental population fell into that category. For the males, who were more heterogeneous, the phrase, 'the average male in our culture', was inserted. Two forms of the scale—male and female—were used for this research.

† Throughout the remainder of this paper, the following symbols will be used:
1. Et means ego-threatening.
2. # ET means absolute number of sentences scored as ego-threatening.
3. ETA means self-acceptance as defined above.

ness (HH)* which enjoins a person's emotional *acceptance-of-others* in terms of their common humanity, no matter how different they may seem from oneself. The major dependent variable in this study, in other words, is not prejudice *per se* but only the effective component of the individual's attitude.

The scale is made up of 15 items† of the following type:

> The white school board in a community builds two new schools and fixes the school lines so that almost all the Negro children go to one new school and all the white children to the other new school. How do you suppose most of the Negroes in the community would react to this?
>
> —— a. While there are some exceptions, many Negroes are mainly concerned with getting money for food, rent, and other things, and so do not have too much interest in the matter of schools one way or the other.
>
> —— b. Every community is different, and it is almost impossible for someone not living in it to know enough about the situation to judge.
>
> —— c. The average Negro parent would not like what the school board has done about drawing school lines.
>
> —— d. The average Negro parent would simply be pleased to have a new school for his children, especially if it were equal to the white school in every way.

The measure of human-heartedness used in this study was derived in this manner: The respondent was asked to rank each of the four choices following an item from 1 ('most likely reaction') to 4 ('least likely reaction'). Each respondent's series of ranks was then compared with a theoretically ideal set of ranks‡ and the absolute difference between ranks was computed. The sum of these differences across the 15 experimental items yielded the respondent's human-heartedness score (HH). This score could range from 0–120 (i.e., 15 items times a maximum difference of 8 points for any item).

---

* Throughout the remainder of this paper, the symbol HH is used to represent an index of a person's level of acceptance-of-others.

† In addition, four control items are included to check on the extent to which response set is operating.

‡ Howard Schuman and the writer *independently* ranked all items as to how the 'most human-hearted person' would assign his ranks. We agreed on 100 per cent of the first and second ranks and 88 per cent of the third and fourth ranks, yielding an overall per cent agreement of 94 per cent.

Psychological anomy

The personality variable chosen for investigation in this research was psychological anomy,* defined as a sense of normlessness, 'the feeling that the world and oneself are adrift, wandering, lacking in clear rules and stable moorings . . . a feeling of moral emptiness' (McClosky and Schaar, 1965, p. 14). This definition is analogous to Seemans's second major usage of the alienation concept—*meaninglessness* wherein 'the individual is unclear as to what he ought to believe—when the individual's minimal standards for clarity in decision making are not met' (Coser and Rosenberg, 1964, p. 530).

McClosky and Schaar (1965) present evidence to suggest that anomic responses are powerfully governed by cognitive and personality factors independent of or in combination with social influences. They conclude that anomy 'results from impediments to interaction, communication, and learning, and is a sign of impaired socialization'. In other words, given that anomic feelings result from a lack of learning, 'whatever interferes with one's ability to learn a community's norms, or weakens one's socialization into its central patterns of belief, must be considered among the determinants of anomy' (p. 20).

In a real sense, the T-group represents for its members a new community or society with a set of norms unlike those to which the members have become accustomed. The individual participant, if he is to benefit from sensitivity training, must be able to see and understand the norms of this new culture. Only then will he be able to decide rationally† whether they are personally relevant and functional and if so, to truly internalize these new learnings.

The high anomic person might experience difficulty in understanding and internalizing the dominant norms of the T-group. Furthermore, due to the relatively short duration (two weeks) of the experiment and the here-and-now focus of the T-group, no change was expected in a person's level of anomy.

The study

Subjects

The laboratory population studied in this research were the participants

---

* The scale used to measure this variable is a nine-item Guttman scale developed by McClosky and Schaar (1965). The items are of the following form:

(a) People were better off in the old days when everyone knew just how he was expected to act.

(b) It seems to me that other people find it easier to decide what is right than I do.

† W. G. Bennis, E. H. Schein, D. E. Berlew and F. I. Steele, (1964) discuss this point in terms of a possible meta-goal of sensitivity training—'expanded consciousness and sense of choice'.

in the Osgood Hill* 1965 summer program in sensitivity training. The program was two weeks in length (June 25–July 7), and the participants 'lived in' in the sense that they slept on the premises and ate virtually all their meals together.

There were 50 participants—30 females and 20 males. They ranged in age from 23 to 59, with a mean age of 33 years. The majority had at least a B.S. degree and a few had advanced degrees. The majority came from the New England area, but several came from Miami, Cleveland, and Chicago. There were eight Negroes in the population, and the trainers made certain that each of the five T-groups† that were formed had at least one Negro and an even proportion of males and females.

Occupationally, the males were a relatively heterogeneous group that included several businessmen, teachers, policemen, clerics, graduate students, government employees, a male nurse, and dentist. The females were much more homogeneous, the majority of them being associated with the nursing profession (students, teachers, practising nurses, and nursing supervisors).

Experimental design and procedure

One of the problems facing the researcher interested in evaluating the effects of sensitivity training is that of finding a relevant control group. The participants in a laboratory are, in one sense, a self-selected group—a circumstance which negates the relevance, for control purposes, of just any group of warm bodies.

Thus the experimental design utilized in this study was one in which the subjects served as their own controls. Herbert Hyman (H. Hyman, C. R. Wright and T. K. Hopkins, 1962, p. 42) utilized this approach in his evaluation of the effects of citizenship camps, as did Carl Rogers in his attempts to evaluate the effects of psychotherapy. As Hyman points out:

> With such a procedure, matching of experimental subjects and controls presents no difficulty, for the same persons constitute both groups. By determining how much instability there is in the group's attitudes, opinions, or other characteristics *during a normal period of time* we could then estimate how much of the change manifested during the experimental period exceeds the normal change resulting from other factors.

Within this design, the total available experimental group (N = 50) was randomly split into two groups of unequal size. The smaller group (N = 14)

* Osgood Hill is in Andover, Massachusetts. It is owned and operated by Boston University. The author wishes to acknowledge the cooperation and assistance provided by the entire staff group of Osgood Hill in the successful completion of this study.

† Two of the trainers were females—one of whom was a Negro—and the remaining four were males. (One group had two trainers.)

was tested (O_{1C}) via mail questionnaires two weeks prior to their arrival at Osgood Hill. The entire group was then tested (for controls: O_{2C} and for experimentals: O_{1E}) upon their arrival, but before the first T-group session. The final 'after' measures (for controls: O_{3C} and for experimentals: O_{2E}) were obtained the morning of the next to last day of the laboratory.* This timing was necessary in order to provide a feedback session to all participants prior to their departure at the end of the laboratory.

This design can be depicted in the following manner:†

June 11	*June 25*	*July 5*
$O_{1C} \dfrac{\text{controls}}{2 \text{ weeks}}$	$O_{2C} \dfrac{\text{controls}}{\text{T-group}}$	O_{3C}
(N = 11)		
	$O_{1E} \dfrac{\text{experimentals}}{\text{T-group}}$	O_{2E}
	(N = 30)	

Results

Control group

Table 1 presents the test-retest scores for the control group (O_{1C}, O_{2C}) and the initial test scores for the experimental group (O_{1E}). A series of t tests were performed that compared scores for O_{1E} versus O_{1C} and O_{2C} in order to determine empirically the degree of similarity between experimentals and controls. None of the resulting t's reached statistical significance, with p's being greater than 0·50. On the basis of these results, it is assumed that the members of the control group represent a population comparable with the experimentals on the major variables.

It can also be seen from Table 1 that among the members of the control group $\overline{Ap}$ increased slightly, $\overline{\# ET}$ increased slightly, and $\overline{ETA}$ and $\overline{HH}$ both decreased slightly. In using a t test for dependent samples (Blalock, 1960), it was observed that none of the resulting t's reached the 0·60 level of significance. On the basis of these results, it is assumed that the controls do not change significantly from O_{1C} to O_{2C} on any of the major variables. It is assumed, therefore, that any changes found among experimentals cannot be attributable to the main effects of instrument instability and/or practice.

---

* All administrations, other than 0_{1C}, were conducted by the author on a group basis.

† Of the available control group of 14, two persons never arrived and one returned an unusable questionnaire, leaving a final control group of 11. Of the available experimental group of 36, one missed the pretest and five returned unusable questionnaires, leaving 30 for the final experimental group.

Experimental group

It was hypothesized that $\overline{Ap}$ and $\overline{\# ET}$ would not change as a result of sensitivity training. Examination of Table 2 reveals that $\overline{Ap}$ and $\# ET$ decreased slightly over this two-week period. Using a t test for dependent samples, it was found that for ΔAp (change in $\overline{Ap}$), $t = 0.84$ with an associated $p < 0.40$ two-tail (N = 30); and for $\Delta \# ET$ (change in $\# ET$),

Table 1—*Before–af terscores for control group* (O_{1C}, O_{2C}) *and before scores for experimental group* (O_{1E})

(N=11)		$O_{1E}{}^a$ (N=30)
O_{1C}	$O_{2C}{}^a$	
(a) $\overline{Ap} = 5 \cdot 5$	$\overline{Ap} = 5 \cdot 8$	$\overline{Ap} = 6 \cdot 5$
(b) $\overline{\# ET} = 11 \cdot 0$	$\overline{\# ET} = 12 \cdot 0$	$\overline{\# ET} = 13 \cdot 5$
(c) $\overline{ETA} = 66 \cdot 0$	$\overline{ETA} = 65 \cdot 0$	$\overline{ETA} = 55 \cdot 0$
(d) $\overline{HH} = 46 \cdot 5$	$\overline{HH} = 47 \cdot 5$	$\overline{HH} = 46 \cdot 2$

(a) $\overline{Ap}$ represents mean level of anomy. Scores ranged from $1 \cdot 10$, with a low score representing a low level of anomy.

(b) $\overline{\# ET}$ represents the mean absolute number of statements scored as being ego-threatening, with the range from 5 to 23.

(c) $\overline{ETA}$ represents mean level of self-acceptance, i.e., the number of ego-threatening statements accepted divided by absolute number of ego-threatening statements. Scores ranged from 0 to 100 per cent, with a low score indicating a low level of self-acceptance.

(d) $\overline{HH}$ represents mean level of human heartedness. Scores ranged from a low of 18 to a high of 80. The lower the score, the closer the respondent's set of ranks was to the theoretically perfect set of ranks and, therefore, the higher his level of human-heartedness.

a $O_{2C} + O_{1E}$ were gathered at the same point in time, just prior to the first T-group session.

$t = 0.70$ with an associated $p < 0.45$ two-tail (N = 30). We are unable to reject the null hypothesis of no difference and can therefore assume that sensitivity training had no appreciable effect upon an individual's level of anomy (Ap) or upon the absolute number of ego-threatening statements generated by an individual on our sentence completion test.

The next major hypothesis concerns Δ ETA* (change in self-acceptance).

* ΔETA refers to change in self-acceptance score—ETA score after the laboratory minus ETA score before the laboratory.

The prediction here was that self-acceptance would increase as a result of sensitivity training. Examination of Table 2 reveals that ETA went from a mean of 55·0 per cent to a mean of 67·0 per cent. The differences between these means (t test for dependent samples) is significant at the 0·01 level one-tail (N = 30, t = 2·58, $p < 0·01$). It is therefore concluded that as a result of sensitivity training, an individual exhibits a greater willingness to accept the personal relevance of ego-threatening material; i.e., his ETA increases.

With respect to ΔHH* (change in human-heartedness), it was predicted that an individual's level of human heartedness would increase. Operationally, this means that his 'after' HH score would be lower than his 'before' HH score. Table 2 reveals that HH decreased from 47·2 to 42·0. The difference between these means (t test for dependent samples) is significant at the 0·01 level one-tail (N = 30, t = 2·54, $p < 0·01$). In other words, the rankings an individual assigned after the laboratory corresponded more closely with expert rankings than those he assigned before the laboratory— he was found to be more human-hearted.†

Table 2—*Before–after scores for experimental group* (N = 30)

	T-group (2 weeks)	
	O_{1E}	O_{2E}
	$\overline{Ap}$ = 6·5	$\overline{Ap}$ = 5·9
	$\#\,\overline{ET}$ = 13·5	$\#\,\overline{ET}$ = 13·2
	$\overline{ETA}$ = 55·0	$\overline{ETA}$ = 67·0
	$\overline{HH}$ = 47·2	$\overline{HH}$ = 42·0

Conditioning influence of anomy

We turn now to an examination of the conditioning influence of anomy with respect to the observed changes in ETA and HH. It was predicted that those E's low in anomy (Ap) would change more on ETA and HH than

* ΔHH refers to change in human-heartedness score—HH score after the laboratory minus HH score before the laboratory.

† The critical test here is whether ΔETA and ΔHH among the experimentals differ from ΔETA and ΔHH among the controls. A Mann-Whitney U-Test (Siegel, 1956, pp. 116–127) was therefore performed on the difference between the changes. This analysis yielded a Z = 1·76 for the ΔETA's (N_1 = 11, N_2 = 30, p = 0·05 one-tail) and a Z = 1·76 for the ΔHH's (N_1 = 11, N_2 = 30, p = 0·04 one-tail). In other words, *not only* do the experimentals change while the controls do not, but the *experimentals also change significantly more* than the controls.

those high in anomy (Ap). The skewed nature of the distribution of Ap scores (the majority of respondents scored either 1 or 8, 9, 10, with virtually no scores in the middle) suggested that the most relevant test of these hypotheses would be to split the group at the median Ap score and to compare the magnitude and direction of ETA and HH differences among groups. Utilizing the Mann-Whitney U-test, it is observed that those below the median in Ap increased significantly more on ETA than those above the median in Ap ($N_1 = 19$, $N_2 = 19$,* $Z = 1\cdot77$, $p < 0\cdot04$ one-tail). A similar trend was found with respect to HH scores ($N_1 = 19$, $N_2 = 19$, $Z = 1\cdot56$, $p < 0\cdot06$ one-tail). In absolute terms, those low in Ap increased seventeen per cent on the average. With respect to HH, those low in Ap decreased six points on the average, while the high Ap's decreased only two points. In summary, strong support is provided for the hypothesized conditioning influence of Ap on changes in self-acceptance (ETA), and marginal support is provided with respect to changes in human-heartedness (HH).

Central hypotheses

In the light of the results of these preliminary analyses, we are now in a position to examine the central hypotheses of this study:

1. Those who increase in self-acceptance will increase more in human-heartedness than those who either do not change or decrease in self-acceptance.†

2. Changes in self-acceptance will lead to change in human-heartedness.

With respect to the first, of the 38 members of the total experimental group, 23 increased on ETA, six did not change, and nine decreased in ETA. The sample was therefore split into $+ \Delta$ETA (positive changers in self-acceptance, $N = 23$) and 0ΔETA (zero or negative changers in self-acceptance, $N = 15$). On the average, the $+ \Delta$ETA group decreased five points in HH, a result which is statistically significant at the $p < 0\cdot01$ level one-tail ($N = 23$, $t = 2\cdot80$). The 0ΔETA group also decreased in HH an average of three points, but this change does not reach significance ($N = 15$, $t = 1\cdot03$, $p < 0\cdot20$ one-tail). However, the difference between these changes is *not* significant (Mann-Whitney U-Test, $N_1 = 15$, $N_2 = 23$, $Z = 1\cdot0$,

---

* For the purposes of this and the following analyses, the eight of 11 control group members who returned usable responses after the laboratory (O_{3C}) were added to the 30 experimentals. These eight persons changed as much (percentagewise) in ETA and HH after the laboratory as did the experimentals. In addition like the experimentals, they did not change in Ap or # ET. This raises our available population from $N = 30$ to $N = 38$.

† The *initial* correlation between ETA *versus* HH was $R = -0\cdot32$ ($N = 41$, $p < 0\cdot05$ one-tail). The minus sign is explained by the fact that a high level of HH is represented by a low score.

$p < 0.16$ one-tail). The hypothesis in its present form cannot be un-equivocally supported.

In order to shed some light on the reasons for this result, individual change scores on ETA were examined more closely. There appeared to be a sharp discontinuity in the distribution of scores. Several persons increased a moderate amount in ETA (8 to 14 per cent), but then the next highest change was 21 per cent. There were 13 persons who increased 21 per cent or more in self-acceptance. When we examined this group of high $+$ ΔETA's *versus* the remainder of the sample, the following results emerged: The high $+$ ΔETA group decreased an average of 8·0 points on HH (N $= 13$, $t = 3·0, p < 0·01$ one-tail), while the remainder of the sample decreased an average of 2·0 points on HH (N $= 25$, $t = 1·3$, $p < 0·12$ one-tail). A Mann-Whitney U-Test on the difference between these differences yielded a Z $= 1·76$ (N$_1$ $= 13$, N$_2$ $= 25$, $p < 0·04$ one-tail). In other words, those who increase a great deal in self-acceptance (ΔETA > 21 per cent) will increase significantly more in human-heartedness than those who decrease in self-acceptance or increase only a moderate amount.

One way to test the hypothesis that changes in self-acceptance lead to changes in human-heartedness is to utilize the method of partial correla-tion.* The three-variable† model to be tested can be depicted in the follow-ing manner:

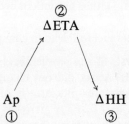

Within the framework of this research, we should like to know the direc-tion of the causal arrow in the relationship between ΔETA and ΔHH. In order to infer that ΔETA is causing ΔHH, the following mathematical condition must be satisfied‡ (Simon, 1954; Blalock, 1960):

* The utilization of partial correlations to infer causality rests upon several assump-tions. In addition, all other possible models must be eliminated. A complete discussion of these assumptions and the methods for eliminating irrelevant models can be found in Simon (1954) and Blalock (1960).

† Anomy (AP) was chosen as the third variable because, as discussed earlier, it was unaffected by the training experience but was related both to changes in self-acceptance and changes in human-heartedness. Other ways exist to prove causality but, for these, different experimental designs are required.

‡ Numerical subscripts are used for simplicity: 1 $=$ Ap; 2 $=$ ΔETA; 3 $=$ ΔHH.

The correlation of Ap *versus* ΔHH with the effect of ΔETA removed should be less than the zero order correlation of Ap *versus* ΔHH; i.e., $R_{13 \cdot 2} < R_{13}$.

Table 3 presents the data from which the required zero order correlations are computed. The dichotomous nature of the Ap scores suggested that a tetrachoric correlation method would be most appropriate. Under appropriate conditions (Guilford, 1956), this method 'gives a coefficient that is numerically equivalent to a Pearson r and may be regarded as an approximation to it'. In every case, the high *versus* low split was based upon those above and below the median.*

Substitution of the zero order correlations into the partial correlation of formula (Blalock, 1960) yields an $R_{13 \cdot 2} = + 0 \cdot 09$ and the mathematical condition stated above is therefore satisfied.† It is important to note that this analysis does not enable one to rule out a direct effect of sensitivity training on HH. Nor does it eliminate the possibility that sensitivity training influences another variable which may be termed 'feelings-orientation' which, in turn, influences ETA and HH. All it suggests is that some change in HH does result from a change in ETA.‡

Trainer ratings

Trainers were asked, at the end of the laboratory, to characterize the nature of each individual's participation during the T-group session on a scale from 1 (Group Process Orientation) to 7 (Personal Development). In addition, the trainers rated for each individual, the 'Salience of the Topic of Race Relations' (i.e., per cent of time spent discussing the Topic).

It was hypothesized that changes in self-acceptance (ΔETA) would be associated with an 'individual orientation' leaning toward Personal Development. Again this hypothesis is supported only when we compare the high + ΔETA group with the remainder of the sample. The average trainer rating for the high + ΔETA's was 5·2 (i.e. leaning toward Personal Development), as compared with 3·8 (i.e., leaning toward Group Process)

* Median AP = 5·0.
Median ETA = + 8; i.e., 8 per cent increase in self-acceptance.
Median HH = 2·0, i.e., 2-point decrease in HH score.
† A more conservative approach here is to split the total sample at the median ΔETA score and compute the tetrachoric correlation between Ap *versus* ΔHH within each subsample. The split was made, and the results are almost identical with those obtained when the partial correlation formula was used.
‡ A Kruskall–Wallis one-way analysis of variance (Siegel, 1956, pp. 184–193) among the five T-groups on all major variables was performed, and none of the resulting HH's reached the 0·50 level of significance two-tail. From this result, it can be assumed that there was no significant trainer effect, nor can the observed changes be attributed to some other factor unique to any one of the T-groups.

for the remainder of the sample. This difference is significant ($N^* = 30$, $t = 2 \cdot 16$, $p < 0 \cdot 02$ one-tail).

No directional hypotheses were made concerning the effect of 'Salience of the Topic' on an individual's change in human-heartedness. The 20 persons for whom these ratings were available were split into two groups— high (20 to 50 per cent of time) *versus* low (0 to 20 per cent) salience, and

Table 3—*Contingency tables necessary to compute tetrachoric correlations between Ap, ΔHH and ΔETA*

A	Low Ap	High Ap
High ΔHH	13	10
Low ΔHH	6	9
	^{R}Ap, ΔHH $= -0 \cdot 255$ (R_{13})	
B	Low Ap	High Ap
High ΔETA	13	6
Low ΔETA	6	13
	^{R}Ap, ΔETA $= -0 \cdot 550$ (R_{12})	
C	High Ap	Low Ap
High ΔHH	15	8
Low ΔHH	4	11
	^{R}ΔETA, ΔHH $= 0 \cdot 575$ (R_{23})	

changes in HH within the two groups were examined. The low-salience group decreases an average of eight points in HH, while the high-salience group decreases an average of only one point in HH ($N_1 = 10$, $N_2 = 10$, $Z = 1 \cdot 65$, $p < 0 \cdot 10$ two-tail, Mann–Whitney U-Test). In other words, there appears to be somewhat of a negative relationship between the amount of time spent discussing the topic of race relations and the change in human-heartedness.†

Discussion

Generalizability of results

One question which comes up immediately is the extent to which the findings of this study are generalizable. It was pointed out earlier that the members of the experimental population all shared a certain level of 'motivation to attend a laboratory'. It is not yet known what personality

* The sample is reduced here because one set of trainer-rating forms was never returned to the researcher.

† The correlation between 'Salience of Topic' and initial HH score was zero, as was the correlation between 'Individual Orientation' and the initial ETA score.

variables, for example, differentiate those who are 'motivated to attend' from those who are not. Even if knowledge of these parameters did exist, it would then have to be demonstrated that they have relevance in terms of differential learnings resulting from training. This broad issue is beyond the scope of this study. However, several related sub-issues are manageable.

Concerning the distribution of initial self-acceptance scores, a reasonably normal distribution of scores with a mean value close to 50 per cent was observed. Unfortunately, no norms exist to indicate what the expected average score might be. Two comparison samples, however, are available: the average ETA score among the college sophomore group studied by Dorris *et al.* (1954) was 53 per cent, and among a pretest group of 30 Sloan Fellows at M.I.T. (with a simplified index of self-acceptance being used), the mean score was 50 per cent. In addition, the results of the present study suggest that even some of those who were initially very low in self-acceptance could be 'reached' by sensitivity training.

Concerning human-heartedness scores, Schuman and Harding (1963) found in their main standardization sample that the average HH score (with a simplified measure being used) leaned toward the 'unhuman-hearted' end of the scale. The distribution of initial scores observed in this study was skewed in the other direction—toward the human-hearted end of the scale. The atypical* educational level of the Osgood Hill sample, with the majority having at least a bachelor's degree, helps to explain this difference. It may be that a certain level of education is a necessary prerequisite to learning via sensitivity training. This proposition is as yet untested empirically.

What kind of sensitivity training

Another question of importance deals with the impact of different emphases in sensitivity training.† The results of this study highlight the importance of a 'personal development' as opposed to a 'group process' orientation. The greatest increasers in self-acceptance and, consequently, in human-heartedness were those whose predominant focus during the T-group sessions was in more personal areas.

From a pragmatic viewpoint, if one wishes to use sensitivity training as a means to reduce ethnic prejudice, then, within the Schein and Bennis (1965) framework, the individual should be viewed as the client, and learning about self and others should be stressed at the levels of awareness and changes

---

* The terms 'typical' and 'atypical' used in this section, have as their frame of reference a random sample of adults drawn from the general population'.

† Schein and Bennis (1965) present a three-dimensional schema for classifying the goals of a laboratory in these terms: What is the learning about? Who is the ultimate client? What is the level of learning?

4

attitudes.* Furthermore, given the specific goal of prejudice reduction and a personal focus, a shorter laboratory might be feasible. Much research is needed to determine the optimal mix of group process *versus* personal development orientation, the relative impacts of various kinds of supplementary cognitive inputs, and the effect of laboratory duration on the amount of change observed.

One of the most interesting findings in this study involved the strong conditioning influence of anomy with respect to changes in self-acceptance. The success of sensitivity training as an educational strategy rests upon an individual's ability to see and understand the dominant norms of self-exposure, openness, and feedback which develop within the T-group. What remains to be demonstrated by future research is the role of anomy as a conditioning variable for learning criteria other than increased self-acceptance.

The roles played by discussion of the topic of race relations and the presence of Negroes in the T-group are still unclear. Pure discussion does not help those who are doing the talking. This situation does not mean that the observed changes in human-heartedness could have occurred without any such discussion. The nontalkers† may have benefited immensely from listening to the more vocal members of the group. On the other hand, the talkers may have been 'intellectualizing'—a technique commonly employed in T-groups to keep the discussion on a less threatening level. This negative effect of participation has been observed by other researchers,‡ and further research is necessary to better understand the dynamics of the relationship between participation (amount and content) and change.

Concerning the effect of racially mixed groups, it may be that for a majority of the white participants the T-group experience was the first opportunity they ever had to meaningfully interact with a Negro. During the T-group discussions, many insights may have occurred that served to highlight a feeling of 'oneness' or common humanity. For example, 'He (a Negro) has feelings and emotions just the same as I!' Research is needed to examine in greater detail the specific patterns of interaction (e.g., Negro to white) and discussion content within a mixed T-group and their effects on the attitudes people have toward one another, as well as the effects of an all-white group.

* For an excellent description of this form of sensitivity training, see Irving R. Weschler, Fred Massarik and Robert Tannenbaum. The self in process: A sensitivity training emphasis, in *Issues in human relations training*, No. 5 in NTL's Selected Reading Series. Washington, D.C.: National Training Laboratories 1962. Pp. 33–46.

† 'Nontalker' does not mean 'silent member', but refers instead only to the substance or content of an individual's discussion. The most vocal member, in terms of total participation, may never have mentioned the topic of race relations.

‡ Personal communication from David Kolb of M.I.T. concerning some research he is conducting an individual change within T-groups. 1965.

Change in self-acceptance versus *change in human-heartedness*

One of the central hypotheses in this study was that those who increase in self-acceptance will increase more in human-heartedness than those who decrease or do not change in self-acceptance. The data suggest that this hypothesis, in its original form, was too broad. It appears instead that some minimum increase in self-acceptance (20 per cent in this study) is necessary in order for any significant change in human-heartedness to be immediately observable.* Perhaps, where sensitivity training really 'took' (in the sense of great increase in self-acceptance), those involved may have been better able to immediately make the mental transfer from self-acceptance to human-heartedness. The others may have needed some period of incubation in order for this transfer to occur.

Support for this interpretation is provided by Katz (D. Katz, I. Sarnoff and C. M. McClintock, 1956, 1957) who found that as a result of a self-insight manipulation no changes in prejudice were observed immediately after the experimental induction, but that highly significant shifts occurred several weeks afterwards. In other words, a 'sleeper effect' appeared to be operating. The written case study utilized by Katz *et al.* (1956) to increase self-insight is certainly less intensive than a two-week sensitivity training laboratory and may well be less powerful. It is possible, therefore, that changes in human-heartedness will persist after the laboratory and, in fact, may become more marked among the group who experienced only moderate increases in self-acceptance.† This hypothesis could not be tested because it was necessary to provide a full feedback session‡ for the laboratory participants prior to their departure.

Finally, the reader has undoubtedly noticed that by changing a few words, e.g., 'T-group' to 'therapy group' and 'trainer' to 'therapist', this study could have been concerned with the effect of client-centered psychotherapy upon prejudiced attitudes. Both the T-group and the therapy group provide the elements of psychological safety, support, and opportunities for reality testing assumed necessary to effect an increase in an individual's level of self-acceptance and consequently, by our model, to decrease one's level

* The risk of maximizing change variations by examining a small subgroup of the total population is reduced considerably by the findings concerning individual focus during the T-group sessions. The great changers in self-acceptance were also those whose focus during the T-group was in more personal areas.

† The Bunker studies (1963, 1965) discussed earlier suggest that many of the learnings derived from sensitivity training *do* remain with an individual over a long period of time.

‡ The reason for this was only partially based upon ethical considerations. Of equal importance was the fact that the data which were fed back to the participants became topics for discussion in the few remaining T-group sessions and therefore, hopefully enhanced the learning value of their training experience.

of ethnic prejudice. To the extent that future research and practical experience substantiate the conclusions drawn from the present study, a step has been taken toward solving a problem posed by Adorno (T. W. Adorno, E. Frenkel-Brunswick, D. J. Levinson and R. N. Sanford, 1950, p. 976) some 17 years ago.

Although it cannot be claimed that psychological insight (self-insight) is any guarantee of insight into society, there is ample evidence that people who have the greatest difficulty in facing themselves are the least able to see the way the world is made. Resistance to self-insights and resistance to social facts are contrived, most essentially, of the same stuff. It is here that psychology may play its most important role. Techniques for overcoming resistance, developed mainly in the field of individual psychotherapy, can be improved and adapted for use with groups and even for use on a mass scale.

References

Adorno, T. W., E. Frenkel-Brunswick, D. J. Levinson and R. N. Sanford (1950) *The authoritarian personality*. New York: Harper and Row.

Bennis, W. G., E. H. Schein, D. E. Berlew and F. I. Steele (1964) *Interpersonal dynamics*. Chicago: Dorsey.

Blalock, H. M. (1960) *Social statistics*. New York: McGraw-Hill.

Bunker, D. (1963) 'The effect of laboratory education upon individual behaviour.' *Proc. of the 16th Annual Meeting*, Industrial Relat. Res. Ass., December, pp. 1–13.

Bunker, D. (1965) 'Individual applications of laboratory training.' *J. appl. Behav. Sci.*, **1** (2), 131–148.

Coser, L. A. and B. Rosenberg (Eds.) (1964) *Sociological theory—A book of readings*. New York: Macmillan.

Dorris, R. J., D. Levinson and E. Hanfmann (1954) 'Authoritarian personality studied by a new variation of the sentence completion technique.' *J. abnorm. soc. Psychol.*, **49**, 99–108.

Gordon, T. (1950) 'What is gained by group participation?' *Educ. Leadership*, (January), 220–226.

Guilford, J. P. (1956) *Fundamental statistics in psychology and education*. New York: McGraw-Hill.

Harding, J. and H. Schuman (1961) 'An approach to the definition and measurement of prejudice.' Unpublished manuscript, Harvard University.

Hyman, H., C. R. Wright and T. K. Hopkins (1962) *Application of methods of evaluation*. Los Angeles: Univ. of California Press.

Johnson, P. C. (1949) *Statistical methods in research*. New York: Prentice-Hall.

Kahn, R. (1963) 'Aspiration and fulfillment: Themes for studies of group relations.' Unpublished manuscript, Univ. of Michigan.

Katz, D., I. Sarnoff and C. M. McClintock (1956) 'Ego defense and attitude change.' *Human Relat.*, **9**, 27–45.

Katz, D., I. Sarnoff and C. M. McClintock (1957) 'The measurement of ego defense as related to attitude changes.' *J. Pers.*, **25**, 465–474.

McClosky, H. and J. H. Schaar (1965) 'Psychological dimensions of anomy.' *Amer. soc. Rev.*, **30** (1), 14–40.

Miles, M. B. (1960) 'Human relations training: Processes and outcomes.' *J. Counsel. Psychol.*, **7** (4), 301–306.

Schein, E. H. and W. G. Bennis (1965) *Personal and organizational change through group methods: The laboratory approach.* New York: Wiley.

Schuman, H. and J. Harding (1963) 'Sympathetic identification with the underdog.' *Pub. Opin. Quart.*, 230–241.

Sheerer, E. T. (1949) 'The relationship between acceptance of self and acceptance of others.' *J. Consult Psychol.*, **13**, 169–175.

Siegel, S. (1956) *Nonparametric statistics for the behavioral sciences.* New York: McGraw-Hill.

Simon, H. A. (1954) 'Spurious correlation: A causal interpretation.' *J. Amer. Stat. Ass.*, **49**, 467–479.

Steele, F. I. (1965) 'The relationships of personality to changes in interpersonal values effected by laboratory training.' Unpublished doctoral dissertation, Massachusetts Institute of Technology.

Stock, D. (1949) 'An investigation into the interrelations between the self-concept and feelings directed toward other persons and groups.' *J. consult. Psychol.*, **13**, 149.

CHAPTER 3

The T-group as a Vehicle of Organizational Change

For a large number of participants T-group training means a one- or two-week residential experience with a group of managers or administrators from a wide variety of organizations. They are taken out of their organizational environment and role and put through an isolated experience that is likely to change their attitudes and behaviour and, consequently, their conception of their job. Over the last few years many people have questioned this approach because, they argue, changing only one aspect of the organizational system, namely the manager, attempts to affect the social environment of the organization on 'too narrow a front'. Pugh (1965) extends this argument, 'it is not the individual but his network of social relationships which is basic, and attempts to alter it through the individual must remain only marginally effective. Indeed there is the suspicion that if a really major change were brought about . . . this could result in *increased* tension and conflict in the "back-home" situation.'

In short, the problems of re-entry can be great and, in at least one third of the cases (Miles, 1965; Bunker, 1965), this is not achieved with success. It has been suggested by some (Miles, 1965; Bamforth, 1965; Smith and Moscow, 1966) that a more effective way of increasing and insuring the transfer of T-group learnings is to encourage organizations involved in this type of training to establish 'custom-built' training programmes. As Bamforth (1965) suggests after an in-company T-group programme lasting seven years; 'it became clear as time went on that the use of group training in a work situation was more effective and appropriate . . . than the heterogeneous groups (groups composed of strangers from a wide variety of organizations), which led to "classroom encapsulation"'. He went on to say that the work groups made it possible to explore 'reality relationships' such as those between boss, subordinates and colleagues.

85

We wish to turn at this stage, therefore, to a consideration of organizational change through the laboratory methods. A number of studies of the effects of these programmes have been undertaken, which provide additional information for evaluation, although few of them are as methodologically sound as some of the foregoing studies of individual learning and follow-up change.

Argyris (1965) has developed a set of categories to measure what he terms interpersonal competence for use in evaluating the impact of the T-group on group and organizational behaviour. These categories are dichotomized into positive and negative aspects of group/organizational functioning. Within the former he lists at the *individual and interpersonal level*: owning up to, openness, and risk-taking; within the latter; not owning up to, not being open and rejecting risk-taking. On the *group norms* level the positive categories are individuality, concern and trust; on the negative side, conformity, antagonism and mistrust. These categories, which are further refined into feeling and ideational levels, have been used with respectable reliability in a number of studies of T-group and discussion/case study groups.

Argyris (1964) has used them to evaluate the effects of five T-group type meetings on the behaviour of a board of directors. Scores on the first three sessions were compared with scores during the training activity and scores derived from board meetings conducted during the twelve months following the T-groups. Antagonism scores were seen to have decreased throughout the period and there were significant positive changes in 'concern for others', 'feelings and ideas', 'openness' and 'helping others'. Argyris concludes, with reservations, that a comparison between scores for board meetings immediately before the change session with meetings conducted 8 and 12 months after the intervention, indicates a significant and desirable growth in interpersonal competence. One of the interesting things about this study is that Argyris is not simply relying on paper and pencil tests of perceived behaviour as do many of the other studies. His focus is clearly upon a specific organizational group, its training experience and its subsequent performance as rated by two independent observers working from tape recordings. Unfortunately, as no control was used, one cannot rule out change resulting from system development, the presence of the experimenter (rather than the nature of the experiment), or other situational factors. It is worth noting, however, that the direction of change is in line with change facilitated by other T-group experiences in other situations.

Morse and Reimer (1956) were responsible for a field experiment which used a trained matched-control group for comparison with T-group trained subjects. The clerical staff from four comparable divisions of a firm were assessed and all the supervisory staff in these four divisions received training; two groups in laboratory methods, which emphasized the importance of participative decision-making, while the other two were given a lecture and discussion course on the need to coordinate and centralize the decision-making within the organization. The authors found a marked increase in productivity in all four divisions of the company with a marginally greater increase for the divisions trained to centralize decision-making. However, an assessment of labour turnover figures revealed a sharp increase in turnover in the division trained to centralize decision-making, but no change in the T-group trained divisions. Thus, in the former divisions, as Smith and Moscow (1966) have interpreted in a recent article, 'a high increase in productivity was linked to a marked decrease in morale' while in the latter 'a slightly lower increase in productivity was achieved with no less morale'. The evidence, however, is more useful for a consideration of the consequences of different managerial styles than for a real evaluation of laboratory training, since there is no evidence that similar results would not have been arrived at had the T-group trained supervisors acquired their participative style through lecture/case discussion methods.

Underwood (1965) also reports a field experiment in which the effects of T-group training were measured, in this case with engineering and manufacturing staff in an electronics company. The training programme consisted of one two-hour session per week of T-group training for 15 supervisors drawn from several departments and organizational levels over a 15-week period. A 15 subject matched-control group (by department, supervisory level, age and sex) was selected for comparison. Positive and negative changes were measured by reports from the trainees' work associates, who were not informed about the research design or the training programme. The observers or work associates were asked to report anonymously to the author any changes in the subjects' characteristic behaviour during the 15 weeks of the training programme and the 15-week period following the programme. He found that nine of the T-group trained subjects as compared with seven of the control group subjects were observed to show change one or more times. Although this was not a large difference—no statistical treatment was performed on the data—he did find a large difference in the frequency of incidents reported between the two groups. Observers of the participants of the T-group programme reported 25 changes in the 30 week period whereas the observers of the control group reported only 11 changes in the same 30 week period; a T-group training to control group change ratio of 2·3 : 1. The observers then codified the changes as either more or less effective supervision. In the T-group trained group 15 of the 25 observers were said to increase leadership and supervisor effectiveness of the subjects, 7 to decrease effectiveness and 3 had no bearing on leadership. The control group showed eight increases, two decreases and one no influence. One interesting feature of the research design is that the *observers* are asked to classify the new behaviour and not the researchers as in the previous studies; for the first time in a study of this kind associates not only report changes but, in effect, say what they think of them in terms of effectiveness. This really highlights the potentiality of bias in measures of *perceived* change; in other studies the associates report, and the researchers classify new behaviour according to *their* frame of reference. The difficulty is that the researchers' values can sometimes be out of line with the values of the organization. Underwood's study attempts to avoid this difficulty. As he himself writes:

'The experimental subjects were reported to show decreased effectiveness in the personal category in a substantial number of reports. An analysis of these changes reveals a heavy emotional loading in the nature of the change. It is speculated that these subjects were venting emotion to a greater degree than usual and to the ovservers, *operating in a culture which devalues such expression* this behaviour yielded a negative evaluation.'

By implication one could say that whilst openness, acceptance, expression of feelings, and a generally more democratic approach may be valuable from the point of view of the T-group trainer it is not necessarily seen as such by the organization. As with some of the other studies, the organizational climate or culture seems to be a critical factor in the transfer of training. While the size of the sample population used by Underwood is relatively small and the results far from conclusive, this study certainly appears to highlight the importance of the situation in which the laboratory trained person is required to operate.

A further study involving the use of laboratory training within an organization development programme was conducted by Buchanan and Brunstetter (1959). In one department of a large aircraft company 224 supervisors and higher management participated in a series of T-groups. A matched control group was provided by a second similar department of the company. Sometime after the training programme the trained and the non-trained control supervisors were asked to rate which of a list of organizational functions (45 in all) were being performed more or less effectively than a year previously. They found that the trained supervisors reported significantly greater improvement in their department than did the control group subjects. In addition, the improvement reported from the list of organization functions were on items closely related to the training programme such as 'improved effectiveness of meetings', 'better use of delegation', and so on. These results should be treated with caution since they are self-report measures only and it is possible that participants who believe in a training programme and who have assimilated its peculiar language will tend to give higher ratings after than before in order to confirm their own beliefs.

Friedlander (1967) reports the results of an evaluation of what he terms organizational training laboratories. The nature of this training in general refers to laboratory sessions where all members of a particular work group attend, the purposes being: (1) to identify problems facing the work-group system and the reasons for their existence; (2) to invent possible solutions to the problems in the form of needed system changes; and (3) to plan implementation of these solutions through regular and newly-constructed channels. Within this context, Friedlander notes, the group explores numerous inadequacies in interpersonal and intergroup processes which directly or indirectly influence the total work system.

Over a two-year period 12 groups of civilians employed in a services' research and development station were studied. These 12 groups composed of from five to fifteen members and represented four levels in the organizational hierarchy. They met regularly, usually weekly, and were essentially task-oriented work groups. Four of the groups eventually participated in organizational training laboratories; the others did not, thus providing the project with four training groups and eight comparison groups (Friedlander does not consider them as controls since he considers the term 'a soothing misnomer which tends to gloss over a myriad of variables that might otherwise be quite relevant').

Proceeding inductively from interviews and discussions, together with a scanning of the professional literature, Friedlander used a factor analysis to arrive at underlying dimensions of group phenomena. These dimensions were tapped by a specifically devised instrument the Group Behaviour Inventory (Friedlander, 1966). The G.B.I. was administered twice to each of the 12 groups. For the four training groups the second administration followed the training by six months. For the eight comparison groups, the second administration followed the first administration by six months.

Two separate analyses of covariance were performed on each of the six group dimensions. In the first set, the four trained groups were compared with the eight comparison groups. In the second set, the groupings were ignored and changes in the mean of 31 individuals who participated in training were compared with the changes in the mean of the 60 individuals who did not participate. The results of the two analyses were similar. On the group level significant changes occurred involving team effectiveness in problem solving (Factor I), mutual influence among group members (III), and members sense of personal involvement and participation in group meetings (IV). Dimensions where no significant improvement occurred included feelings of approachability toward the chairman (II), intergroup trust and confidence (V), and the general evaluation of group meetings (VI).

Friedlander concludes that significant improvements in effectiveness and the interaction process in work groups do occur as a result of participation in organizational training laboratories, and that these improvements take place in areas which are of direct personal and organizational relevance to members of the on-going work groups. In addition, they endure for a period of at least six months beyond the training experience. Friedlander's findings, however, are somewhat baffling in at least three respects: (1) significant increases in mutual influence and participation were not paralleled by gains in trust; (2) greater team effectiveness was achieved without concomitant increases in the evaluation of group meetings; and (3) there was a heightened sense of involvement and participation with no significant improvement in members' rapport with their leader.

Finally, Wilson, Mullen and Morton (1968) report the results of a comparison between what they term organization training laboratories and sensitivity or T-group training. As Morton puts it 'the Organization Training Laboratory attempts to change not only the individual but the organization climate in which the individual must continue to live'. In the organization training laboratory apparently the face-to-face feedback process focuses on 'managerial styles' rather than on 'personal behaviour' type characteristics which may or may not be related to management (Morton and Bass, 1964). As Wilson and coworkers conceive it organization training emphasizes team decision-making and problem-solving. It is concerned expressly with how effectively a team uses its material and human resources. It does not avoid individual learning but this is acquired in a work-oriented context that encourages transfer or learning back to the world of work. The authors argue that team training experience may have more impact on individual behaviour on the job, where the impact of T-group training may have a broader and more intense impact on the individual and all of his interpersonal relationships. Using a questionnaire designed to determine managers' perception of the value of training experience to themselves as individuals and to themselves as managers, Wilson and co-workers sought to compare the impact of traditional laboratory training as compared with organization training laboratories. The results as presented in Table 1 suggest that these courses were approximately of equal value to the managers as individuals. However, when the focus shifted to the individual as a manager or as one responsible for building team effort the results clearly favour the organization training method. Differences are statistically significant, with the exception of the cases of managers quoting

Table 1—*The proportion of managers who considered their training experience of considerable value after attending a sensitivity training programme or an organization training laboratory*

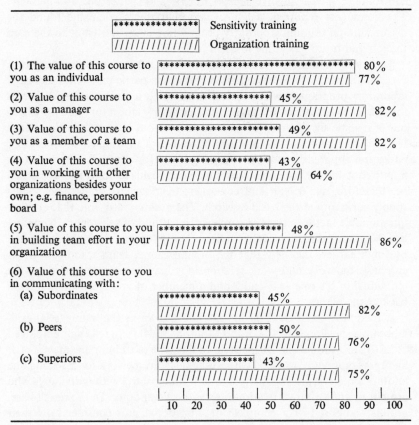

**************	Sensitivity training
///////////////	Organization training

(1) The value of this course to you as an individual — 80% / 77%

(2) Value of this course to you as a manager — 45% / 82%

(3) Value of this course to you as a member of a team — 49% / 82%

(4) Value of this course to you in working with other organizations besides your own; e.g. finance, personnel board — 43% / 64%

(5) Value of this course to you in building team effort in your organization — 48% / 86%

(6) Value of this course to you in communicating with:
  (a) Subordinates — 45% / 82%
  (b) Peers — 50% / 76%
  (c) Superiors — 43% / 75%

10 20 30 40 50 60 70 80 90 100

working with other organizations besides his own, for example finance, personnel. The questionnaire requested reports on activities initiated or discounted since the laboratory training. The twenty-eight persons from the normal laboratories reported thirty-nine activities; twenty-one persons from the organization training laboratory reported ninety-three activities.

Wilson and coworkers note that those from the normal laboratory, who made comments, reported primary changes in the areas of better listening, sensitivity to self, better understanding of self and others, and being more considerate. Only in the category of sensitivity itself did the persons from the normal laboratories give more reports than the persons from the organizational training laboratory. In addition, a proportionally larger number from the organizational training laboratory reported 'being less controlling', 'greater involvement of others' and 'better decision-making'. The comments reported, again suggest that the participants found the organizational training laboratory programme of greater value to them on the job and of no less value to them personally.

These results must be treated with extreme caution for several reasons. First of all, nearly two years elapsed before the participants in the normal laboratory programme were required to complete a questionnaire. Whereas those who had attended the organization training laboratory had only been out of it some six months. As we have pointed out in our discussion of the work of Argyris these findings demonstrate that the impact of laboratory education apparently continues on a high level for a period in excess of six months but during the tenth month a fade-out begins to appear. It could well be, therefore, as Wilson and coworkers acknowledge that these results simply substantiate the basic research. The authors also note that another questionable factor in their research is the method of self-report. Nonetheless the general direction of the findings clearly support the ideas elaborated by Pugh earlier, the view that the organizational team training with its emphasis on work and work relationships may be more effective for the individual in his role as a leader and a member of an organizational team back at the plant.

A modification of the T-group method known as the 'managerial-grid' laboratory developed by Blake and Mouton (1964) is increasingly employed as an organizational change method. In this type of training the members of an organization are provided with a diagnostic framework for assessing one another's behaviour. The first phase of training starts with individuals who are not in authoritative relationships with one another. In the next phase, groups composed of a complete organizational unit consider how their phase 1 experience (groups of initial strangers) affects the way in which *they* work together. Barnes and Greiner (Blake, Mouton, Barnes and Greiner, 1964; Greiner, 1967a, 1967b) undertook an evaluation of the managerial-grid in a large American petrochemical company of 800 managers. They reported a number of major changes in the company's performance, which included increased profits, reduction of controllable costs, and more positive managerial attitudes. There was, however, no control data for untrained companies or companies trained by some other method in the same market situation. In addition, many substantive changes within the organization were occurring at the same time, such as 600 men being declared redundant (which obviously affected wages saved and may have had other side effects). These changes also resulted in collaboration with a management consultant, which may have been as important as the actual training in contributing to change.

Smith and Honour (1969) improved upon the above study in at least one respect by establishing control conditions. They examined changes within a British factory after managerial-grid training and compared these with concurrent changes at a second untrained factory within the same organization. There were 49 trainees in the first factory and 51 untrained controls in the second, matched for age and seniority. Questionnaires were completed before and four months after training. The trainees were also interviewed at various intervals after training. Just over one-half of the trainees reported improvement in their relationship to their subordinates, whereas the subordinates who we might expect to be more objective saw the changes in only one-third of the instances. Changes were particularly noted in group meetings and committees within the company. The untrained managers showed much lower change rates. Overall the study confirmed that the predicted changes did occur, but only among a minority of those trained. No attempt was made in this study to assess the change in profitability or cost-control as a result of grid training. Both the Barnes and Greiner and Smith and Honour studies used for the most part a recall method, whereby trainees were asked to recall after training what their situation was like before training. We must consider the possibility of the findings being biased as a result of this methodological approach. The possibility exists that a 'halo' of favourable response to the training may have led the trainees 'to paint the pre-training situation blacker than it really was'. With grid-training the research evidence remains scattered and only partially conclusive.

Conclusion

The studies of the use of T-groups as tools of organization change are much less complete and more difficult to compare than those evaluating individual change. This stems not only from the lack of willingness by companies to conduct experiments and controlled evaluation in organization change, but also from the inherent difficulty in measuring and comparing the effectiveness of different organizations who tend to use different criteria for effectiveness. The findings cited above are no more than encouraging, more complete and organized data is needed in this area. Buchanan (1965) has pointed out 'what is needed is more attention to strategies of organization development and to adapting laboratory training theory and methodology to fulfil the strategy, and to devising ways of assessing the impact of such programmes.'

References

Argyris, C. (1964) 'T-groups for organization effectiveness.' *Harvard Business Review*, **42**, 71.

Argyris, C. (1965) 'Explorations in interpersonal competence—II.' *Journal of Applied Behavioral Science*, **1** (3), 255–269.

Bamforth, K. (1965) 'T-group method within a company.' In G. Whitaker (Ed.), *T-group Training: Group Dynamics in Management Education.* Oxford: Blackwell, 69–77.

Blake, R. R. and J. S. Mouton (1964) *The Managerial Grid.* Houston, Texas: Gulf Publishing Co.

Blake, R. R., J. S. Mouton, L. B. Barnes and L. E. Greiner (1964) 'Breakthrough in organisation development.' *Harvard Business Review*, **42**, 133–155.

Buchanan, P. C. and P. H. Brunstetter (1959) 'A research approach to management development—Part II.' *Journal of the American Society of Training Directors*, **12**, 18–27.

Buchanan, P. C. (1965) *Evaluating the Effectiveness of Laboratory Training in Industry.* Washington, D.C.: National Education Association.

Bunker, D. R. (1965) 'Individual applications of laboratory training.' *Journal of Applied Behavioral Science*, **1** (2), 131–148.

Friedlander, F. (1966) 'Performance and interactional dimensions of organizational work groups.' *Journal of Applied Psychology*, **50**, 257–265.

Friedlander, F. (1967) 'The impact of organizational training laboratories upon the effectiveness and interaction of on-going work groups.' *Personnel Psychology*, **20** (3), 289–309.

Greiner, L. E. (1967a) 'Antecedents of planned organizational change.' *Journal of Applied Behavioral Science*, **3**, 51–86.

Greiner, L. E. (1967b) 'Patterns of successful organization change.' *Harvard Business Review.*

Miles, M. B. (1965) 'Changes during and following laboratory training: A clinical-experimental study.' *Journal of Applied Behavioral Science*, **1** (3), 215–243.

Morse, N. and E. Reimer (1956) 'The experimental change of major organizational variable.' *Journal of Abnormal and Social Psychology*, **52**, 120–129.

Morton, R. B. and B. M. Bass (1964) 'The organizational training laboratory.' *Training Directors Journal* (October).

Pugh, D. (1965) 'T-group training from the point of view of organization theory.' In G. Whitaker (Ed.), *T-Group Training: Group Dynamics in Management Education.* Oxford: Blackwell, 44–50.

Smith, P. B. and T. F. Honour (1969) 'The impact of phase 1 managerial grid training.' *Journal of Management Studies*, **6**.

Smith, P. B. and D. Moscow (1966) 'After the T-group is over . . . .' *New Society* (December).

Underwood, W. J. (1965) 'Evaluation of a laboratory method of training.' *Journal of the American Society of Training Directors*, **14**, 34–40.

Wilson, J. E., D. P. Mullen and R. B. Morton (1968) 'Sensitivity training for individual growth—routine training for organization development.' *Training and Development Journal*, **22** (1), 47–54.

The Impact of Organizational Training Laboratories upon the Effectiveness and Interaction of Ongoing Work Groups*

Frank Friedlander

School of Management,
Case Western Reserve University

Introduction

Action taken to resolve problems which hinder the effectiveness of work groups is a topic touched upon only occasionally in the research literature. For the most part innovations in group training efforts, such as group problem-solving and sensitivity training, have fallen apparently outside the boundaries of industrial psychology, despite the fact that much of this training currently occurs in industrial settings. On the other hand, a number of studies have been reported in such journals as *Human Relations* and the *Journal of Applied Behavioural Research*. In part, this may be because group training programs deal with the social and environmental factors, and not merely with individual differences in characteristics. It may also be because group training involves efforts toward change, and not merely acceptance and measurement of a *status quo* situation. In an article relevant to these issues, Sanford (1965) strongly advocates programs and studies aimed toward understanding the conditions and processes of developmental change, the social settings in which these changes occur and, in particular, the settings that have been designed to modify people in some way.

This article is concerned with an evaluation of the impact of change programs which will be called here *organizational training laboratories*. The nature of this training quite naturally varies among groups in some ways. In general, however, the laboratory sessions last approximately four to five days and are attended by *all* members of a particular work group. The purposes of the sessions generally are (a) to identify problems facing the work-group system and the reasons for their existence, (b) to invent possible solutions to the problems in the form of needed system changes, and

* Originally published in *Personnel Psychology*, 1967, **20**, 289–309.

(c) to plan implementation of these solutions through regular and newly-constructed channels. Within this problem-solving context, the group explores numerous inadequacies in interpersonal and intergroup processes which directly or indirectly influence the total work system.

It is important to note that these training sessions deal with the intact work group as an integrated system into which is introduced procedural and interpersonal change, rather than with a collection of strangers representing different organizations—or unrelated components of the same organization. This difference is relevant to the expected training impact and, therefore, to the research design and criteria.

Much of the previous emphasis in training seems to have been upon evoking changes in the *individual* primarily in the isolated island of his training context. The organizational training laboratory is directed at helping the individual bridge the hazardous, yet critical transition from his trainee role to the 'real life' role of his back-home environment, and at preventing dissipation of the training effects. Since much of the discussion centers upon the relevant work problems which the group actually faces, and since the members of the training group are also the members of the organizational work group, ideally there is a perfect consolidation of the training and organizational membership roles. The back-home and the here-and-now are one and the same.

To the researcher, this shift in emphasis implies not only a criterion of more enduring change, but perhaps a qualitatively different one. Research emphasis is not only upon behavioural change in the individual, but also upon change of the individual within his organizational context, and changes in the organizational context or organic system of which the individual is one interacting part.

Although back-home criterion for evaluating laboratory training is frequently an implicit assumption made by both the consultant and the researcher, it is seldom made explicit in the design of the training or in the design of the research. 'Change process', as Mann (1962) points out, 'needs to be concerned with altering both the forces within an individual and the forces in the organizational situation surrounding the individual.' This point is dramatically emphasized by Bennis, Benne and Chin (1962) in their discussion of programs and technologies of planned change:

Isolating the individual from his organizational context, his normative structure which rewards him and represents a significant reference group, makes no sense. In fact, if it sets up countervailing norms and expectations, it may be deleterious to both the organization and to the individual.

It is usually assumed that changes in individual behaviour 'will lead to increased effectiveness in the back-home situation; and this, rather than change *per se*, is the "raison d'etre" for the training group' (Stock and Thelan, 1958).

Those who have concerned themselves with back-home impact have reported mixed results. Trainees attending as a team have been found to change more than trainees attending as individuals (Lippitt, 1949). Similarly, Riecken (1952) found that those who attended work camp, and who had continuing contact with others from developmental experiences, were most likely to retain attitude changes. On the other hand, Bennis (1963) uses the term 'fade-out' to describe lack of durability of training results when participants return to their company. Shepard (1960) reports that the impact of laboratory experience was greater on personal and interpersonal learning than in changing the organization. Harrison (1962) reports that trainees increased their use of emotional and interpersonal descriptions of each other, but did not increase such descriptions of their fellow employees back home. The thorough and extensive study by Fleishman *et al.* (1955) lends further disturbing evidence—that although training resulted in immediate changes in self-perception, this impact soon gave way to the leadership style of the trainee's supervisor once the trainee returned to his organizational context. Mann (1962) summarizes these disappointing results as follows: 'At best, these studies suggest that this type of training has little or no general effect . . . . Training which does not take the trainee's regular social environment into account will probably have little chance of modifying behaviour. It may very well be that human relations training— as a procedure for initiating social change—is most successful when it is designed to *remold the whole system of role relationships* . . . .'

In a parallel manner research, which ignores the impact of training upon the organization or the ongoing work groups of which it is composed, may be utilizing a criterion of low and temporary relevance. The appropriate research criteria for training that deals with the work groups within an organization is *group* change within the organizational context.

In the light of the above assumptions, the purposes of this research project were to study the impact of several organizational training laboratories upon problems that were of most relevance and utility to the group members of intact organizational work groups who had participated as a group in training laboratories. The data which evolved from this study are also utilized to shed further light on several additional issues concerning potential changes in organizational work groups.

Background

The organizational context in which this project was embedded consists of one of the armed services' largest research and development stations, employing approximately 6,000 personnel. Eighty per cent of the employees are civilians, including about 1,200 scientists and engineers. The organization's mission covers the complete research and development spectrum from basic research through applied research: design, development, test, engineering, evaluation, and limited production. Its products are in all fields of ordnance: rockets, guided missiles, underwater ordnance, propellants, explosives, and aircraft fire-control systems.

In early 1962, a series of individual interviews was held with the members of the Policy Board, the highest level group in the organization. The proposed topic did not concern the Board or its meetings as such. However, it soon became evident that the members were not content merely to discuss the 'planned' topic; instead they dwelled rather consistently and concertedly upon the Board membership and leadership, and the interactions and effectiveness of the Board meetings.

The series of interviews resulted in two decisions—one action-oriented and one research-oriented. In view of the perceived inadequacies that members expressed of the group and its meetings, and in view of the willingness on the part of both group members and the internal consulting staff to do something about these inadequacies, a decision was made to bring in an outside trainer-consultant to work with the group. The second, and parallel decision, was to initiate a research study which might provide an evaluation and an increased understanding of the entire training phenomenon as it would occur in its organizational context.

It became apparent to the initial stage of the research study that at least one group which did *not* participate in the training experience (a comparison group) would be needed with which to compare any changes that might occur in the Policy Board. Over a two-year period the participation of 11 additional organizational work groups was obtained, making a total of 12 groups involved in the study. These 12 groups, described in more detail elsewhere (Friedlander, 1966), represent four levels in the organizational hierarchy. The groups are composed of from five to 15 members, who meet (usually weekly or bi-weekly) and work together regularly for a variety of purposes, including problem discussion and resolution, general co-ordination, information dissemination, decision-making, policy formulation, future planning, etc. As such, the 12 groups represent traditional task-oriented work groups which use typical lateral and hierarchical interaction patterns toward their task accomplishment. Four of the groups eventually participated in organizational training laboratories; the others did not, thus providing the project with four training groups and eight comparison groups.*

* The term 'comparison group', rather than the experimental psychologist's term

Research design

The previously-mentioned series of interviews with members of various work groups resulted in the collection of an extensive amount of material dealing with the problems and the issues which members perceived as important in their work groups. The content of the material concerned such issues as co-operation, competition, openness, initiative, self-awareness, participation, spontaneity, creativity, intimacy, effectiveness, conflict, communication, divergency of ideas, procedural adequacy, authority relations, exploitation, mutual influence, and consensus. Detailed notes were taken during the interviews and the verbatim comments made by group members were re-phrased into questions to form the main body of a questionnaire. Additional group-descriptive variables were obtained through discussions with members of several different groups. Relevant group-descriptive dimensions, issues, and hypotheses recurrent in the professional literature provided a third source of information. In addition to evaluations of adequacy and effectiveness of the group and its meetings, the variables encompassed perceptions of the actual network of feelings—both in terms of the perceptions of one's own position in the network as a member, and of the perceptions by members of relationships existing between other members of the group.

Directly quantifiable data were also collected for each individual concerning the number of meetings he had previously attended, the number of topics he had submitted for the agenda, the number of problems he felt needed discussion at the next meeting, the percentage of time he had talked, and his estimate of the percentage of time the chairman had talked. A nine-adjective semantic differential of the concept 'X Department Staff Meetings' were also included.

In an effort to reduce these items to a comprehensive set of dimensions, a factor analysis was performed from which six underlying dimensions of group phenomena evolved. A detailed account of the construction, development, and factor analysis of the items is described elsewhere (Friedlander, 1966). However, since these six dimensions were utilized as principle variables in the current research, a brief description of each is provided:

I. *Group Effectiveness*: This dimension describes group effectiveness in

---

'control group' is used throughout this paper since there is virtually nothing controlled in these eight groups. While it is true that they did not participate in a planned training experience, it is also likely that many events occurred in the eight groups during this period which had a positive or negative impact upon characteristics relevant to this study. Perhaps the term 'control group', as used by the field researcher, is a soothing misnomer which tends to gloss over a myriad of variables that might otherwise be quite relevant.

solving problems and in formulating policy through a creative, realistic team effort.

II. *Approach to* vs. *Withdrawal from Leader:* At the positive pole of this dimension are groups in which members can establish an unconstrained and comfortable relationship with their leader—the leader is approachable.

III. *Mutual Influence:* This dimension describes groups in which members see themselves and others as having influence with other group members and the leader.

IV. *Personal Involvement and Participation:* Individuals who want, expect, and achieve active participation in group meetings are described by this dimension.

V. *Intragroup Trust* vs. *Intragroup Competitiveness:* At the positive pole, this dimension depicts a group in which the members hold trust and confidence in each other.

VI. *General Evaluation of Meetings:* This dimension is a measure of a generalized feeling about the meetings of one's group as good, valuable, strong, pleasant, or as bad, worthless, weak, unpleasant.

The questionnaire from which this data was obtained is described here as the Group Behaviour Inventory (GBI). Group members were introduced to the study at one of their regular meetings. After a discussion period where questions were answered, a copy of the GBI was distributed to each member of the group to be completed at his leisure in the privacy of his own office. Each member was asked to affix an identification code number of his own choice to the GBI so results of a planned second administration of the questionnaire might be compared to the first one. The GBI was administered twice to each of the 12 groups. For the four training groups, the second administration followed the training by six months. For the eight comparison groups, the second administration followed the first administration by six months.

Inquiries, methods and results

The remainder of this paper will incorporate selected issues which the research project attempted to explore, the methodologies used to explore each issue, the results of the analyses, and a brief discussion of the possible relevance of the results.

Issue 1—General impact of organizational training laboratories

What changes took place within the four work groups which participated in organizational laboratory training relative to any changes that took place

within the eight work groups which did not participate in organizational training laboratories—for each of the six group dimensions?

In order to shed light on this question, analyses of covariance (ANCOVA) were performed. In a statistical sense, the procedure tests whether, after training, differences between training groups and non-training groups remain after a statistical adjustment has been made for differences before training. In a sense, the ANCOVA attempts to approximate a situation in which each of the 12 groups is equated before training has occurred (Winer, 1962).

Two separate ANCOVA's were performed on each of the six group dimensions. In the first set, the four training groups were compared with the eight comparison groups. In the second set, the groupings were ignored and changes in the mean of the 31 individuals who participated in training were compared with the changes in the mean of the 60 individuals who did not participate. The results of the two analyses were similar. The extent and direction of change in the four training groups *vs.* the eight comparison groups are depicted in Figure 1.

It is immediately apparent from Table 1 that group dimensions in which a significant change occurred involved team effectiveness in problem solving (I), mutual influence among group members (III), and member's sense of personal involvement and participation in group meetings (IV). Dimensions where no significant improvement occurred included feelings of approachability toward the chairman (II), intragroup trust and confidence (V), and the general evaluation of group meetings (VI). Thus, a random group which had participated in laboratory training might phrase its perceptions as (1) we now expect and achieve greater participation in group meetings, (2) we now have a greater influence with each other, and (3) we now are a more effective team in solving problems; but (4) our chairman is no more approachable than he was, (5) we are just as much a collection of competitive individuals as we were, and (6) our group meetings are no more worthwhile than they were.

This pattern of change represents some interesting interdimensional relationships. Group effectiveness (I) and evaluation of meetings (VI) might well be considered syntality dimensions in that they are measures of the group acting as a whole. Yet, in only group effectiveness (I) did members of training groups perceive significant change. This might be considered as a change in effective synergy (Cattell, Saunders and Stice, 1953), which is that portion of group energy devoted to attaining group goals. The change also represents perceived improvement in productive performance. As a function of laboratory training, greater team effectiveness was evidently achieved without concomitant increases in evaluation of group meetings

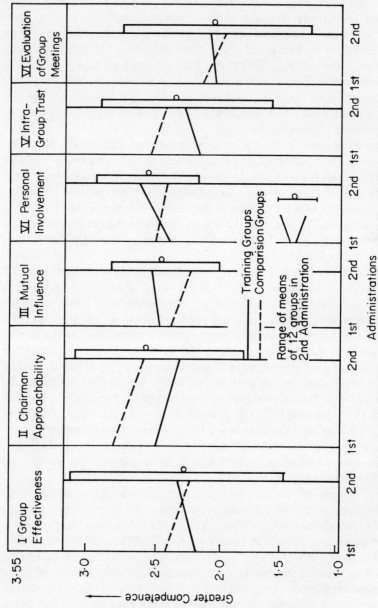

Fig. 1. First and Second Administration Scores on Six Group Dimensions.

Table 1—*Comparisons of relative gains for training members* (*T*) vs. *comparison members* (*C*) *in each of six group dimensions by analysis of covariance*

| | Relative gain[a] | | Difference in gain (T–C) | F-level[b] | |
| | Trainees | Com- parisons | | Indivi- duals | Groups[c] |
Group dimension					
I. Group effectiveness	2·40	2·14	0·26	5·01*	3·98*
II. Leader approach- ability	2·51	2·47	0·04	0·14	0·21
III. Mutual influence	2·55	2·32	0·23	6·53*	4·94*
IV. Personal involve- ment	2·64	2·44	0·20	7·15**	6·76**
V. Intragroup trust	2·36	2·34	0·02	0·03	0·00
VI. Evaluation of meetings	2·09	1·93	0·16	1·15	0·79

[a] Relative gains are represented by the adjusted means in the ANCOVA. All signs are necessarily positive as a result of the computational method rather than indicating that no decrement occurred.

[b] The F-levels for the column marked 'Individuals' indicate the significance of the ANCOVA in which the 31 trainees were compared to the 60 comparison members as *individuals*. The column marked 'Groups' indicates the significance of the ANCOVA in which the four training groups were compared to the eight comparison groups. In the latter method, all groups received the same weight regardless of differences in size of membership.

[c] Relative gains for the four training groups and the eight comparison groups are not shown. These were highly similar to relative gains by individuals.

* $p < 0.05$.

** $p < 0.01$, d.f. = 1·88.

(VI). Furthermore, these increases in effective synergy were not supported by similar increases in the maintenance synergy of increased trust and reduced competition (V).

In accordance with the literature in the area of group change and group dynamics, changes in all six of the group dimensions might have been hypothesized. For example, durable modifications in group ideology and social practice are frequently considered in terms of increased mutual influence (III), heightened involvement and participation (IV), and increased trust (or decreased competition) (V) among group members (Lewin, 1947, pp. 330–344; Coch and French, 1948). While the laboratory experience did result in significant increases in mutual influence and participation, no parallel gains in trust were found. The implication that increased trust is correlated with gains in effectiveness, mutual influence, and participation is not upheld in this study. Similarly, in this study it was found that laboratory training can result in a heightened sense of involvement and participation (IV) despite no significant improvement in members' rapport with their leader (II). Among groups which have participated in training laboratories, the coaction of heightened involvement, participation, and expectations (IV) on the one hand, and reduced leader approachability (II) on the other hand, may lead to the eventual frustration of group members and a declination in their involvement.

The combination of increased mutual influence (III) and greater member involvement (IV) after training participation implies that there is far more nteraction among members in the group setting. But this interaction without concurrent improvement in intragroup trust (V) suggests that members are tackling group problems more as a collection of competitive individuals —each utilizing his own skills, rather than an interaction of the unified group, typified by intragroup trust and confidence—drawing upon the total-group competence.

These results, in general, point to the complexity of the training impact upon group members. Concomitant changes in all dimensions do not seem to occur. In particular, group members who have participated in training laboratories perceive themselves as a more effective problem-solving team despite the finding that certain hypothesized changes in the inter-personal processes do not appear to be significantly modified.

Issue 2—Diversity of impact of training upon individuals on each of the six group dimensions

What is the impact of training in terms of changes in the ranking of individuals on each of the six group dimensions?

The previous analysis (Issue I) indicated that laboratory experience resulted in significant improvements in group effectiveness (I), mutual influence (III) and personal involvement (IV). That analysis was concerned primarily with changes in *average group* competence in training and control members. However, it is also possible that the impact of laboratory experience has diverse impacts across *individuals* who participate. Hypothetically, if this diversity is such that gains and decrements in group competence (as perceived by each individual) cancel out each other, no *average* change across trainees will have occurred. Yet, it is possible that every individual has changed his perception of his group; i.e. half in a positive direction and half in a negative direction. In order to test this possibility, correlations between pre and post-scores on each of the six dimensions were computed separately for those who participated in laboratory experience and those who did not.

Correlation coefficients for training members and comparison members, as well as the differences in coefficients for each dimension, are listed in Table 2. The magnitude of the correlation is indicative of the consistency of the rank order of individuals before training as compared to after training.

Table 2—*Pre and post-correlation coefficients for trainee members and comparison members*

Group dimension	Comparisons	Trainees	Difference in correlation $(C–T)^a$
I. Group effectiveness	0·80	0·55	0·25*
II. Leader approachability	0·81	0·50	0·31*
III. Mutual influence	0·71	0·54	0·17
IV. Personal involvement	0·80	0·43	0·37**
V. Intragroup trust	0·68	0·57	0·11
VI. Evaluation of meetings	0·64	0·42	0·22

^{a} Tests of significance were computed after r to z transformations of all correlation coefficients.
* $p < 0.05$.
** $p < 0.01$; Comparisons, $N = 60$; Trainees, $N = 31$.

The correlations for control members, in effect, are a measure of the (test–retest) reliabilities of the six dimensions.* It is immediately apparent from Table 2 that group members who participated in organizational training laboratories during the six-month period experienced a diversity of impacts, whereas group members who did not participate in such training maintained an unusually stable ranking on the six dimensions. This difference in stability (or change) among individual rankings was significant in the case of group effectiveness (I), leader approachability (II), and personal involvement (IV). Trainees changed significantly more in relative perception of their group on these dimensions than did the comparison members. This diversity is understandable in that laboratory experience can be expected to affect different individuals in different ways; in part as a function of each person's specific needs, and also in his mode of interaction in the training experience. The impact of laboratory experience upon perceptions of mutual influence (III), intragroup trust (V), and evaluation of meetings (VI) was somewhat more consistent when compared to that of comparison members; but no significant differences between trainee and comparison members were found on these dimensions. This seems to be due to less consistency on these dimensions among comparison members rather than to significantly greater consistency among training participants.

In dimensions of group effectiveness (I) mutual influence (III), and personal involvement (IV), it will be remembered that the analysis of

* Of the first six factors, the test–retest reliabilities of scales V and VI are somewhat low. However, since the six-month interval is longer than usual for test–retest reliabilities and since the internal consistency reliability of these scales is relatively high, the reliabilities are viewed as acceptable.

Issue I indicated a significant training impact. The results of this section can now be incorporated with the previous analysis to indicate that, although the impacts of training in group effectiveness and mutual influence are diverse across individuals, they are definitely positive in direction. The impact upon mutual influence (III) was significantly positive and consistent.

Finally, in perception of leader approachability (II), no significant changes occurred in the *average* competence of trainees as a result of laboratory experience, but the training impact was significantly diverse to have resulted in a larger number of both positive and negative changes. The 0·81 correlation for comparison members in perception of leader approachability and the significant decrement in this dimension for comparison members (Figure 1) imply a *deterioration* which is disturbingly consistent across group members who did not participate in laboratory experience.

Issue 3—Possible Biases in the Selection of Training and Control Groups

Prior to training, did the competence of training groups differ from that of comparison groups?

In a field study of this kind, the researcher obviously has little prerogative in selecting matched groups for training and control purposes. He must generally abide by the decisions of the organizational groups with which he deals. The question then arises as to the similarity of the training and comparison groups prior to training.

To explore this question, analyses of variance were performed which indicated that the comparison groups had significantly greater competence than the pre-training groups on three of the six group dimensions: group effectiveness (I), approachability of the chairman (II), and intragroup trust (V). These data are indicated in the first three columns of Table 3. Statistical (covariance) methods were used to compensate for these initial differences. However, such methods are not equivalent to experimental methods in which all groups are matched on each dimension prior to training.

Perhaps the more relevant question concerns the reasons for greater competence in the comparison groups (and less competence in the pre-training groups) before training. Note the words 'before training', rather than 'before the research project'; the administration of the GBI to the comparison groups actually was part of the research project. Obviously it is impossible to measure group adequacy before measuring group adequacy —it would have been neat to have done so, for then some light would have been cast upon the effect of the administration of the GBI.

If the assumption can be made that comparison groups were, in fact, more competent than pre-training groups, then a bias in selection of groups did exist. Such a bias might well be attributed to a selection process in

Table 3—*Mean raw scores in six group dimensions before and after research project for four training groups and eight comparison groups*

Group dimension	Before research project			After research project			Changes	
	Trainees	Comparisons	T–C	Trainees	Comparisons	T–C	Trainees	Comparisons
I. Group effectiveness	2·08	2·35	−0·27*	2·31	2·28	0·03	0·23*	−0·07
II. Leader approachability	2·46	2·78	−0·32*	2·37	2·62	−0·25*	−0·09	−0·16**
III. Mutual influence	2·44	2·40	0·04	2·61	2·37	0·24*	0·17*	−0·03
IV. Personal involvement	2·53	2·57	−0·04	2·68	2·51	0·17	0·15*	−0·06
V. Intragroup trust	2·13	2·58	−0·45**	2·25	2·45	−0·20	0·12	−0·13
VI. Evaluation of meetings	2·04	2·13	−0·09	2·08	2·02	0·06	0·04	−0·11

* $p < 0.05$.
** $p < 0.01$; Comparisons, N = 60; Trainees, N = 31.

which groups that perceive themselves as less effective gravitate toward
training as a mechanism to alleviate procedural and interpersonal inadequacies. If this is the case, then the questionnaire is merely validly reflecting
these inadequacies.

An alternative explanation, which incorporates and builds upon the
above concepts, suggests that differences between comparison and training
groups are artifactual and are due to researcher–participant interactions. It
is quite possible that the process of reading, considering, and responding to
items in a questionnaire serves as important stimuli upon each group
member, and that the nature of these stimuli differs for pre-training
members as opposed to comparison members. For example, in this study
pre-trainees (1) had already planned to participate in a training laboratory
when they completed the GBI, (2) had therefore considered at least some of
the issues raised by the items in the GBI, (3) had hopes that something was
going to be done about these issues, and (4) had perhaps reacted with greater
acceptance and realism, and with less defensiveness, to the GBI items.
Comparison members on the other hand (1) had probably not considered
the issues raised by the questionnaire, (2) were informed that they were
participating as a comparison group (although the word comparison was
not used), (3) had reacted to the lack of previous confrontation and to their
label of 'comparison group' with a desire and a need to demonstrate the
competence of their group to themselves and to the researcher. Furthermore, since no training was planned—nor was any likely to be planned—
increased dissonance of the comparison groups would have resulted from
their admission to the researcher and to themselves of any inadequacies with
no corresponding remedy (laboratory training).

Issue 4—Possible artifacts in measuring the relative changes of the
training groups *vs.* the comparison groups

*What changes occurred in the comparison groups when considered separately
from the training groups? Did these changes affect measurement of the
training impact?*

A casual glance at Figure 1 will show that the mean competence for the
comparison groups declined on all six dimensions.

*Did the significant relative improvements that were found in Issue I occur
within the training groups only because of this 'unfair' comparison with
comparison group decrements?*

Separate analysis indicates that the apparent decrements of the comparison groups did not differ significantly from a zero change for five of the
six dimensions, but a significant decline did occur on the chairman
approachability dimension (II) ($p < 0.01$). For the training groups, gains in

dimensions I, III and IV do differ significantly from zero and thus are of consequence whether compared to the decrement in comparison groups or compared to a zero change.

As mentioned, during the course of a six-month period, the comparison groups declined significantly in the extent to which they perceived their chairman as approachable. This decline presumably occurred as a result of events which took place during the six-month interval. Similar findings of an increase in competence for training groups and a corresponding *decrease* for comparison groups is not uncommon. Miner (1960) reports that supervisors attending a course in psychology showed significant gains in attitude toward the human relations aspects of their jobs, while a control (comparison) group from the same department *evidenced a significant decline*. The author reasons that 'the training acted in such a way as to ward off or minimize those factors operating to produce an increase in negative attitudes . . .'. In other words, he suggests that *all groups would have declined* in attitude had not training occurred for some groups. This explanation would seem to assume that some negative event had transpired within the context in which *both* training and comparison groups operated, and yet no such event is noted. It is also difficult to explain the decline in chairman approachability (II) in the current study as one which might also occur if divorced from the research project itself. To do so would imply that groups in their natural organizational settings undergo continual deterioration on at least one dimension; that of chairman approachability. Rather, this decline might be viewed as a function of participation by comparison groups in a research project—without their concurrent participation in the corresponding laboratory experience.

In Issue 3 of this report, the suggestion was offered that the tendency for comparison groups to describe themselves as more adequate in the first administration of the GBI was a function of researcher–participant interactions and the realization that no laboratory training would be forthcoming. But what happened to these auspicious descriptions as the comparison groups reassembled continuously over a six-month period and were confronted recurrently with whatever inadequacies they gradually perceived? Our hypothesis is that the opportunity to express their reactions (concerning the group and its meetings) to the feelings that had been aroused over a six-month period materialized *in the form of the second administration of the GBI*. Prior to the research study, members had an unclear perception of the role of the group leader, or of their expectations of this role as it affected them in terms of chairman approachability. The first administration of the GBI queried comparison group members with blunt questions as sensitive issues which they were unprepared to confront at that time. But after six months of observing those inadequacies which did occur, expectations and standards of the leadership role became clearer. Since current leadership practice did not conform to these expectations, comparison group members now perceived significantly greater inadequacies in the rapport and approachability of their chairman.

Discussion

This study has indicated that significant improvements in effectiveness and interaction processes of work groups do occur as a result of participation in organizational training laboratories. These improvements take place in areas which are of direct personal and organizational relevance to members of the ongoing work groups and endure for a period of at least six months beyond the training experience. The specific problem areas in which significant positive changes occurred were group effectiveness, mutual influence among members, and personal involvement and participation. Those areas which showed no significant changes were leader approachability, intragroup trust, and the evaluation of group meetings. In general, these findings point to the complexity of the impact of organizational training laboratories upon ongoing work groups.

A further analysis has indicated that training participation not only has an impact upon the work group as a unit, but also upon individuals (relative to each other) within the group. Changes in perceptions of those individuals who participated in training laboratories were more diverse over the six-month period than were the changes of perceptions of those who did not participate. Although the diversity in change was apparent on all six dimensions, it was statistically significant in group effectiveness, leader approachability, and personal involvement.

Several questions were raised as a result of some of the unforeseen findings of this study. It was noted that groups which did not participate in training were significantly more competent than training groups on several dimensions *prior to the training*. This difference may be attributed to the training selection process in which groups that perceive themselves as less competent gravitate toward training. An alternative hypothesis is that pretraining differences were due to researcher–subject interactions. It was suggested that comparison group members were not playing the role assigned to them by the researcher (Back, Hood and Brehm, 1964). Rather, they reacted to the first administration of the GBI with a need to demonstrate the competence of their group to themselves and to the researcher. Comparison and training groups differed in this respect in that the former experienced no previous confrontation of the issues raised in the GBI, nor could they expect any remedy for an admission to work group problems.

References

Back, K. W., T. C. Hood and Mary L. Brehm (1964) *The Subject Role in Small Group Experiments.* Durham, N.C.: Duke University.

Bennis, W. G. (1963) 'A new role for the behavioural sciences: effecting organizational change.' *Administrative Science Quarterly,* **8**, 125–165.

Bennis, W. G., K. D. Benne and R. Chin (Eds.) (1962) *The Planning of Change.* New York: Holt, Rinehart and Winston.

Cattell, R. B., B. R. Saunders and G. F. Stice (1953) 'The dimensions of syntality in small groups.' *Human Relations,* **6**, 331–356.

Coch, L. and J. R. P. French (1948) 'Overcoming resistance to change.' *Human Relations,* **1**, 512–532.

Fleishman, E. A., E. F. Harris and H. E. Burtt (1955) *Leadership and Supervision in Industry.* Columbus: Bureau of Educational Research, Ohio State University.

Friedlander, F. (1966) 'Performance and interactional dimensions of organizational work groups.' *Journal of Applied Psychology,* **50**, 257–265.

Harrison, R. (1962) 'Evaluations and conclusions.' In C. Argyris, *Interpersonal Competence and Organizational Effectiveness.* Homewood, Ill.: Richard D. Irwin, Inc.

Lewin, K. (1947) 'Group decision and social change.' In T. Newcomb and E. Hartley (Eds.), *Readings in Social Psychology.* New York: Henry Holt.

Lippitt, R. (1949) *Training in Community Relations.* New York: Harper & Brothers.

Mann, F. C. (1962) 'Study and creating change.' In W. G. Bennis, K. D. Benne and R. Chin (Eds.), *The Planning of Change.* New York: Holt, Rinehart and Winston.

Miner, J. B. (1960) 'The effect of a course in psychology on the attitudes of research and development supervisors.' *Journal of Applied Psychology,* **44**, 224–232.

Riecken, H. (1952) *The Volunteer Work Camp: A Psychological Evaluation.* Cambridge, Mass.: Addison-Wesley Publishing Co.

Sanford, N. (1965) 'Will psychologists study human problems?' *American Psychologist,* **20**, 192–202.

Shepard, H. (1960) 'An action research model.' In Esso Standard Oil Company, *An Action Research Program for Organizational Improvement.* Ann Arbor, Mich: Esso Standard Oil Company, Foundation for Research on Human Behaviour.

Stock, Dorothy and H. Thelen (1958) *Emotional Dynamics and Group Culture.* Washington, D.C.: National Training Laboratories.

Winer, B. J. (1962) *Statistical Principles in Experimental Design.* New York: McGraw-Hill.

CHAPTER 4

The T-group Trainer*

In a book concerned with T-group training, *T-Group Theory and the Laboratory Method*, Blake (1964) states that the primary task of the trainer in a T-group is one of 'creating the most productive climate in which the participant can accept responsibility for his own development and can develop valid communications with others'. Tannenbaum, Weschler and Massarik (1961) suggest that to facilitate this the trainer performs several broad functions in the group. First, he provides numerous focal points for discussion and exploration. For example, he may focus attention on his role of authority figure or use research instruments in structuring particular situations for potentially useful insights. Second, he establishes a model of behaviour in the group. He may encourage and accept criticism, express his own feelings, or direct feedback to other people. And finally, he facilitates the flow of communication by initiating, clarifying and encouraging the discussion of essential issues: issues of leadership, group avoidance, interpersonal conflict and intimacy.

The empirical studies of the trainer are of four sorts. The first provide an assessment of the relationship between trainer personality and trainer style; the second, indicate participant perceptual change in reference to the trainer; the third, the trainer's impact on group development; and the fourth, the processes of trainer influence as it relates to participant change.

Relationship between trainer personality and trainer style

There are two studies that evaluate the trainers personality and his style. Deutsch, Pepitone and Zander (1948) looked at a leader of a basic skill training group (the forerunner to a T-group). The study was designed to

* A condensed and revised version of a paper which was published by the authors in *Training and Development Journal* and reproduced by special permission from the March, 1970 issue. Copyright 1970 by the American Society for Training and Development, Inc.

show the interrelationship between the personality needs of the trainer and
his resultant behaviour in the group. His personality was measured by TAT,
Rorschach, Sentence Completion, Ideology Interview and Questionnaire,
and a self-administered life history questionnaire.

His behaviour in the group was assessed by the Workshop Faculty (staff
members of the T-group), without prior knowledge of the clinical results.
The clinical examination indicated:

'Superior intellectual ability, turned creative imagination to immediate and
practical aspects of work, sufficiently socially adaptable but has internal turmoil.
Basically sensitive to others, affilitative and non-aggressive. Skilled in communication, tactfulness and social responsiveness; combined with this ideology
should make for an effective democratic group leader.'

A content analysis of his behaviour in the T-group revealed the following:

'Warm and friendly, gets ideas across easily, never interrupts a group member,
sensitive and careful not to hurt anyone's feelings, no strong emotional displays
such as from moroseness to manicness, extremely unassertive, rarely undertakes
critical analysis, and spontaneous.'

This study illustrates the way in which the trainer's predilections based on
personality characteristics may influence his training philosophy and
behaviour.

Reisel (1959) performed a similar clinical study on two well-established
trainers. A research clinical psychologist carried out the study by observing
each of the subjects as they worked with student T-groups. He attended all
the sessions for both the groups and after each session met individually with
each of the trainers for a clinical interview lasting between 30–45 minutes
(the interviews were taped). In effect, the study attempted to show the
continuous interrelationship between trainer personality and trainer
behaviour in the group. The following excerpts represent the picture drawn
of these relationships:

Trainer I:

'The first trainer's main characteristic was his self-effacing attitude toward
himself and toward his work. He tended to play a warm and benevolent role of
father figure for his group. These characteristic traits, the clinician interpreted,
served to hide a large portion of underlying anxiety over the expression of
hostility. His role of trainer was thusly carried out without the awareness that it
was a means by which he could attract attention and gain vocal vision for purposes
of satisfying his strong needs for affection.'

Trainer II:

'He was characterized by the clinician as having a powerful need to produce.
This trainer was seen as highly ambivalent in his behaviour because of his insati-
able need to be successful. He attempted to behave in a way that would achieve

outward success, as an authoritarian, and at the same time tried to avoid being authoritarian. Consequently he denied the existence of his power in the group but stuck to it unawares.'

The effectiveness of the trainer, it would seem, depends not only on his training, the type of group being trained, or other sociocultural determinants, but also on certain of his personality characteristics. The findings of these two studies are highly tentative, being based on only three cases, but as far as they go, they illustrate that the trainer's personality has an effect on his training style in the group.

Participant perceptual change and the trainer

A second set of studies have attempted to look at T-group members' perceptual change in relation to the trainer. Lohmann, Zenger and Weschler (1959) performed a study to determine whether changes occur in students' self-perceptions and their perceptions of trainers during a T-group. The subjects were male and female college students in three T-groups. They used the Gordon Personal Profile which yields measures of ascendancy, responsibility, emotional stability, sociability, and a total self-evaluation score (a summated score of the previous four measures). Scores were obtained for students' self-perception, students' perception of the trainer, and for the trainer's self-perception. They found that trainers were seen by the students as significantly more adequate at the beginning than at the end of the group. However, the test of another hypothesis indicated a tendency for the students to see their trainer as more adequate than themselves, despite diminished idolization. And lastly, a trend was noted in the direction of the convergence of the students' perception of the trainer and the trainer's self-perception by the end of the group. These findings provide some evidence of the trainer's pre-eminence in the group, especially during the initial stages, and, in fact, although there is a diminished idolization of him, the tendency is to continue to see him as more adequate than themselves.

Vansina (1961) was also interested in the participants' perception of the trainer. He hypothesized that the T-group has an influence on its members' attitudes and opinions, and, since the experience is related to the problem of leadership, these should move closer to those of the trainer. He used two groups of social work students on a four-day residential course. After the introductory session every member of the group, as well as the trainer, described, by means of an item-sort, his image of his actual-self and of his attempted-self (image of ideal leader). This was repeated in the penultimate session when the participants made a new sorting. He found that the participants' attempted-self image became significantly more similar to that of the trainer at the later sorting.

There can be little doubt that the trainer's intervention in the group effects participant change to some degree and in one form or another. This change may take many forms: for example, the trainer may force compliance, serve as a model, or offer help and information. Lohmann and co-workers and Vansina have assessed participant change regarding the trainer, but they did not provide direct information about the meaning of the change and thus the reader has to make inferences from the data. To make such inferences meaningful, a consistent theoretical framework which accounts for the mechanisms and dynamics of the change is needed. This is particularly apparent when one attempts to make predictions about subsequent perceptions or behaviour.

Trainer's impact on group development

In recent years, there has been considerable emphasis on group development *vis-à-vis* the trainer. Stock and Hill (1958) suggested that the trainer's location within the sub-group structure of the group could partially explain why groups develop in given ways. Two groups were observed and a Behavioural Rating System was developed to examine a sample of meetings in terms of quality of work and emotionality. Each of the groups was found to be different in its level of work and expressed emotionality, over the period of group life. Each member was asked to describe his own group-related behaviours and feelings (a series of descriptive statements based on 'most like' and 'least like' himself). These were factor analysed and number of each group's self-perception subtypes were found (for example, Group A was identified as 'interested in maintaining work-oriented, non-personal relationships with others, they are withdrawn, exhibit considerable confusion and anxiety'). Thus, the group's development could be understood in terms of the kind of subtypes that emerge and the amount of consensus within them. It was suggested that the location of the trainer in terms of various emotional and work subgroups (for example, 'if in one or two mutually incompatible and warring subtypes he was blocked in conflict resolution'), the nature of the consensus of these subgroups, and its compatibility with other groups of varying levels of consensus could provide information on group development.

Stermerding (1961) performed a study which reflected the influence of the trainer on group development. He used two Dutch T-groups composed of management consultants and trainers in industry. A tape-recording was made of the groups throughout the experience. The participants were asked daily to fill in forms that required them to state in which of three possible areas they were learning from the group; about themselves, about groups, or about their daily work. They were also given a case study of a decision-making group, at the beginning and at the end of the experience, and asked to describe the kinds of things that were happening in the case. Their replies to the case study were then content analysed into five categories; general normative approach, personality, stereotyping, role functioning, and process-analysis. The trainer behaviour was examined via an analysis of the tape recordings of his interventions. And finally, a trainer assessment form was used by each trainer in evaluating, at the end of the group, their respective groups in terms of movement toward task, maintenance, sensitivity, and over-all effectiveness. A content analysis of the trainer interventions revealed that Trainer A showed a group-oriented approach, while Trainer B directed most of his interventions toward individual group members. Corresponding to this, Group A significantly differed from Group B on a number of process variables: Group A was seen to accentuate the 'group' aspect of learning while Group B emphasized equally the learnings about themselves and their daily work; Group A described the second case study in more process-analytic terms (in their observations of the actual interaction process of the case study) while Group B described it more in terms of role functioning (the relations of an individual in the social context); and finally, Group A was seen by its trainer as moving toward maintenance, sensitivity and overall effectiveness while Group B was seen as moving toward task only. The author draws the conclusion that trainer behaviour and group development are inextricable related. Once again we have some indication of the impact of the trainer in the T-group system, and yet, the link between the trainer and individual learning or group development is still unclear, that is, *how* or by what process does he influence these outcomes?

Psathas and Hardert (1966) investigated the effects of the trainer interventions on the pattern of group behaviour, specifically its normative behaviour. They hypothesized that the trainer interventions 'contain implicit norm-messages indicating to members what norms should be established in the group'. Seven two-week T-groups were studied each containing 12 members. A tape recording was made of the first three and last three sessions for each group and a verbatim record was kept of trainer interventions. At the close of each session the participants and the trainer were asked to write down the most significant trainer intervention. An inventory of norms was established by surveying the T-group literature. A list was then compiled, which grouped the normative items into *ought* and *should* statements, and a list of norm-categories was then established. The results indicate that 'trainer interventions can be reliably classified into these categories' (potentially biased since the authors did the sorting), and thus, 'implicit in trainer interventions, then, is a message concerning what members should or ought to do, and his view of what constitutes appropriate T-group member behaviour'. In addition they found that trainer interventions were consistently judged to fit into four normative categories more than any others; analysing group interaction or process, feelings, feedback and acceptance concern. These categories were consistently high from one time period to another, which the authors suggest reflects the persistent trainer problem of establishing these norms. It is notable, however, that analysing group interaction or process is highest in the early time period whereas acceptance concern is highest in the late time period, which they imply, offers evidence of some pattern in group development.

Although not specifically structured to investigate the trainer *vis-à-vis* group development, Psathas and Hardert's study is highly relevant to this issue. One is forced, however, to question the assumption that a reliable classification of trainer interventions into norm-categories is evidence that the trainer is actually communicating to the members what should or ought to be done. The validity of the assumption can be more directly tested by examining, perhaps, the complete intervention episode (i.e., the trainer's intervention and the subsequent member response).

Another study (Mann, 1966), examines the member-to-trainer relationship in the development of the group. Two self-analytic groups were used for the study. They were composed of university students who met five times a week for 50 minutes each session, for a total of 32 sessions, and were heterogeneous in terms of age, sex and background. Verbatim records and tape recordings were used throughout the groups. A scoring-system was designed to measure 'each act initiated by a group member for the state of his feelings toward the trainer'. The scoring system included 16 categories broken down into three major headings: Impulse area ('member's aggressive and libidinal ties with the trainer'), Authority Relations area ('power and dependency issues'), and an Ego State area ('member's feelings toward himself in the context of the relationship with the trainer'). A scheme was then developed to provide a theory of the development of member–trainer relations, in assessing the similarities and differences on the above variables between the two groups. The five stages of this development are as follows:

Stage 1: *Appraisal:* 'The trainer is the focus for much of the anxiety aroused in members by the new situation; they tend to perceive and use him as an ally in reducing their anxiety and controlling their impulses; they tend to project their ego-ideal onto the trainer, partly as a means of allaying anxiety, but also as a means of setting a satisfying relationship; and he is a source of frustration.'

Stage 2: *Confrontation:* 'Expression of hostile or counter-dependent feelings serves both to challenge the authority of the trainer, and to express the member's exasperation with the trainer's failure to reciprocate affection and esteem. Or, he is at this point serving the purpose of "naming the devil", of crystallizing the vaguely apprehended dangers and uncertainties inherent in a new group.'

Stage 3: *Re-evaluation:* 'The stage is one in which the previous images of the trainer are tested for their continuing usefulness, and an important means of re-evaluation of the image occurs when the members compare the ego state appropriate to the image with how they feel at the moment.'

Stage 4: *Internalization:* 'A shift of the members toward the trainer as internal object. There are two phases in this stage, identification and work. What constitutes success or productive effort? What is work in this group? And how do we go about it?'

Stage 5: *Separation:* 'Anticipation as the group comes to a close, loss and sadness at the losing of the relationship with the trainer.'

He found a number of similarities and differences between the two groups with regard to the above scheme. The primary differences, he suggests, were a result of the way in which each group dealt with the trainer in the confrontation period. Group 2 expressed a great deal of hostility toward the trainer and avoided the issue of appraising him. Group 1, however, confronted the dependency and authority position of the trainer. As a result Group 1 entered the re-evaluation stage and engaged in reparative work, 'to undo and control the aggression of the previous period', whereas Group 2 showed signs of distress and were frightened about the expression of hostility and concerned about its containment. In consequence, Group 2 never entered the internalization stage to any great extent and was left with the need to deal with unresolved issues of anxiety and depression arising out of the confrontation stage. Group 1's reparative work and consequent decrease in anxiety provided it with a period of internalization, although within this stage some anxiety and hostility reappeared.

Mann's study provides a valuable contribution in understanding the importance of the trainer in the T-group. It increases our knowledge of the possible consequences of dealing with authority-based issues and provides an overall schema of group development that encourages a focus on the participant's experience of the learning relationship.

Trainer influence and participant change

A number of points have been made about the variables which need to be considered in describing the trainer's impact in a T-group. No study, however, can escape the obligation to be clear about the conditions necessary to establish a connection between the trainer and the results of his influence on change. The studies discussed in the last three sections, in one form or another, indicate the effect of the trainer in the T-group environment, but none of them state in what form this influence exists and how this relates to participant learning. 'Hopefully, we shall soon have instruments which will permit us to assess trainer style as an independent variable and relate it to kind and extent of outcome' (Harrison, 1966).

Some research of this kind has recently been undertaken. Peters (1966) examined the relationship between trainer identification and personal change. He found that participants who identified with the trainer, assessed by direct, indirect, and projective measures, showed personal learning within the T-group. In respect to trainer identification the participants' self-percept (measured by a semantic differential) converged with their perception of the trainer and the trainer's self-percept. This convergence was noted for most participants in six two-week T-groups. In addition, it was discovered that the more similarities (i.e. same-sex and occupational similarities) between the trainer and the member, the stronger the relationship between convergence and personal change. Peters' interpretation to account for the sex-matching and occupational similarity was that for 'identification to lead to personal change in the T-group may require a model whose attitudes, values and behaviour are relevant, functional and realistically attainable for the person'. That is, that the trainer is a more realistic reference-other or *role-model*.

The study, whilst interesting, has several shortcomings. It assesses personal change by reference to trainer ratings and peer ratings at the end of the group. This has two disadvantages: first, they are post-only measures; and second, neither of these measures of 'change' had been validated unequivocable (Miles, 1959; Bunker, 1965). The control group, as acknowledged by Peters, is more properly what Friedlander (1967) would call a 'comparison group'. Certainly in Peters' case the so-called control group differs markedly from the trained group. The former consisted of graduate students in their early twenties, while the latter consisted on the whole of high status middle-aged administrators (business, school, nursing, government and public administration officials). It would have been better, therefore, to have used a matched control group for comparison.

It is also worth noting that the convergence was clearly significant on only the indirect measurement scale; on the other scales, increases were only of borderline significance.

Nonetheless this study is interesting in that it attempts to link participant change directly to the trainer and to indicate that identification is a relevant learning mechanism in T-groups.

Culbert (1968) investigated the effects of self-disclosing trainer behaviour upon members of two student T-groups. The same trainers participated in both groups. They were provided with 'job descriptions' which set forth guide-lines for their behaviour in each group. These descriptions called for the trainers to behave similarly in both groups, that is, to differ only on the experimental condition of being more self-disclosing (mSD condition) in one group and less self-disclosing (lSD condition) in the other. The first part of the study substantiates that the experimental manipulation was successful. The trainers were judged as more self-disclosing in the mSD condition than in the lSD condition by each of three separate measures.

The data generated by this study showed that the members of the lSD group more often perceived their two-person relationships with the trainers and their specified dyad partners as therapeutic, and the mSD participants more frequently viewed their relationships with *non-critical* others as therapeutic.

As Culbert points out, interpretation as to the desirability of this difference is not clear. It could be argued that the members of the mSD group have learned to create better relationships free from dependence on the trainer. Relationships, that is, that have 'extra-group transferability'. Alternatively, it could be argued, that the lSD participants, in being centrally involved with critical members, may be participating in qualitatively richer relationships than members of the mSD group. Culbert speculates that a very high degree of self-reference behaviour in the mSD group may have been a factor in the lack of two-person therapeutic relationships.

The self-awareness data showed the mSD group as having a significantly higher degree of self-awareness than the lSD group, a difference which narrowed with time. Culbert concludes from this that the results are consistent with *modelling theory*. The subjects of the mSD group appear to have modelled their participation after their self-disclosing trainers. This explanation, Culbert notes, is given further support from clinical impressions reported by the two trainers and the group observer.

In his conclusion, Culbert argues strongly that there is an optimum level of self-awareness for T-group participation and that early attainment of this level is to the group's advantage. It follows from this that self-disclosing trainer participation is called for at least during the early meetings. Upon attainment of this self-awareness level the trainer could productively 'pull in' and be less self-disclosing. It is to be noted, however, that much of this conclusion is speculative in view of the small sample size and in the absence of unambiguous data.

Bolman (1969) added to Culbert's approach in investigating the relationship among certain dimensions of trainer behaviour (similar to self-disclosure) and member learning. He found that one trainer variable was crucial in the learning process, the variable represented by the factor labelled congruence-empathy. It was found that trainer congruence-empathy was positively related to participant learning (as measured by self-rated learning, others' learning, and peer-rated learning). While the data in this study was limited in that it was based only on the perceptions of the group members, it does support the evidence in other social influence situations (Rogers, 1957; Barrett-Lennard, 1962) that change agents who are seen as congruent or honest provide opportunities for individual learning.

Cooper (1969) investigated Kelman's (1961) theory of social influence in respect to the trainer in T-groups. He focused in on two processes of social influence; identification and internalization. It was proposed that the participants' perception of trainer characteristics will determine which process of social influence is likely to result and, consequently, the way in which participants will change. He found that in an identification-based trainer influence process, that is, when the trainer was seen to be attractive: (1) the participant became more like the trainer in his attitudes (as measured by Schutz's (1958) FIRO-B) and behaviour (as measured by tape analysis); (2) changes in the participants' self-concept did not occur; and (3) the participants' work associates did not report them as having significantly changed six to nine months after the T-group (on a measure based on the Bunker (1965) categories). In an internalization-based trainer influence process, that is, when the trainer was seen to be congruent: (1) changes occurred in the participants' self-concept (change toward an increased match between self-percept and ideal-percept, self-percept and other participants' perception of him, and self-percept and actual behaviour); (2) changes in the direction of the trainers' attitudes and behaviour did not occur; and (3) the participants' work associates reported them as having changed six to nine months after the T-group.

Although the data collected by Cooper support the Kelman social influence model, it is important to note some of the assumptions implicit in this study. First, it was assumed that attractiveness and congruence are mutually exclusive dimensions, this, on the surface at least, may not be the case. Second, it was assumed that it is the participants' perception of the trainer's behaviour and not the trainer's actual behaviour that is the primary basis of influence in the relationship.

More fundamentally, an assumption throughout this chapter has been that the trainer is the principal source of influence. At the same time, we must consider whether factors other than the trainer—such as group composition, group format, intragroup dynamics—may be determinants of participant change. In future research we must examine each of these factors by introducing them into the analysis and investigating how the relationship between trainer behaviour and participant change is affected by them.

It cannot be claimed that any of the above studies have exhausted all aspects of trainer influence. They all, however, are provocative of further research.

Conclusion

Much of the trainer research reviewed in this chapter is replete with difficulties which limits the generalizability of the findings in respect to the practical considerations in the organization and conduct of T-group training. There are a number of problems posed by all such studies:

(1) The findings are based, on the whole, on small samples.

(2) Most of the studies rely for their measurements on participant perception of behaviour and not on direct observation of changes in behaviour by unbiased observers.

(3) There is a lack of agreement and clarity about what constitutes the research focus, which is reflected in the widely varying instruments and criteria used.

(4) Little attempt was made to establish a causal relation between observed group or individual changes and the trainer behaviour employed to produce them.

(5) Our survey revealed only one study specifically designed to investigate the effects of the trainer on follow-up change.

References

Barrett-Lennard, G. T. (1962) 'Dimensions of therapist response as causal factors in therapeutic change.' *Psychological Monographs*, **74**, 42.

Blake, R. R. (1964) 'Studying group action.' In L. P. Bradford, J. R. Gibb and K. D. Benne (Eds.), *T-Group Theory and Laboratory Method*. New York: John Wiley & Sons.

Bolman, L. G. (1969) 'Effects of the trainer on his T-group.' Unpublished manuscript, Carnegie-Mellon University.

Bunker, D. R. (1965) 'Individual applications of laboratory training.' *Journal of Applied Behavioral Science*, **1**, 131–148.

Cooper, C. L. (1969) 'The influence of the trainer on participant change in T-groups.' *Human Relations*, **22**, 515–530.

Culbert, S. A. (1968) 'Trainer self-disclosure and member growth in two T-groups.' *Journal of Applied Behavioral Science*, **4**, 47–74.

Deutsch, M., A. Pepitone and A. Zander (1948) 'Leadership in the small group.' *Journal of Social Issues*, **4**, 31–40.

Friedlander, F. (1967) 'The impact of organizational training laboratories upon the effectiveness and interaction of on-going work groups.' *Personnel Psychology*, **20**, 289-307.

Harrison, R. (1966) 'A conceptual framework for laboratory training.' National Training Laboratory working draft.

Kelman, H. C. (1961) 'Processes of opinion change.' *Public Opinion Quarterly*, **25**, 57-78.

Lohmann, K., J. H. Zenger and I. R. Weschler (1959) 'Some perceptual changes during sensitivity training.' *Journal of Educational Research*, **53**, 28-31.

Mann, R. D. (1966) 'The development of the member-trainer relations in self-analytic groups.' *Human Relations*, **19**, 84-117.

Miles, M. B. (1959) *Learning to Work in Groups*. New York: Teachers College, Columbia University.

Peters, D. R. (1966) 'Identification and personal change in laboratory training groups.' Unpublished Ph.D. thesis, Alfred P. Sloan School of Management, M.I.T.

Psathas, G. and R. Hardert (1966) 'Trainer interventions and normative patterns in the T-groups.' *Journal of Applied Behavioral Science*, **2**, 149-170.

Reisel, J. (1959) 'The trainer role in human relations training.' Paper read at the Western Psychological Association meeting, April, 1959.

Rogers, C. R. (1957) 'The necessary and sufficient conditions of therapeutic personality change.' *Journal of Consulting Psychology*, **21**, 95-103.

Schutz, W. C. (1958) FIRO: A Theory of Interpersonal Relations. New York: Rinehart.

Stermerding, A. H. (1961) 'Evaluation research in the field of sensitivity training.' Unpublished manuscript, Leiden: Netherlands Institute of Preventive Medicine.

Stock, D. and W. F. Hill (1958) 'Inter subgroup dynamics as a factor in group growth.' In D. Stock and H. Thelen, *Emotional Dynamics and Group Culture*. New York: New York University Press.

Tannenbaum, R., I. R. Weschler and F. Massarik (1961) *Leadership and Organization*. New York: McGraw-Hill.

Vansina, L. (1961) 'Research concerning the influence of the T-group method on the formation of the participants' social values and opinions.' In *Evaluation of Supervisory and Management Training Methods*. Paris: Organization for Economic Cooperation and Development.

Trainer Self-Disclosure and Member Growth in Two T-groups*

Samuel A. Culbert

Behavioural Science Department,
University of California, Los Angeles

This study compares the effects that 'more' or 'less' self-disclosing trainer behavior had upon members of two T-groups. Part I of the data analysis substantiates that the experimental manipulation took place as intended. Part II shows that while an equivalent number of 2-person 'perceived therapeutic relationships' were formed in each group, Ss in the group with less self-disclosing trainers (*lSD*) more often entered them with their dyad partners and trainers; Ss with more self-disclosing trainers (*mSD*) entered relationships more often with other members. Part III shows that although both groups eventually attained the same level of self-awareness, the *mSD* group did so earlier. A revised prescription for trainer behavior is advanced, suggesting that the trainer might optimally begin his participation with a high rate of self-disclosure and become more selective with time.

Noticeably missing from the literature on T-groups is research on trainer behavior. This gap exists despite widespread acceptance of the T-group trainer as a key factor in group process. The absence of trainer research is no oversight; it bespeaks the complexity of this research topic. Such complexity centers around the need for a methodological strategy that takes account of the particular training orientation being studied. That is, trainer behavior should not be researched without specifically considering both the training goals and the processes the trainer adopts in implementing them.

The orientation of the trainers in the present study is that of Clark (1963). Very briefly, it specifies that shifting 2-person encounters among group participants, encounters of the kind endorsed by Rogers (1961), is the most effective process for bringing about personal growth. Accordingly, the aspect of trainer behavior being investigated here, *trainer self-disclosure*, is evaluated relative to its ability to produce this type of inter-personal encounter, termed 'perceived therapeutic relationships' (PTRs), and the goal that these relationships are hypothesized to bring about in the member,

* Published in the *Journal of Applied Behavioral Science*, **4**, 1968, 47–73. The researcher extends deepest thanks to James V. Clark, Tommy M. Tomlinson and H. Kenneth Bobele, all of whom contributed greatly to the completion of this project.

125

'increased self-awareness'. It is noted that data have already been collected to support the connection between the number of PTRs formed reciprocally, or 'mutually', between pairs of T-group participants and individual increases in self-awareness (Clark and Culbert, 1965).

Also involved in the methodology of this study was a decision on data collection. A strategy needed to be formulated on how much data would be required to measure effectively trainer self-disclosure and the hypothesized dependent variables of PTRs and member self-awareness. Data relevant to each of these variables are generated in voluminous amounts within even a single T-group. Moreover, the exacting methodology used in this study is considered to have a good amount of generalizability. Thus it was decided to extract data from but two T-groups, each corresponding to different degrees of trainer self-disclosure.

Purpose

This study is an attempt to assess the differential effects along two measures of personal learning—one interpersonal and one intrapersonal—between the members of two T-groups where their identical co-trainers, acting consonantly, have been more and less personally self-disclosing. More specifically, the following hypotheses are formulated:

1. Members of a T-group where the co-trainers are 'more personally self-disclosing'* will enter into a greater number of 'mutually perceived therapeutic relationships' than members of a T-group whose trainers are 'less personally self-disclosing'.

   a. Similarly, the members of the group with the more self-disclosing co-trainers will perceive their dyad partner, with whom they have met regularly over the span of the group life, as being more 'therapeutic', in their 2-person relationships, than will members of the T-group where the trainers are less self-disclosing.

   b. Likewise, members of the T-groups with the more self-disclosing co-trainers will perceive these trainers as being more 'therapeutic', in their 2-person relationships, than will members of the other T-group with whom these trainers have been less self-disclosing.

2. Members of the T-group where the co-trainers are more self-disclosing will experience a greater positive change in 'self-awareness', early to late, than the members of the T-group where the trainers are less self-disclosing.

* Quotes are used to designate terms which will be operationalized and subjected to measurement in this study.

Procedure

Subjects

The Ss were 20 upper-division and graduate students participating in two T-groups as course work for academic credit. Each group was composed of six females and four males, none of whom had previous T-group experience. Assignment to the groups was made as follows: each student was given the Jourard Self-Disclosure Questionnaire and paired with another S of the same sex who scored similarly on this premeasure. A matched-pair assignment was made subject to one alteration, that of placing previously acquainted Ss within the same T-group. This was an attempt to minimize intergroup communication, as none of the subjects were to know the 'condition' of their group.

The Ss met twice a week for 2-hour sessions over a semester's span of 14 weeks. One of these weekly sessions was spent in a T-group with the two co-trainers and the other in a dyad pairing with another group member, not a trainer. The same, randomly assigned, dyad pairings were held for the semester's duration. The times and meeting places for these group and dyad meetings were staggered to discourage intergroup communication.

Trainers

The same two male co-trainers participated in both T-groups. Their participation evened out each group into six females and six males. One of these trainers* was quite experienced both in T-group theory and practice, and the other trainer (this researcher) was a relative newcomer to T-group training at the time of the study. Both trainers ascribed to similar philosophies of member learning, following the guide-lines established by Clark (1963).

Conditions

The trainers were provided with 'job descriptions' which set forth guide-lines for their behavior in the group. These descriptions called for the trainers to follow parallel lines of personal conduct in both groups, that is, to differ only on the two experimental conditions of being more self-disclosing (mSD condition) in one group and less self-disclosing (lSD condition) in the other. In both instances, however, the trainers were to do their best to promote member self-disclosure. Once a week, and more often when needed, the two trainers discussed with an observer the problems they were experiencing in holding to these conditions.

* James V. Clark.

Measures

The measures used in this research were of two types, one requiring the Ss cooperation in filling out questionnaires and the other made without S's knowledge, using data collected from tape recordings of the T-group sessions. An overview of these measures and their purposes in this study is contained in Table 1.

Self-disclosure questionnaire. The questionnaire was a 40-item revised edition by Jourard of the Self-disclosure Questionnaire developed by Jourard and Lasakow (1958). It was administered in two forms. The first was the conventional one ('Who Knows You?'), where the respondent

Table 1—*Overview of measures used in self-disclosure study*

Experimental variable	Measure	Purpose	Rater
I. Conformation of experimental conditions	A. Self-disclosure questionnaire (inverted form)	Measure of how well Ss believe they know the two trainers	All 20 Ss
	B. Content categorization	Objective breakdown of self-statements made by trainers by per cent and type	Two specially trained judges (graduate students familiar with group process)
	C. Ratings of five-minute transcripts	Impressions of trainers' in-the-group process	Two clinicians experienced in group process
II. Hypothesis 1: Mutually and one-way perceived therapeutic relationships	A. Relationship inventory	Ratings of degree in which each S views every other S in his group as exhibiting therapeutic behavior toward him	All 20 Ss plus the 2 trainers
	B. Self-disclosure questionnaire (standard form)	S's ratings of degree to which he is known by dyad partner	Ten dyad pairings using all 20 Ss
III. Hypothesis 2: Member self-awareness	A. Process scale speech ratings	Evaluation of changes in member self-awareness from early to late meetings	Three specially trained judges (undergraduate students)

checks off, with respect to specified target persons, what of his own self (personal information) is known by these others. Two administrations of this form were given; one was made prior to the start of the T-groups with the target persons being the S's closest male and female acquaintances, and the second administration came just before the final group meeting with the same two target persons plus the S's dyad partner. Nongroup targets were used to provide a frame of reference for interpreting the scores of the dyad partners. The second form ('Whom Do You Know?'), was a variant of the first one. Each of the questions from 'Who Knows You?' was inverted so that the respondent was checking off what personal information he, as a receiver, had about the target person. This form was administered but once, just prior to the final group meeting and specified as target persons the two co-trainers plus the S's dyad as target partner.

Relationship inventory (RI). The present version of the RI is a 1964 modification of the one Barrett-Lennard (1962) developed two years before. It is a 64-item questionnaire yielding numerical scores on the extent to which one person perceives another as having positive regard, empathy, congruence, and unconditionality of regard toward him. Adding the scores for these four variables yields a fifth RI score, the sum of the other four. A more detailed description of these variables is contained in the Clark and Culbert (1965, p. 185) article as well as in Barrett-Lennard's (1962) monograph.

In this study the RI was used to measure each S's perception of the extent to which he sees himself as receiving the therapeutic qualities of positive regard, empathy, congruence and unconditional regard from a given other within the context of their interpersonal relationship. The RI was filled out by each S *vis-à-vis* every other S, plus the two trainers. These data were collected but once, just prior to the final group meeting. A one-way, 'perceived therapeutic relationship' (PTR), on a given dimension, was defined as an S rating another S above the median on the rating he assigned to all S's for that dimension. A 'mutually perceived therapeutic relationship' (MPTR) was similarly defined; only in this case both members of a 2-person relationship rated each other as being above the medians of the ratings they assigned to others. In order to include the trainers in the calculation of MPTRs, it was also necessary for them to fill out RIs on their individual perceptions of each of the S's in the two experimental groups.

Problem expression scale (PES). This scale was used to operationalize changes in the qualitative variable of 'self-awareness'. It is a seven-point rating scale which was originally designed to measure process changes occurring in individual psychotherapy (van der Veen and Tomlinson, 1962).

The PES has subsequently been used in research on group therapy (Truax, 1961) and for research in sensitivity training (Clark and Culbert, 1965).

The previous methodology is identical with that previously used in the just-mentioned T-group research. Thirty speech segments were selected for each S on a random basis from tape recordings of the T-group sessions, 15 early and 15 late. Inasmuch as each S did not participate equally in every session, and sometimes not at all, segments were selected from four early sessions (Sessions 1–4) and four late ones (Sessions 11–14). Segments from sessions 5 and 10 were used for Ss who did not produce a large enough participation sample in the selected sessions.

The 720 speech segments (from two groups of ten Ss plus two trainers with 30 segments each) were coded and typed on index cards. These cards were randomized and submitted in staggered order to three judges who had been trained along the lines prescribed in a manual developed for PES raters (Bobele, 1965). Each judge worked independently, assigning numerical ratings to each segment. The particular rating for a given segment corresponded to that one of seven stages of the PES scale which, in the judge's opinion, best described the entire speech segment. Segments which appeared to be mostly at a given stage, but showed some of the next higher stage, received a rating of 0·5 higher than the given stage.

Content analysis of trainer speech segments. A content categorization of a random sample of speech segments spoken by the two co-trainers was made in order to determine the extent to which the experimental manipulation was carried out. This particular analysis was adapted from the originally developed by Bugental (1948), fully operationalized by Weschler and Reisel (1959), and described in a manual by Reisel (1959). Two phases of the system are relevant to this study. First there is the determination of *thought units*. A thought unit is defined as a series of words expressing a single idea or thought; basically it is equivalent to a simple grammatical sentence. Second is the assignment of thought units to *content categories*. There are three types of categories having to do with self-references which, for these purposes, imply self-disclosure. The first type of self-reference refers to a trainer talking exclusively about himself. In this case he is either the subject or the subject and object of the thought unit being categorized. Such thought units are assigned to the content category 'S'. The second type of self-reference refers to the trainer discussing the way some group member or group incident affects him. Such thought units are collected under the symbol '→ S'. The third type of self-reference refers to the trainer discussing the effect his participation is having either on the group or on some subset of group members. These thought units are collected under the symbol 'S →'.

As mentioned above, this content analysis was applied to the random sample of speech segments made by the two co-trainers. In all, 120 speech segments were analysed, 15 early and 15 late for each trainer in each of the two experimental conditions. Two judges were selected on the basis of having clinical or sensitivity training backgrounds. As with the judging of PES ratings, these judges underwent a mutual training period but made their ratings independently.

Ratings of five-minute transcripts. This measure was used to collect data bearing on the impressionistic meaning the experimental manipulation held for two experienced clinicians heretofore not involved in this experiment.* Utilizing a table of random numbers, five-minute segments of unedited group process were transcribed. A total of 30 segments were selected, 15 from each experimental group. Within each group, five segments were selected from the first three, the middle three, and the last three meetings. At least one segment was selected from each meeting, and an equal number of segments were selected from early, middle, and late thirds of the meetings. Random numbers completely determined this selection, subject to the frequency requirement that a minimum of three trainer speech statements be contained within each five-minute block.

A list of 21 bipolar adjectives of the seven-point semantic differential variety was constructed (see Table 6). The 21 items were selected for their relevance either to the trainer job descriptions governing the experimental conditions or for their relevance to the Rogerian conceptualization (Rogers, 1959) regarding the process of a 'helping' relationship.

The five-minute segments (coded for group, meeting, and speaker) were then submitted to the two clinicians, who independently rated each segment along the adjectives of the bipolar check list. The instructions for making these ratings were identical with those typically used in Semantic Differential research (Osgood, Suci and Tannenbaum, 1957). The raters were requested to focus on the combined effect of the trainers' behavior, making a single rating based on their impressions of the two trainers acting in consort.

Results

The results of this study can be most clearly presented in three parts. The first part contains data relevant to discerning the extent to which the experimental manipulation was carried out as intended. The second and third parts contain data bearing on the two member variables, 'perceived

* Gerard V. Haigh and Karl Pottharst.

therapeutic relationships' and 'self-awareness', hypothesized to be affected by the manipulation. The overview contained in Table 1 should be helpful in assisting the reader to follow this presentation.

Part I: Confirmation of experimental conditions

Self-disclosure questionnaire. This questionnaire was used, in the inverted form, to provide a measure of how much personal information the Ss (of both conditions) believed they knew about their trainers. The total ratings for each experimental group are illustrated in the first two columns of Table 2. The third column contains the total number of points assigned to dyad partners on this questionnaire and provides a reference point for interpreting the meaning of these data. Although the number of points

Table 2—'*Whom do you know?*': total number of points assigned by members of each experimental group (*N* = 10)

	Trainer 1	Trainer 2	Dyad partner
mSD	68	55	285
lSD	16	19	256

Notes: James V. Clark was trainer 1 and the researcher was trainer 2.

assigned to the trainers of the *mSD* group is greater than the number assigned to the trainers of the *lSD* group, these ratings are far below the number of points assigned to dyad partners, and in both cases indicate a relatively low knowledge of the trainers. A Mann–Whitney U (Siegel, 1956) was computed, comparing the two experimental groups on the combined ratings each S made of the two trainers. The U of 86·5 was significant at the 0·01 level (2-tailed test) and supported the experimental intent that the trainers would be viewed as more self-disclosing by the Ss of the *mSD* condition.

Content categorization. 'Early' and 'late' trainer speech statements were content-analysed to provide an objective breakdown both of the percentage and the variety of self-statements made by the co-trainers in each of the experimental groups. Since two judges were used in making these categorizations, percentages of interjudge agreement were calculated. Both the separation of speech segments into thought units and the content categorization of thought units were performed with high levels of agreement—88 per cent and 79 per cent, respectively. Moreover, no systematic differences were detected when agreement as to content categorization was broken down by experimental condition, trainer, or time: each subpercentage was above 77 per cent.

The between-groups comparison of thought unit categorization is presented in Table 3. Percentage-wise, the combined trainer effort was as desired, producing almost twice the percentage of thought units categorized as self-references in the mSD condition than in the lSD condition. A two-by-two chi-square made by dichotomizing thought units into self- and non-self-references for each of the two experimental groups was highly significant ($\chi^2 = 35 \cdot 87$, $p < 0 \cdot 001$), statistically supporting the aforementioned inspection of Table 3.

Table 3—*Breakdown of content categorization of trainer speech segments: Experimental group $\times$ trainer $\times$ time*

| | mSD | | lSD | | lSD (corrected[a]) |
	Self-references	Non-self-references	Self-references	Non-self-references	self-references
Trainer 1					
Early	43 (0·402)	64	19 (0·380)	31	23·43
Late	79 (0·494)	81	42 (0·334)	84	69·64
Trainer 2					
Early	67 (0·670)	33	7 (0·117)	53	8·62
Late	59 (0·444) $\chi^2 = 8 \cdot 07*$	74	20 (0·220) $\chi^2 = 0 \cdot 69$	71	33·16
Total for both trainers	248 (0·496) $\chi^2 = 35 \cdot 87**$	252	88 (0·261)	249	134·85

Note: The numbers in parentheses are percentages of the total number of thought units represented by the number above.
[a] Corrected for differential frequency of trainer intervention.
* $p < 0 \cdot 005$.
** $p < 0 \cdot 001$.

The above categorization is best considered as a measure of the intensity of self-references and differs from the absolute quantity of trainer self-references made in the two experimental groups. This point is illustrated by the fact that while the trainers intervened more frequently in the lSD group than in the mSD group (the ratio between their combined frequencies was on the order of 3 : 2), they spoke longer in the mSD group: an average of 8·33 thought units per ratable intervention to an average of 5·61 thought units per ratable intervention in the *lSD* group. A 'corrected' trainer self-reference count was calculated for the *lSD* group so that quantity of these references might be compared (see last column in Table 3). Comparison of this estimate with the quantity of self-references in the *mSD* group is again consistent with the experimental intent to vary trainer self-disclosure. (The figures in each row of column 5 are lower than those in the same row in column 1).

Table 4—*Percentage[a] of self-reference in content categorization: trainer $\times$ experimental group $\times$ time*

	Trainer 1			Trainer 2		
	S	→S	S→	S	→S	S→
mSD Early	0·187	0·177	0·037	0·240	0·330	0·100
mSD Late	0·313	0·157	0·025	0·098	0·142	0·203
lSD Early	0·180	0·160	0·040	0·033	0·067	0·017
lSD Late	0·119	0·159	0·056	0·044	0·088	0·088

[a] Percentages are based on samples from the trainers' total participation.

Examination of the intragroup self-references (see Table 3) made by the two trainers shows statistically significant opposing trends between trainers in the *mSD* condition ($\chi^2 = 8·07$, $p < 0·005$), and similar trainer trends within the *lSD* condition, where χ^2 is nonsignificant. Overall, trainer 2 did the better job of holding the experimental conditions although his percentage of self-references decreased over time in the *mSD* group and increased in the *lSD* group. Trainer 1 began with comparable frequency in both experimental groups, making about four self-references for every ten thought units. However, with time, he participated with greater differentiation, making fewer self-references in the *lSD* group and more in the *mSD* group.

A breakdown of the specific types of self-references made by these trainers is contained in Table 4. The three types of self-references include the trainer talking exclusively about himself (S), the trainer discussing the way some group member or group incident affects him (→ S), and the trainer discussing the effect his participation is having either on the group or on some subset of group members (S →). The data for trainer 1 show that he uniformly avoided self-references of the S → variety in the *mSD* group and that he increased his combined percentage of self-references in this group. His increase in self-references was primarily accounted for by an increase in the S type reference. Trainer 2's percentage of self-references remained relatively constant in the *lSD* condition, while his percentage decreased considerably, over time, in the mSD condition. This decrease is noticeably accounted for by a shift from the S and → S types of thought units to the S → variety. However, when the data for the two trainers are combined, as in Table 5, these individual trainer differences cancel out, with the combined distribution of self-references remaining relatively constant within each group from early to late meetings.

Table 5—*Percentage of thought units content-categorized as self-references: experimental group × time*

	mSD				lSD			
	S	→S	S→	Total	S	→S	S→	Total
Early	0·213	0·251	0·068	0·536	0·100	0·109	0·027	0·236
Late	0·215	0·153	0·105	0·471	0·089	0·129	0·069	0·286
Total	0·214	0·192	0·088	0·494	0·092	0·122	0·055	0·266

Five-minute transcripts. Two experienced clinicians gave their impressions of the way the co-trainers performed in each of the experimental groups. Four sets of medians were compiled, one from each judge's ratings for each experimental group. The selection of median ratings was made on the rationale that the rating distributions would not necessarily be symmetrical. While the two judges' median ratings were not correlated ($r = 0·012$, $SD_1 = 0·650$, $SD_2 = 0·809$), they were in agreement. The percentage of agreement, using an agreement interval of 1·00, was 71 per cent. Those ratings not within this interval were split; i.e., the medians of each judge's ratings were higher than those of the others about half of the time.

The judges' median ratings were next combined to obtain an average median rating for each of the bipolar scales, on each of the experimental groups. These averages are presented in Table 6. The differences between groups on average median ratings for 15 of the 21 bipolar pairs were less than 0·5 apart. The trainers' behavior on these dimensions, then, is likely to have been similar in each experimental group. Three adjective pairs have a between-groups difference between 0·5 and 1·0. The inference from these data is that the trainers are likely to have performed differently on these dimensions in each of the two groups and were thus viewed by the judges as more 'genuine', more 'involved', and more 'personal' in the mSD group. Three adjective pairs have quite large between-groups differences, greater than 1·0. Thus, it is highly probable that the trainers were viewed as more 'vulnerable', as showing more 'feelings', and as being more 'self-disclosing' in the mSD group than in lSD group. Five of these six afore-mentioned differences are highly consistent with the experimental intent to have the trainers behave comparably in the two groups, except on the dimension of self-disclosure. The exception is on the dimension of 'genuine–artificial' where a 'less self-disclosing' trainer should be able to be viewed as equally

Table 6—*Average of median ratings assigned by judges after reading five-minute transcripts of trainer behavior*[a, b]

Dipolar adjective[c]	mSD	lSD	0·5 →	1·0 >	1·0
			Differences		
*Direct–indirect	6·02	5·60			
*Genuine–artificial	5·13	4·44		X	
Attentive–inattentive	5·09	5·13			
*Vulnerable–invulnerable	5·03	3·75			X
Important–unimportant	4·94	4·76			
Expresses warmth–coolness	4·46	4·04			
*Effective–ineffective	5·07	5·19			
Likable–not likable	4·32	4·14			
*Understanding–not understanding	5·07	5·19			
Aware–unaware	5·34	5·43			
*Interpretive–noninterpretive	4·86	4·88			
Here-and-now–there-and-then	5·27	5·57			
Analyzes–does not analyze	4·55	4·98			
Shows feelings–hides feelings	5·31	3·96			X
Directive–nondirective	4·64	4·80			
Involved–uninvolved	5·68	5·13	X		
Strong–weak	5·17	4·87			
Self-disclosing–self-concealing	5·44	3·65			
Accepting–rejecting	4·75	4·58			X
*Facilitating–hindering	5·16	5·35			
*Personal–impersonal	5·13	4·30	X		
N=30					

[a] Ratings were made on a 7-point scale, range 1·0 to 7·0 with midpoint (neutral) at 4·0. However, the average of the median ratings has a range of 0·5 to 6·5 and a midpoint of 3·5.

[b] Values of 3·5 or greater are in the direction of the first adjective presented in the bipolar pair.

[c] Those adjective pairs preceded by an asterisk were reversed in order of presentation on the rating sheets used by the judges.

genuine to a 'more self-disclosing' trainer. The lack of between-groups differences of 0·5 or more seems consistent with the experimental intent for at least 14 of the 15 adjective pairs. The one possible exception is on the dimension 'expresses warmth–expresses coolness'. It seems probably that a 'more self-disclosing' trainer should be able to avail himself of more opportunities to express warmth than a 'less self-disclosing' trainer.

Part II: Hypothesis 1: *Mutually and one-way perceived therapeutic relationships*

The Relationship Inventory was used to measure how each group participant viewed every other group member on exhibiting therapeutic behavior in their relationship. Hypothesis 1 predicted that the members of the *mSD* group would form a greater number of MPTRs than the members of the *lSD* group. Comparison of the two 'total' rows in Table 7 shows that this was not the case. These two rows are quite similar. The limiting number of such relationships was 60 (six MPTRs for each of ten group members); about one-third of this limit was attained on each dimension in each group. The remaining entries in Table 7 do not show so much similarity as the

Table 7—*Number of mutually perceived therapeutic relationships formed among group members*

		Positive regard	Impathy	Con-gruence	Uncond. regard	Total
mSD	Dyad partners	2	0	1	1	2
	With trainers	7	7	7	6	7
	All others	12	11	10	12	13
	Total	21	18	18	19	22
lSD	Dyad partners	3	2	2	4	3
	With trainers	6	10	9	8	10
	All others	12	9	10	6	8
	Total	21	21	21	18	21

totals, although none of their differences is statistically significant. This lack of significance may be more a function of a small N than a reflection of a homogeneous population. The maximum possible number of MPTRs for members with trainers was 10. Table 7 shows that the members of the *lSD* group formed more MPTRs with their dyad partners and trainers while the participants in the *mSD* group formed more MPTRs with other group members who were not so central to the experimental design.

Hypothesis 1a predicted that the members of the *mSD* group would perceive their dyad partner as being more 'therapeutic' in their 2-person relationships than would the participants in the *lSD* group. The data in Table 8 do not support this hypothesis. Again, because of the small N, statistical inference is not possible. The limiting number here is also 10.

Hypothesis 1b predicted that the members of the *mSD* group would perceive their T-group trainers as being more 'therapeutic' in their 2-person relationships than would the participants in the *lSD* group. The data in Table 8 not only fail to support this hypothesis but indicate that the converse

Table 8—*Number of one-way perceived therapeutic relationships formed among dyad partners and by members with trainers*

		mSD	lSD	χ^2
Positive regard	Dyad partner	6	7	
	With trainers	12	9	0·40
Empathy	Dyad partner	5	6	
	With trainers	12	20	7·65**
Congruence	Dyad partner	5	6	
	With trainers	13	17	1·20
Uncond. regard	Dyad partner	6	8	
	With trainers	13	14	0·11
Total	Dyad partner	5	7	
	With trainers	12	19	5·16*

* $p < 0.02$ (two-tailed).
** $p < 0.005$ (two-tailed).

better describes what took place. An χ^2 test was applied to the dichotomized distribution of the frequency with which the trainers were perceived as 'therapeutic' and the frequency with which they were not so perceived. The limiting number for each group was 20 (ten members, each rating two trainers). Two of these χ^2s were significant: the one for empathy and the one for overall total. Thus it seems that the Ss in the *lSD* group viewed their 2-person relationships with the trainers as therapeutic, taken as a total, and empathic, as a specific component, significantly more often than did the Ss in the *mSD* group.

The source of the between-groups differences in 'therapeutic' relationships formed by the members with their trainers is given clarification by Table 9. The breaking down of data into relationships formed with each individual trainer makes it apparent that the 'with trainer' differences noted

Table 9—*Breakdown of relationships members formed with group trainers*

			Positive regard	Empathy	Congruence	Uncond. regard	Total
mSD	One-way perceived	Trainer 1	8	9	10	8	9
	as therapeutic	Trainer 2	4	3	3	5	3
	Mutually perceived	Trainer 1	5	5	5	4	5
	as therapeutic	Trainer 2	2	2	2	2	2
lSD	One-way perceived	Trainer 1	7	10	10	8	10
	as therapeutic	Trainer 2	2	10	7	6	9
	Mutually perceived	Trainer 1	4	5	5	4	5
	as therapeutic	Trainer 2	2	5	4	3	5

in Table 9 are due primarily to the relationships members formed with trainer 2. Inspection shows that trainer 2 was more often perceived as 'therapeutic' in the lSD condition than in the mSD condition, while trainer 1 was perceived rather uniformly in the two groups. Dichotomized χ^2s, with Yates' correction for small numbers (Walker and Lev, 1953) applied only to the 'one-way' data of trainer 2, are significant both for 'empathy' and 'total': $\chi^2 = 7 \cdot 91$, d.f. $= 1$, $p < 0 \cdot 01$, and $\chi^2 = 5 \cdot 21$, d.f. $= 1$, $p < 0 \cdot 05$, respectively. This finding parallels the significant χ^2s presented in Table 8.

Part III: Hypothesis 2: Member self-awareness

Member self-awareness was measured by the Problem Expression Scale (PES). The correlations among the three judges for their ratings of 720

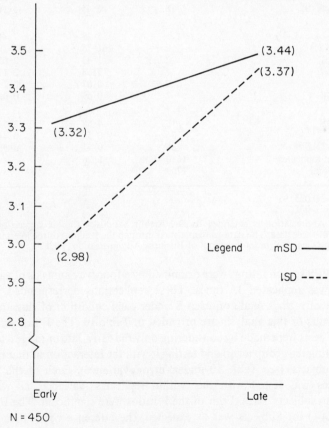

N = 450

Fig. 1. Mean PES Ratings, Early and Late, for Experimental Groups.

speech segments were within the range typically obtained for such ratings: for judges 1 and 2, r = 0·66; for judges 1 and 3, r = 0·62; and for judges 2 and 3 r = 0·59.

Figure 1 is a graph of the overall mean PES ratings for the two experimental groups. While initially the mean for the mSD group was significantly greater than the mean for the lSD group (U = 8968·5, z = 3·258, 2-tailed $p < 0.0014$), the means for these two groups converged with time.

Table 10—*Four-way analysis of variance for PES ratings (Ss only): experimental group × early–late × judges × subjects*

Source	d.f.	MS	F
Between			
Groups (G)	1	16·25	2·52
Subjects (S)	18	6·45	5·11**
Within			
Early–Late (E–L)	1	35·28	7·71*
Judges (J)	2	161·75	292·29**
E–L×J	2	1·43	2·03
G×E–L	1	9·68	2·11
G×J	2	0·07	0·13
G×E–L×J	2	0·69	0·98
Error			
E–L×S	18	4·58	3·63**
J×S	36	0·55	0·44
E–L×J×S	36	0·71	0·56
Within replicates	1680	1·26	
Total	1799		

* $p < 0.025$.
** $p < 0.001$.

Note: Appreciation is extended to Dr. Arthur Sandusky for his suggestion as to analysis of these data. The data were analyzed through the facilities of the Western Data Processing Center, Graduate School of Business Administration, UCLA.

The PES speech ratings were examined by a four-way analysis of variance which was replicated 15 times. These replications corresponded to the number of ratings made on each S under each condition of this analysis. The results of this analysis are provided in Table 10. The F ratios for the 'within' tests were made by considering only the early–late or judges' term(s) (neglecting the group term) and testing it with the interaction of that term(s) with 'subjects' (see Table 10 under 'error' variance). Each of the 'error' variances was tested with the 'within replicates' variance, as was the 'between subjects' term. Four of the F ratios were significant. The F (5·11, $p < 0.001$) for Subjects was as expected, the inference being that the Ss were significantly different in the ratings assigned to their verbal output.

The F for Early–Late was 7·71, $p < 0.025$, the inference being that PES changes take place within Ss as a result of the T-group experience, regardless of experimental condition. The F for Early–Late × subjects was 3·63, $p < 0.001$, the inference being that individual Ss change differently over time. The F for Judges was quite large, 292·29. This ratio is significant at a very high level of confidence, the 'inference' being that the three judges rated differently. However, while these judges rated differently they did so consistently as is borne out in their significantly high correlations with one another. The nonsignificant Fs for the two-way and three-way interactions with judges is also consistent with this interpretation.

The F for Between Groups was not significant. This result, however, is somewhat secondary in that the U testing of the early between-groups difference, noted previously and illustrated in Figure 1, was significant. Similarly the nonsignificant F for Group × Early–Late is of no central importance inasmuch as an early between-groups difference has already been identified.

The 'between-subjects' changes in PES ratings are displayed in Table 11. The larger early–late difference experienced by the *ISD* group is reflected in the data showing positive PES changes for all but one of this group's participants, S-10, whose performance remained just about constant. In the *mSD* group, which did not show a very large early–late group effect, Ss varied more widely in their PES changes than the Ss in the *ISD* group. Over both groups, only four Ss (two male and two female) had significantly positive PES changes. In each of these cases the S's early performance was at or below his group's 'early' mean. Only one S had a significant decrease in PES ratings. This was S-10 in the *mSD* group, who began her participation at the highest PES level obtained by a participant of either group, early or late, but over time lowered her PES 'style' until it more closely approached the *mSD* group mean.

Discussion

Part I of the results presents data which are wholly consistent with the experimental intent to vary trainer self-disclosure. The trainers were judged as more self-disclosing in the *mSD* group than in the *ISD* group by each of three perspectives from which their behavior was measured. In the *mSD* condition the participants claimed to know more personal information about the trainers than the participants in the *ISD* group claimed to know; two judges more often assigned randomly selected coded trainer statements from the *mSD* group to content categories labeled 'self-referents' than they assigned such statements taken from *ISD* group; and a pair of experienced clinicians, in rating their impressions of trainer behavior as

Table 11—*Early–late between-subjects changes in PES ratings*

	Subject	Early	Late	Change	U
mSD	1	3·51	2·93	−0·58	76
	2	2·52	3·33	0·81	56*
	3	2·74	3·54	0·80	83·5
	4	3·28	3·56	0·28	94
	5	3·37	3·13	−0·24	91·5
	6	3·41	3·98	0·57	72
	7	3·52	3·54	0·02	108
	8	3·16	3·02	−0·14	101
	9	3·31	3·74	0·43	90
	10	4·34	3·64	−0·70	54·5*
	T-1	2·90	2·94	0·04	106·5
	T-2	2·95	2·91	−0·04	110·5
lSD	1	2·97	3·18	0·22	96
	2	2·97	4·00	1·03	54·5*
	3	2·90	3·29	0·39	83
	4	2·81	3·39	0·58	75
	5	3·21	3·38	0·17	109
	6	2·94	3·72	0·78	53·5*
	7	2·80	3·71	0·91	56·5*
	8	2·77	3·06	0·30	87
	9	2·85	3·12	0·27	95·5
	10	3·53	3·47	−0·06	110
	T-1	2·61	2·67	0·06	111·5
	T-2	2·12	2·34	0·22	105

N = 15 Statements × 3 Judges = 45

* $p < 0.05$ (2-tailed).

Note: T-1 and T-2 are trainers 1 and 2. These ratings were influenced by the experimental instruction guiding their performance. The lack of any change is interpreted as evidence of their performance consistency.

contained in five-minute transcriptions of group process, differentially and similarly perceived the trainers' participation to be consistent with the 'more' and 'less' self-disclosing job descriptions the trainers had been instructed to follow. Thus, not only was the experimental manipulation successful, but the data further suggest that trainers have stylistic options in the way they choose to conduct their T-groups.

The Part II relationship data (RIs) show each group forming about one-third of the statistically possible MPTRs on each of the four dimensions of positive regard, empathy, congruence, and unconditional regard, plus the sum of these four. Following from the reasoning of Clark (1963), this indicates that an equivalent amount of therapeutic potential was developed in both experimental conditions. However, between-groups differences did appear when the relationship data were examined with respect to 'critical' others.* The members of the *lSD* group more often perceived their 2-person relationships with the trainers and their dyad partners as therapeutic, and the *mSD* participants more frequently viewed their relationships with non-critical others as therapeutic.

Interpretation as to the desirability of this difference is not clear. On one hand, the members of the *mSD* group, in being centrally involved with non-critical others, seem to have learned to form MPTRs independently of the major structure of this laboratory design. This suggests that they have learned to create therapeutic relationships on their own, with implications of extra-group transferability. On the other hand, the *lSD* participants, in being centrally involved with critical members, may be participating in qualitatively richer relationships than the ones possible with noncritical group members. A possible lead in understanding these RI data comes from comparing the between-trainers differences in PTRs and their styles of self-disclosing as tabulated in content categorization. While both trainers were viewed with a high frequency as therapeutic by the members of the *lSD* group, definite differences were noted in the *mSD* condition. Here trainer 2 was viewed as therapeutic both less often than was trainer 1 and less often than how he was viewed by the *lSD* group. Table 3 presents data which are parallel to this effect and lead to the speculation that trainer 2's very high early percentage of self-references in the *mSD* group may have been a factor in his lack of 2-person therapeutic relationships there. That his percentage of self-references declined considerably with time suggests that trainer 2 was, at some level of awareness, responding to group pressures aimed at getting him to disclose less.†

Alternative explanations exist; one plausible explanation has to do with the types of disclosures made by trainer 2. Table 4 shows trainer 2 making many more 'interaction' self-references and fewer 'self-only' references in the *mSD* condition than trainer 1. Thus it is not possible to determine whether it was trainer 2's high frequency of self-disclosure or high frequency of interactional disclosures, in the *mSD* group, which kept him from taking part in more of these relationships.

Likewise, one may speculate as to the cause of dyad partners' being perceived as therapeutic less often in the *mSD* group than in the *lSD* group.

---

* It is reasoned that the two trainers and the dyad partner comprised three 'critical' relationships for each group participant. The relationships with the trainers are considered critical because of the trainers' professional training and leadership positions in the group, and the relationships with the dyad partners are considered critical because of the captive way in which these pairings were structured.

† This corresponds with the impressions reported by both trainers. They claimed to experience *mSD* participants as attempting to get them to disclose less and *lSD* participants as attempting to get them to disclose more.

If the members of the *mSD* group either disclosed more or disclosed with a greater number of interaction references than members of the *lSD* group, then the lesser number of therapeutic relationships formed within the *mSD* dyad pairings would be consistent with the above line of explanation. Unfortunately limited amounts of data were collected measuring self-disclosure by group members. The Self-Disclosure Questionnaire was used but did not yield between-groups differences in disclosure to dyad partners. Without data which specifically tap the amount and the type of member self-disclosure that took place, no conclusions can be formed about the specific way in which trainer self-disclosure influences the participation styles of group members or the group's overall effectiveness. However, it is quite possible that self-disclosure enhances a trainer's overall effectiveness at the cost of his taking part in 2-person therapeutic relationships. In fact, as will be discussed below, this is exactly what appears to have taken place in the *mSD* group taking part in this experiment.

The Part III self-awareness data (PES ratings) showed the *mSD* group as having a significantly higher *early* PES mean than the *lSD* group, a difference which dissipated with time. Supplementary analysis* indicates that the elevated early mean is probably not the result of differences in group composition; more likely it reflects a greater amount of emotionality and spontaneity among members of the *mSD* group. This suggests that the early difference is a reflection of an accelerated PES mean for early meetings of the *mSD* group rather than a depression of this mean in the *lSD* group. While no conclusive causal determinant can be deduced from this analysis, the data are consistent with a 'modeling' theory. That is, based on their greater variability and higher peaks in PES performance, the Ss of the *mSD* group appear to have modeled their participation after their self-disclosing trainers. This explanation is given further support from clinical impressions reported by the two trainers and the group observer.†

A desirability interpretation for the self-awareness data hinges on whether there is any advantage to having high early PES ratings in addition to high late PES ratings. Evaluation of this issue (and the issue of 'critical' or 'noncritical' relationships) would be most meaningfully accomplished were

---

* Estimates of the mean PES ratings for the two groups were compared on a meeting-by-meeting basis. They indicated that the effect of the more self-disclosing trainers was almost immediate. In meeting 1, the mean rating for the *mSD* group begins higher than the mean rating for the *lSD* group, but comparable with the overall mean for early meetings of the *lSD* group. Almost immediately the mean ratings for the *mSD* group increase and show a far greater variability than is present in the sample of mean ratings from the *lSD* group. This differential variability persisted throughout late meetings. Further analysis-comparing log transformations of the PES variances for individual members—failed to turn up member between-groups differences.

† These impressions are reported in greater detail in Culbert (1966).

we to use longitudinal criteria. But no longitudinal data were generated, and one can only speculate as to whether the PES data produced by the *mSD* or by the *lSD* condition best favor an extension of member learning and growth to extra-group situations and relationships.

The type of self-awareness measured by PES ratings specifically entails an individual's first accepting the idea that he is centrally involved in his problems and then progressing through stages where he views his reactions to his problems and his contribution in effecting them. At higher levels he comes to understand the specific inputs of his own personality dynamics and finally comes to see his best personal alternative for dealing with a given problem. Thus one might speculate that speech statements earning higher PES ratings indicate that the speaker is gaining more preparation and practice for understanding involvements which extend beyond the T-group laboratory. The position advanced here interprets the total amount of self-awareness that takes place in a T-group to be an index of member gains and group productivity. One way to estimate this quantity is to measure the area under the trapezoid constructed by dropping two perpendicular lines from the gradient which connects the early and late mean PES ratings and anchoring them to the abscissa of the graph. According to this criterion, Figure 1 (which graphs the early-late PES means obtained in the present study) clearly predicts that the group receiving the more self-disclosing trainer participation will have the greater extra-laboratory gains.

Given the results of this study, a revision is suggested for the originally stated hypotheses which took a monolithic position with respect to trainer self-disclosure. The finding that the mean PES ratings produced by the *lSD* group eventually caught up with the mean ratings produced by the *mSD* group is believed to be due to a ceiling effect which places an upper limit on PES ratings. Such an effect has been noted by two other researchers who have used the PES scale to measure self-awareness.* However, even if a ceiling effect has operated to limit the upward rise of the early–late gradient for the *mSD* group, it still is not clear whether this ceiling represents an artifact of the PES rating scale or indicates that there is an upper level of self-awareness—about which individuals vary—that makes for the most profitable examination of problems, or both. If, as this researcher believes, there is some mean PES rating which characterizes the optimum level of self-awareness for T-group participation, the present data indicate that it can be achieved with or without high amounts of trainer self-disclosure. Since, as argued, the early attainment of this level is to the group's advantage, it seems that self-disclosing trainer participation is called for at least during early meetings. Such trainer participation might optimally stress

* Tommy M. Tomlinson and James V. Clark.

'interactional' types of disclosures. The data from the *ISD* condition suggest that upon attainment of this self-awareness level the trainer could just as productively 'pull-in' and be less self-disclosing. Gradual curtailment of trainer disclosures would give members the option of developing therapeutic relationships with 'critical' as well as 'noncritical' members. Hence, this revised prescription favors high early and selective late trainer self-disclosure. The trainer then would initially be providing an active model for self-disclosing participation. His gradual pulling back would free members to concentrate on their involvements with one another as well as with the trainers, as they see fit. Ideally this would provide them the independent experiences which would best transfer beyond the boundaries of the T-group laboratory.

In summary, three main effects of more self-disclosing trainer participation have been pointed to by the data generated in this study. First, this type of trainer participation resulted in group members' forming therapeutic relationships outside the three 'critical' ones promoted by the laboratory structure and favored by the *ISD* members. Second, either too much self-disclosure or too much of one or both types of 'interactional' self-disclosure by trainer 2 (especially during early meetings) may have keyed off resistances prompting some group members to avoid 2-person therapeutic involvement with that trainer. And third, more self-disclosing trainer participation apparently accelerates ratings of self-awareness and stimulates the members to approach more quickly their upper potential on the PES scale.

References

Barrett-Lennard, G. T. (1962) 'Dimensions of therapist response as causal factors in therapeutic change.' *Psychol. Monogr.*, **76**, No. 43 (whole no. 562).
Bobele, H. K. (1965) 'A rater's guide to the problem expression scale.' Unpub. mimeo. manuscript, Grad. School of Bus. Administ., UCLA.
Bugental, J. F. T. (1948) 'An investigation of the relationship of the conceptual matrix to the self-concept.' Unpub. doctoral dissertation, Ohio State University.
Clark, J. V. (1963) 'Authentic interaction and personal growth in sensitivity training groups.' *J. humanist. Psychol.*, Spring, 1–13.
Clark, J. V. and S. A. Culbert (1965) 'Mutually therapeutic perception and self-awareness in a T-group.' *J. appl. Behav. Sci.*, **1** (2), 180–194.
Culbert, S. A. (1966) 'Trainer self-disclosure and member growth in a T-group.' Unpub. doctoral dissertation, UCLA.
Jourard, S. M. and P. Lasakow (1958) 'Some factors in self-disclosure.' *J. abnorm. soc., Psychol.*, **56**, 91–98.
Osgood, C. E., G. J. Suci and P. H. Tannenbaum (1957) *The Measurement of Meaning*. Urbana: University of Illinois Press.

Reisel, J. (1959) 'A search for behavior patterns in sensitivity training groups.' Unpub. doctoral dissertation, UCLA.

Rogers, C. R. (1959) 'A theory of therapy, personality and interpersonal relationships, as developed in the client-centered framework.' In S. Koch (Ed.), *Psychology: A Study of a Science*, Vol. III. New York: McGraw-Hill.

Rogers, C. R. (1961) *On Becoming a Person*. Boston: Houghton Mifflin.

Siegel, S. (1956) *Nonparametric Statistics*. New York: McGraw-Hill.

Truax, C. B. (1961) 'The process of group psychotherapy.' *Psychol. Monogr.*, 75, No. 14 (Whole No. 511).

van der Veen, F. and T. M. Tomlinson (1962) 'Problem expression scale.' Unpub. manuscript, Wisconsin Psychiat. Inst., Univer. of Wisconsin.

Walder, Helen M. and J. Lev (1953) *Statistical Inference*. New York: Holt.

Weschler, I. R. and J. Reisel (1959) *Inside a Sensitivity Training Group*. Instit. of Industrial Relations Monogr., UCLA.

CHAPTER 5

T-group Composition

Are T-groups more effective when composed of people who are similar or dissimilar to one another? This is the question that researchers in the area of group composition are trying to answer. Bennis and Shepard (1956), Schutz (1958), Harrison and Lubin (1965) and Harrison (1965) claim that heterogeneous groups present multiple learning opportunities for participants since they can model their behaviour on a range of styles present in their immediate group. In addition, it has been suggested that these groups are likely to induce change that is more generalizable since it is argued that heterogeneous groups more accurately reflect the variability and diversity of society at large. Stock (1964) in her review of research argues, on the other hand, that similarity of member orientation can facilitate communication and empathy and thus lead to a better climate for learning.

Harrison (1965), Harrison and Lubin (1965) and Pollack (1967) have provided us with the most systematic research in this area in recent years. Since their work relies partly upon the seminal findings of Lieberman (1958) and Schutz (1961) we shall briefly review their work before examining in some detail the work of Harrison and Pollack.

Lieberman (1958) utilized the RGST (Reaction to Group Situation Test) to compose two T-groups and to assess the magnitude of participant change. One group contained individuals who showed a marked preference for each of the five modalities of fight, pairing, dependency, counter-dependency and flight. The second group was similar to the first in all respects except that it excluded individuals high on the pairing dimension. Focusing on the participants high on counter-dependency, he found that they changed *least* in the group which excluded pairers. Further, he found that in this group authority issues remained the group preoccupation throughout its life. A climate obtained of continuous counter-dependent struggle. In the other group, the 'pairers' appeared to provide an acceptable

149

model such that the counter-dependents could experiment with a more co-operative style. This study sought to demonstrate that a group composed heterogeneously would constitute a learning environment in which a wider range of behaviours could be made available for members to explore.

Schutz (1961) composed groups homogeneously with respect to the members' 'expressed behaviour' and the 'behaviour they wanted from others' in the interpersonal areas of inclusion, control and affection (as measured by the FIRO-B—an attitude questionnaire devised by Schutz (1958)). He predicted that such compositions would lead to a high degree of recognition of within-group behavioural styles. On balance, he found that homogeneous groups could identify characteristics of their own group significantly better than chance. An interesting finding, though impression-istic, was that there were marked behavioural differences between groups. Each seemed to settle on a particular topic and each went into the topic to a greater depth than is usual in groups of this type. He concludes 'the pos-sibility thus emerges of composing groups with certain characteristics for a given purpose. For example, a training group to be introduced to a variety of group phenomena might better be made heterogeneous on the FIRO-B scales while the therapy or other type of grouping in which it is desirable to explore a single area in some detail could be composed homogeneously'.

Harrison and Lubin (1965) composed two different kinds of homogeneous groups based upon the individual's preferences for utilizing particular types of concepts in describing himself and others (Person Description Instrument—Harrison (1964)). The usefulness of the instrument was con-sequent upon their findings that individuals could be differentiated along two basic dimensions: an interpersonal or an impersonal/task orientation. The groups were homogeneously composed, one group consisting entirely of individuals high on interpersonal orientation and the other consisting of individuals high on the impersonal/task dimension. Rating was done by staff members who scored the expression of feelings, the perceived degree of intimacy obtaining in the groups, and the extent of learning achieved. Harrison and Lubin's basic hypotheses were: that the person-oriented group members would learn more than the impersonal-oriented members; that they would develop better personal relations; be more cohesive and be better able to understand and to cope with interpersonal issues. Two of the hypotheses were confirmed, the person-oriented group was more expressive and was more intimate, but there was no confirmation of the third hypo-theses. Indeed the results almost reached significance in the opposite direction—the impersonal group was rated as *learning* more. Harrison and Lubin reason that the 'personal' group did not have sufficient confrontation with alternatives. The 'personal' group members if anything, they suggest, were too comfortable in the T-group. The authors further argue that the impersonal-oriented members probably felt severe cultural shock in the T-group setting and were thus forced to reconsider their basic approach. The T-group experience itself was the necessary and sufficient confrontation for them and consequently lead to their learning more than their relatively unconfronted colleagues in the personal-oriented group. An important variable expressly considered by the authors, could have been the behaviour of the trainers in the respective groups. The impersonal-oriented group would possibly represent a greater challenge to trainer skill and, thus, would elicit greater if different efforts to facilitate learning. The personal-oriented group, on the other hand, would be likely to be more trainer-seductive: warm, intimate and expressive.

In another study Harrison (1965) re-analysed some data originally collected by Stock and Luft at Bethel. Midway through the experience individuals were removed from their regular T-groups to new groups which met for five sessions. Individuals were identified by staff members as being high, moderate or low in their preference for structure. The groups were then composed as follows: A homogeneous group consisting of individuals all high in preference for structure; a homogeneous group with everyone low in preference for structure; a homogeneous group with everyone moderate in preference for structure; and a heterogeneous group composed of half of the members being high in preference for structure and half being low in preference for structure.

Harrison found that members of the heterogeneous groups increased significantly more in terms of understanding themselves and others than did members of the homogeneous groups, when participant ratings were used as a measure. There was a tendency, though not statistically significant, for the members of the heterogeneous groups to be rated as being more effective in helping the group along than being able to express themselves more openly. The heterogeneous group did have more instances of conflict, but this apparently produced a confrontation with alternatives *sufficient* to enable participants in this group to learn more. The homogeneous groups, on the other hand, tended to create atmospheres which tended to confirm rather than confront the individuals' basic orientations.

Harrison (1965) reports a further study conducted by N.T.L. in 1964. Personal styles of members were identified by observation in an early phase of the laboratory, and 'controlled climate' learning groups were composed for the benefit of two types of problem members—the passive, low affect members were grouped with active, negative affect members in an attempt to provoke the former into an expression of anger and irritation. And passive, high affect members were placed with active, positive affect members to provide a protected atmosphere in which they could explore the possibility that expressed emotionality need not be destructive.

Each learning group was divided into homogeneous sub-groups which met by themselves during some parts of the programme to explore common problems. The passive, high affect members were able to be more active and apparently to make more progress than they usually do in more heterogeneous groups. The mixture of passive, low affect members with those high in preference of fight and counter-dependency met with only moderate success from a learning point of view, though the induction of group climate generally occurred as designed. These members were sometimes passively led by the most counter-dependent ones, with the result that the hoped for increases in the activity level of the former did not take place. Where a group climate was not *too* high in fight and counter-dependency, on the other hand, the more passive members often did use the chance to explore alternatives. Harrison concludes that the staff agreed that it was feasible to plan the emotional climate of learning groups through group composition based on simple observational procedures and that the opportunities for learning may thereby be improved for relatively passive members.

The only large scale study that has directly focused upon the homogeneity–heterogeneity issue in T-groups is that done by Pollack (1967). Using a subject population of 150 students, 77 males and 73 females, Pollack composed 16 groups such that four were homogeneous and 12 heterogeneous on Schutz's FIRO-B (1958).

The composition was based upon the expressed and wanted control behaviours of the FIRO-B. The control dimension was chosen as the critical compositional variable because it is a variable mentioned often in the literature as being critical to the development of groups, notably in Tuckman's review of group development (1965). Not only was the control dimension selected as the compositional variable it was also chosen as the primary index of change, though the Adjective Check List was also utilized as a correlate.

Pollack composed four different types of homogeneous groups:

(1) High expressed–high wanted;
(2) High expressed–low wanted;
(3) Low expressed–high wanted;
(4) Low expressed–low wanted.

The twelve heterogeneous groups were composed of individuals who manifested high, moderate and low scores on expressed and wanted control. As Pollack notes it would have been preferable to have more homogeneous groups, but this was not possible because the subjects, psychology students for the most part, did not score frequently at the extremes of the relevant dimensions.

It was predicted that members of heterogeneous groups would show more positive changes than members of homogeneous groups on the FIRO-B insofar as the difference between expressed and wanted behaviour of the three interpersonal needs of inclusion, control and affection would be reduced. When all three need areas were taken together this prediction was upheld, though when considered individually, none of the differences in each of the need areas attained significance in inter-group comparisons.

A further hypothesis was tested which predicted that members of heterogeneous groups would manifest more changes on the scales most concerned with interpersonal functioning as measured by the Adjective Check List: affiliation, nurturance, self-confidence, succourance and defence. The results show that none of the comparisons undertaken reached significance. No differences were found in the changes shown by either the homogeneous *versus* the heterogeneous groups, or in the entire sample as a whole.

A final prediction was that while members of homogeneous groups might feel at the beginning of their groups that their groups were more cohesive, attractive and effective than members of heterogeneous groups, this difference would dissipate and not be statistically significant at the conclusion of the T-group experience. A related prediction was that members of heterogeneous groups would show significantly greater increases in their ratings than members of homogeneous groups. As the T-group neared its conclusion, members of heterogeneous groups would manifest significant increases on items of the T-group rating scale, devised by Blake, Mouton and Frutcher (1962). These predictions were upheld.

The basis for Pollack's study is an attempt to relate the composition of groups to Harrison and Lubin's (1965) confrontation–support model of change. While the findings are consistent with the theory, they cannot be seen as offering support for the theory, since the number and kinds of confrontations occurring in the groups were not directly studied. Nonetheless Pollack claims that there were some subjective indications that heterogeneity did lead to more confrontation.

In view of the somewhat mixed findings it could be argued that as composition increases through a range from minimum to maximum heterogeneity there will be a corresponding increase in participants learning. Up to a certain point, however, further increases in heterogeneity will be associated with decreasing success. At some unspecified point a psychological law of diminishing returns begins to operate. If this line of argument is followed, and it has theoretical and empirical support in the related field of psychotherapy (Carson and Heine, 1962), group composition becomes not an either/or issue, rather it is the degree of heterogeneity which becomes critical.

Personality variables, composition factors and outcomes

Several other researchers have focused on issues relevant to composition, but not necessarily pertinent to the homogeneity/heterogeneity dichotomy. Swanson (1951), for example, investigated the relation between personality and group interaction using projective tests and interaction records. Watson (1950, 1953) has been similarly involved in attempting to use psychoanalytic theory to predict group behaviour, but as yet has produced little in the way of detailed support for her ideas.

Bennis and Peabody (1962) provide support for their ideas concerned with the impact of personality variables upon sub-group formation. They hypothesized that dependents would join up with dependents, counter-dependents with counter-dependents and personals—people who have a high need to be intimate—with other personals. In a relatively simple design, trainers were asked to rate their T-group members in the three dimensions indicated and each member was asked to indicate those three members with whom he got along least well. The authors conclusion, that there is a tendency for members to choose like-minded people and to reject unlikes, is supported significantly in the cases of counter-dependents and personals, less so in the case of dependents.

Other writers, notably Miles (1960) and Steele (1968) have tried to relate personality variables, composition inputs, to change in performance outcomes. In a very thorough study involving many factors, Miles concludes that the three personality factors he utilizes, namely ego strength, flexibility and the need for affiliation, have no direct relation to change. How these variables interact with other variables—commitment, involvement, feedback, trainer behaviour—is critical.

Steele (1968) in a paper reprinted here, investigated the possibility that learning from immediate experience requires a scientific posture toward the world and that this posture may be much more difficult for some personality types than for others.

Conclusion

There would appear to be fairly strong evidence that composition can critically influence the course of development in the T-group. Less strongly supported is the notion that composition influences the outcomes though all the evidence is directional. It would seem that though we can safely predict the climate given a rather crude manipulation of composition (Lieberman, 1958; Schutz, 1961; Harrison and Lubin, 1965; Greening and Coffey, 1966), we are not yet in a position to determine who will change and in what direction.

References

Bennis, W. G. and H. A. Shepard (1956) 'A theory of group development.' *Human Relations*, **4**, 415–437.

Bennis, W. and D. R. Peabody (1962) 'The conceptualization of two personality orientations and sociometric choice.' *Journal of Social Psychology*, **57**, 203–215.

Blake, R. R., J. S. Mouton and B. Frutcher (1962) 'A factor analysis of training group behaviour.' *Journal of Social Psychology*, **58**, 121–130.

Carson, R. C. and R. W. Heine (1962) 'Similarity and success in therapeutic dyads.' *Journal of Consulting Psychology*, **26**, 38–43.

Greening, T. C. and H. S. Coffey (1961) 'Working with an "impersonal" T-group.' *Journal of Applied Behavioral Science*, **2**, 401–411.

Harrison, R. (1965) 'Group composition models for laboratory designs.' *Journal of Applied Behavioral Science*, **1**.

Harrison, R. (1964) Unpublished.

Harrison, R. and B. Lubin (1965) 'Personality style, group composition, and learning.' *Journal of Applied Behavioral Science*, **1**, 286–301.

Lieberman, M. (1958) 'The influence of group composition on changes in affective approach.' In Stock and Thelen (Eds.), *Emotional Dynamics and Group Culture*. Washington, D.C.: NTL-N.E.A.

Mathis, A. G. (1958) ' "Trainability" as a function of individual valency pattern.' In D. Stock and H. A. Thelen (Eds.), *Emotional Dynamics and Group Culture*. Washington, D.C.: National Training Laboratories, N.E.A.

Miles, M. B. (1960) 'Human relations training: processes and outcomes.' *Journal of Counseling Psychology*, **7**, 301–306.

Miles, M. B. (1965) 'Learning processes and outcomes in human relations training.' In E. Schein and W. G. Bennis, *Personal and Organizational Change Through Group Methods*. London: John Wiley.

Pollack, H. (1967) Unpublished Ph.D. thesis. University of California.

Schutz, W. C. (1958) FIRO: *A Theory of Interpersonal Relations*. New York: Rinehart.

Schutz, W. C. (1961) 'On group composition.' *Journal of Abnormal and Social Psychology*, **62**, 275–281.

Steele, F. I. (1968) 'Personality and the "laboratory style".' *Journal of Applied Behavioral Science*, **4**, 25–45.

Stock, D. (1964) 'A survey of research on T-groups.' In L. P. Bradford and co-workers, *T-group Theory and Laboratory Method*. London: John Wiley.

Tuckman, B. (1965) 'Development sequence in small groups.' *Psychological Bulletin*, **63**.

Watson, J. (1950) Unpublished. University of Michigan.
Watson, J. (1953) 'The application of psychoanalytic measures of personality to the study of social behaviour.' Paper read at the American Psychological Association Meeting.

Personal Style, Group Composition, and Learning*

Roger Harrison

Department of Industrial Administration, Yale University

Bernard Lubin

Indiana State Department of Mental Health

Part I

This is an investigation of differences in interpersonal behaviour and learning in a sensitivity training laboratory between highly person-oriented and highly work-oriented participants (identified through the Person Description Instrument III). Second, it is a study of the effects of a training design that involves both heterogeneous and homogeneous training groups.

It was expected, and confirmed at satisfactory levels of significance, that the person-oriented members would be seen as behaving more expressively and warmly and that they would be more comfortable and would feel stronger interpersonal ties within their homogeneous group than would the work-oriented members. It was expected, but with results approaching significance in the opposite direction, that person-oriented members would be seen as learning more than would the work-oriented members.

It is hypothesized that the person-oriented group found the laboratory a kind of psychic home without much challenge, whereas the work-oriented members experienced 'culture shock', and that this in fact pushed them toward change.

Part II

To test the learning model, data were examined from a laboratory in which each participant was assigned to a heterogeneous training group and to an experimental group composed in terms of preference for high, low, or moderate structure. The statistical and impressionistic data collected through member ratings of one another and through interviews with staff

* This study was carried out under Grant M-6466(A) of the National Institute of Mental Health. It was published in *Journal of Applied Behavioral Science*, 1965, **1**, 286–301. A more detailed technical report of this study is available from the author(s).

and participants strongly suggest that homogeneous groups do not provide the confrontation needed for optimum learning. The superiority of the mixed high- and low-structure (and more stressful) groups in terms of member learning suggests that feelings of completion, cohesion, and emotional satisfaction may not be the appropriate criteria for evaluating the impact of a training group experience.

Part I

This is a study of the relationship between personal styles in interpersonal perception, and behaviour in unstructured training groups. It also explores some effects of homogeneous and heterogeneous grouping on behaviour and learning of the participants.

The theory on which this study was based has been presented and explored in previous publications (Harrison, 1962, 1964*, 1965). The theory postulates a close relationship between cognitive structure and interpersonal behaviour. By assessing a person's preference for certain kinds of concepts to describe himself and others, we discover those aspects of the interpersonal world to which he is ready to respond. Those concepts which he neglects or avoids in describing self or others are held to represent areas of indifference or aversion, aspects of the interpersonal world with which the person is less inclined to deal actively.

People notice in a situation those phenomena with which they are used to dealing; working with those aspects of the situation, they can bring to bear their own particular skills. By passing over and not attending to those aspects of the situation for which they do not have adequate concepts or behaviour skills, they reduce the complexity of the world to something more manageable. They focus on those areas where they have most competence.

Previous studies (Harrison, 1962, 1964†) have produced the Person Description Instrument III, which may be scored for preference for person-oriented versus work-oriented concepts. The individual describes three persons: himself and two close associates, using 27 semantic differential scales. He then goes back and picks out nine of the 27 scales which he feels best describe the person. Scales dealing with such personal characteristics as warmth and sympathy, openness and genuineness, control relations, and comfort in interaction with others contribute to the person-oriented score. Scales dealing with competence and ability, responsibility and dependability, energy and initiative are scored as work-oriented.

* The structure and measurement of interpersonal perception. The work is the subject of a forthcoming report.
† *Ibid.*

Objectives

We desired to investigate the differences in interpersonal behaviour and learning in a sensitivity training laboratory between highly person-oriented and highly work-oriented participants. We reasoned that persons with a strong preference for person-oriented concepts would exhibit relatively high comfort and effectiveness in the training situation. Those with a high preference for task-oriented constructs would find it difficult to understand and to react appropriately to much of the emotional and feeling-based behaviour which it is the task of the training group to expose and understand. We expected that the person-oriented members would relate more effectively to others, that they would more easily express their own feelings, and would find it easier to develop close, intimate relationships with others. Because of these initial advantages in adapting to the learning situation, we expected that the person-oriented members would learn more in the training laboratory.

A second objective of this study was to evaluate a sensitivity training design involving both heterogeneous and homogeneous training groups. It was hoped that homogeneous groups would give their members a unique opportunity to explore the consequences of the styles of perception and interpersonal behaviour which they held in common. We felt that we could learn more about the consequences of extremely personal or work-oriented styles of person perception by observing the operations of groups of people who shared an extreme style.

The study

The 69 persons (49 men and 20 women) in the 1962 Western Training Laboratories at Lake Arrowhead, California, were assigned to six heterogeneous groups for the morning sessions and reassigned to homogeneous groups for equal periods in the afternoon. The members with whom we are concerned belonged to two homogeneous groups composed on the basis of the Person Description Instrument III. One contained the ten members scoring highest on person orientation; the other contained the ten scoring highest on task orientation. For the morning sessions, these members were distributed evenly throughout the six heterogeneous morning groups.

To assess interpersonal behaviour and learning, sociometric questions were administered toward the end of the laboratory. Staff members also made ratings on each participant.

The ratings of interest to our study were along three dimensions:

1. The extent to which the individual openly expressed his feelings.

2. The extent to which others saw the individual as a person with whom they could establish close, warm relationships.
3. The extent to which the individual was seen as having learned in the training laboratory.

For each person, ratings on these dimensions are available both from those who saw him in the heterogeneous morning group and those who saw him in the homogeneous afternoon group. The following hypotheses were tested:

1. Members of the person-oriented group would be more expressive of feelings than members of the task-oriented group.
2. Members of the person-oriented group would establish closer, warmer relations with others than would members of the task-oriented group.
3. Members of the person-oriented group would be seen as learning more than members of the task-oriented group.
4. Members of the person-oriented group would experience more comfortable and more intimate relationships in their homogeneous afternoon group than would members of the task-oriented group.

The most rigorous test of the first three hypotheses is one making use only of the data obtained from persons who saw the participants in the heterogeneous morning groups. These data from participants and staff members were tested by the Mann–Whitney Test.

Results

Hypotheses 1 and 2 were confirmed at satisfactory levels of significance for the ratings from participants. The differences in trainer ratings were in the same direction, but reached only the 0·10 level of significance. It was concluded that the person-oriented members were indeed more emotionally expressive and more warm toward others in the training laboratory than were the work-oriented members. (The ratings from the homogeneous afternoon groups were overwhelmingly in the same direction.)

The results for Hypothesis 3, that person-oriented members would be seen as learning more than work-oriented members, were opposite to the predicted direction. They approached but did not quite reach the 0·10 level of significance (2-tailed test). This almost significant reversal of our hypothesis signaled the likelihood that our theory was inadequate. This finding is further discussed below.

The results for Hypothesis 4 were confirmed at high levels of significance. When choosing persons in the laboratory whom they saw as particularly expressive and with whom they felt they could be particularly close, person-oriented members were much more likely to choose members of their own homogeneous group than were the task-oriented members. The person-oriented members made about 60 per cent of their choices from within their homogeneous group on both questions, while the work-oriented members chose only 15 per cent of their own members on the expressiveness question, and 30 per cent on the intimacy rating.

The quantitative findings thus clearly indicated that the person-oriented members were seen by others as behaving more expressively and warmly, and that they were more comfortable and felt stronger interpersonal ties toward the members of their homogeneous group than did the work-oriented members. These findings were further confirmed by the descriptions obtained from staff members working with the homogeneous afternoon groups. The person-oriented group was described by its staff as made up of members who valued and sought close personal relationships with others. They experienced the group as a place in which they could be much more themselves than they could in other settings, and for some the homogeneous afternoon group became the major laboratory learning experience. The group was described by the staff member as reaching a depth and degree of intimacy which he had rarely experienced, although he had seen groups in which there was more movement and change for individuals.*

In contrast, the work-oriented group members were described as 'hard-working, overcontrolled achievers'; they had a 'strong need for control' and showed considerable 'constriction of emotionality'. They tended to be threatened by the expression of feelings by others, and they found it hard to experience and express their own emotional reactions. However, although the group experienced great difficulty in dealing with interpersonal relationships and feelings, it did move gradually toward greater freedom and expressiveness (Greening and Coffey, 1964).

The observations of the staff thus strongly confirmed the indications of the rating data. Our results support the hypothesis of a close relationship between concept preference in interpersonal perception and the actual behaviour that a person exhibits in his relations with others. This finding is of significance for both theory and practice.

Implications

In theory, our findings support those cognitive models of personality (Kelly, 1955; Harvey, Hunt and Schroder, 1961; Witkin, Dyk, Paterson,

---

* The staff member in this group was Harrington Ingham.

Goodenough and Karp, 1962; Harrison, 1965) which take the view that a person's relationships with the world are structured by a framework of 'constructs' or dimensions along which he orders salient properties of people and things. According to these theories, a person's ability to respond to phenomena is determined and limited by the constructs he has available for ordering and making sense of the phenomena. If a person does not have constructs which are adequate to particular kinds of phenomena, he cannot respond to events of those kinds in an organized fashion. In our study, the person and work-oriented members did indeed tend to respond to others along the dimensions or 'channels' which were provided for them by the constructs which they used in describing others and themselves. In the case of the work-oriented group, members were uncomfortable, cautious, and relatively less competent in responding to others along dimensions which were not so salient for them in their perceptions of others. (Since this training laboratory did not expose members to task demands, we have no way of knowing whether the person-oriented members would have been equally cautious and inept when it came to getting work done.)

For the practitioner, our findings suggest the possibility of selecting members who will respond in different ways in training groups and other interpersonal situations, and thus create different kinds of emotional climates and learning situations for one another.

In this connection, we should examine more carefully the unexpected differences in learning between the two experimental groups. Homogeneous training groups have been experimented with and defended on the grounds that they provide an increased learning opportunity for their members by confronting them with a group composed of others who 'mirror' their own style. In our study, however, the person-oriented group was lower than (but resembled in their ratings of learning) a mixed group of members who did not attain high scores in either direction on the Person Description Instrument III. The work-oriented members, on the other hand, received higher scores on learning than either the person-oriented or mixed groups, and the difference was nearly significant in the direction opposite to our prediction. This suggests that if the homogeneous grouping had any effect on the learning of the person-oriented members, it was probably a negative one.

The descriptions by the training staff of the two groups would support the interpretation that the person-oriented group was considerably less challenged by their learning experience than were the task-oriented members. From their workaday worlds they entered a protected situation in which their personal styles and preferences were confirmed, first, by the methods and values of the laboratory and of the training staff, and even more strongly by the confirmation they received from other members of their homogeneous group. It is probably not an exaggeration to say that for them the laboratory was a kind of psychic home, a place where they could relax and be themselves. This is not to imply that these members did not work hard or that they did not learn. It is likely, however, that the learning was more an elaboration of previous personal styles than it was a questioning of basic orientations or a real 'shaking up' and confrontation, as training experiences frequently are.

The work-oriented participants, on the other hand, were seen by the staff as 'out of step' with the values and norms of the laboratory. Their characteristic styles of relationship and of interpersonal perception were disconfirmed and proved inadequate by their experiences.

The work-oriented participants thus appear to have been more strongly confronted, challenged, and pushed toward change by their training experience. They experienced not only the pressures to conformity which are exerted by other members in a culture which values emotional expressiveness and personal closeness, but also the discomfiture involved in finding themselves ill-equipped to cope with the phenomena around them. In other words, we may hypothesize that the work-oriented members underwent a kind of 'culture shock' in their laboratory experience. At the same time, their homogeneous group experience may have provided them with the knowledge that they were not alone in their confusion and ineptitude, and it may have provided a respite from confrontations which was needed to maintain their anxiety at an optimum level for learning. This is suggested by Greening and Coffey's (1964) description of their training styles as staff members in this work-oriented group. The members' discomfort with emotionality was strongly communicated to the staff, and the latter responded by being gentle, permissive, and supportive. This support in going slowly may be badly needed by members who, unlike the person-oriented group, are daily having their values and interpersonal competence thrown into question not only by events in the laboratory but also by the expressed goals, methods, and values of the training staff and by the removal of accustomed structural and emotional supports due to the design of the laboratory.

A model for learning

This is indeed reasoning after the fact; it is detailed here because it gives rise to the central learning model which is explored in this paper and the paper which will follow.

According to this model, two processes are central in laboratory learning (and perhaps in any learning): confrontation with opposites, and support for one's current personal style. By confrontation we mean that, whatever a person's current orientation, he is faced with evidence that its opposite is viable and effective and that the opposite is held by other persons with whom he must come to terms in some way. This condition was met for the work-oriented participants in our study, but it was not met for the person-oriented members, who found both the laboratory and their homogeneous group especially supportive of their customary styles and orientations.

By support for one's current orientation, we mean the assurance that others, whom one can respect, hold views and ways of operating similar to one's own. In this way, a continuous tension between poles is maintained. The person neither 'loses himself' nor can he fail to take account of opposing orientations.

This model will be further elaborated and tested in Part II.

Part II* (Roger Harrison)

Part II investigates the effects on change and learning of polar confrontation with contrasting persons. The data were collected during Stock and Luft's (1960) study of the T-E-T Design but were not analyzed or reported in that paper. In this study, participants were identified after the third training group meeting by staff ratings as preferring 'high structure', 'low structure', or 'moderate structure'.

Designs and data collection

The design of the three-week laboratory was to have a relatively long period of group activity (11 sessions), followed by recomposition into E-groups for six sessions, and a return to T-groups for four sessions. Data were collected from the T-groups after the third, tenth, and fourteenth T-group meetings. These special E (for 'Experimental') Groups were composed as follows:

1. Homogeneous in preference for high structure.
2. Homogeneous in preference for low structure.
3. Half high and half low structure.
4. Homogeneous in preference for moderate structure (three groups).

Repeated participant ratings of one another's behaviour were collected throughout this laboratory. The mean ratings for each participant were

* Appreciation is due to the staff members of Session I, 13th Annual Summer Laboratories in Human Relations Training, National Training Laboratories. This group designed the laboratory and collected the data which are analyzed and re-examined in this report: Howard Baumgartel, F. Kenneth Berrien, Hubert S. Coffey, Joseph Luft, Dorothy Stock and Thomas H. Van Loon.

distributed to staff members in the laboratory by Baumgartel (1961). These data, which provided the only record of which the author is aware of the differential progress of participants with differing orientations throughout a laboratory, were reanalyzed to see whether they were consistent with the hypothesis of learning through confrontation of opposites.

Hypotheses

We tested two specific hypotheses:

1. The high-structure group would be seen as learning more in the laboratory than the low-structure group.
2. The mixed high- and low-structure E-group would have a greater effect on the learning of its members than any of the homogeneous E-groups, whether high- or low-structure, or homogeneously moderate in composition.

The high- and low-structure groups in Part II are similar to the work-oriented and person-oriented groups respectively in Part I. Stock and Luft (1960) describe the dominant characteristics of high- and low-structure members as follows:

'High structure'... refers to a constellation of characteristics including preference for clarity and order; ... less interest in personal feelings; ... a readiness to accept self and others as is; ... and a tendency to defer to persons perceived as power or authority figures.

'Low structure'... refers to a constellation of characteristics including... a readiness to explore the emotional atmosphere of the group, to recognize positive and negative feelings, and to examine interpersonal relationships...

We see the low-structure members as entering a sympathetic culture, while the high-structure members are entering an alien and confronting culture. High-structure participants are more deviant when compared with the norms and standards of a training laboratory, and so they may be expected to experience more dissonance and disagreement with others about group and interpersonal issues. Because of this confrontation, we would expect them to change more toward laboratory norms than the low-structure participants, whose behaviour is initially closer to the norm (Hypothesis 1).

When members enter a homogeneous E-group, we should expect them to build a climate which institutionalizes norms with which they are mutually comfortable. We should expect them to have no need for confrontation in those areas on which the group is homogeneous. For the high-structure group, these norms would include the avoidance of the expression of emotionality and the avoidance of close examination of interpersonal processes in the group, along with a norm for 'getting things done'.

For the low-structure participants, shared orientations would include the valuing of close, friendly interpersonal relationships, along with a good deal of free discussion of feeling.

The mixed high- and low-structure group, on the other hand, should be characterized by a good deal of tension between opposing camps. We should expect a good deal of 'fight' in such a group, along with rapid changes in group climate, as first one faction and then the other obtains the upper hand. In this group, alone of all the E-groups, confrontation should be expected to be at a maximum. While each member would have support from a subgroup for his own orientation, he would also be under attack from those in the opposing group. Thus, each member's personal style would be both confirmed and challenged by the experience. While the lack of more moderate members might make a true resolution of differences difficult, we would expect the conditions in this group to be more favourable for personal learning and change than in any of the homogeneous groups.

The data were obtained from ratings of each member by each other T-group member on the following six-point scales:

1. How well does this person understand himself in his relation to this group?
2. How effective do you think this person is in helping the group along?
3. In your opinion, how able is this person to express himself freely and comfortably in the group?
4. To what extent do you think this person really understands your ideas and feelings?

The specific predictions corresponding to the two hypotheses in this re-analysis of the data were:

1. Even before the E-group experience (T3 to T10), high-structure members would be rated as changing more on all questions than low-structure members.
2. Members of the mixed high- and low-structure E-group would be rated as changing more after the E-group experience than members of homogeneous E-groups (T10 to T14).

Results

Although the data from all four questions are in the predicted direction, the results are statistically significant only on the first and fourth questions:

understanding self in relationship to the group, and understanding others. The changes on these two questions are shown in Figure 1.

Stock and Luft (1960) interviewed participants and staff members in the E-groups. Their results confirm that the groups did indeed create climates and norms which tended to confirm rather than confront the basic orientations and personal styles on which the members were selected. The high-structure members felt themselves to be highly compatible; they engaged in a lively but somewhat shallow discussion; and they tended to avoid examination of their interrelationships and feelings about one another. The low-structure group, on the other hand, were preoccupied with self-analysis; they spent so much time examining their interrelationships that the group tended to stagnate for lack of action; and they consistently avoided conflict and the expression of irritation and anger.

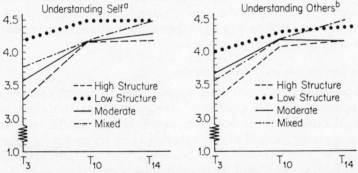

[a] Note: Difference, high vs. low structure, T_{10}–T_3, significant $p < 0.05$. Difference, mixed groups vs. other groups, T_{14}–T_{10}, significant $p < 0.02$.

[b] Note: Difference, high vs. low structure, T_{10}–T_3, significant $p < 0.01$. Difference, mixed group vs. other groups, T_{14}–T_{10}, significant $p < 0.03$.

Fig. 1. Mean Participant Ratings of E-group Members by Their Heterogeneous T-groups.

In striking contrast, the mixed high- and low-structure E-group was seen as having 'little tolerance for conflict; no one took a stand that persisted for more than a few comments at most, and the group seemed unable to deal with their feelings. The group was process-centered, but there was much fight, and they had a hard time getting down to anything' (Stock and Luft, 1960).

Thus the statistical findings and the impressionistic reports were both consistent with the predictions and with our learning model. Work- and structure-oriented participants find their personal styles greatly in conflict with the demands of the T-group and the laboratory, and hence they experience more pressure to adapt by changing their behaviour. Low-structure participants, on the other hand, find themselves more 'in tune' with the norms of laboratory training, and consequently they are less radically challenged by the experience.

When high- and low-structure participants were mixed, the group tended to polarize. Each member experienced the behaviour of the other sub-group as confrontation with an opposite orientation. At the same time, he received support for his values from his own homogeneous subgroup. Thus, members remained in tension between competing and irreconcilable ideas as to how the group should operate. It is important to note that neither staff nor participants felt that these issues were resolved. On the other hand, the evidence suggests that members did not give up, but continued to fight it out during the six sessions the E-group met. Far from suffering from their unresolved conflicts, the members of the mixed high- and low-structure E-group exhibited greater increases in understanding of self and others on return to their T-groups than did those who had experienced the more comfortable homogeneous groups.

Some implications and further questions

These results, along with those reported in Part I, strongly suggest that homogeneous groups in which members support one another's basic inter-personal orientations do not seem to provide the confrontation with alternate perceptions and ways of behaving which are needed for optimum change and growth. Groups in which conflict is 'built-in' by the composition appear, on the other hand, to stimulate their members to work toward more effective ways of dealing with people different from themselves. The optimum amount of confrontation is by no means clear. It may be that greater amounts can be tolerated for short periods of time than in a longer experience. A highly polarized E-group in this study might have produced discouragement on the part of the members if it had been the only learning group for them, instead of being a stimulating interlude. The optimum conflict is probably also a function of the psychological integration or ego strength of the participants.

Furthermore, while our data do not support the use of homogeneous groups to facilitate change, it still seems reasonable that under some circumstances such groups are useful for providing support. This could be particularly true for members whose orientations are deviant from laboratory-supported values (e.g., the work-oriented group in the Harrison and Lubin study). Such persons, if not supported in their group, sometimes receive so much pressure from others that they are forced into withdrawal or other defensive maneuvers which inhibit learning.

The practically significant finding in this study is that of the superiority of the mixed high- and low-structure E-group for the learning of its members. This finding casts doubt upon the standards used by participants and often by staff to evaluate the success of T-group experiences. Ordinarily, we regard a T-group in which 'everything comes out all right in the end' as more 'successful' than one in which polarized subgroups of members continue to slug it out until the final gong, with no significant resolution of the initial differences. The results from this study are of course based upon a comparison of groups in only one training laboratory. If these findings may be trusted, however, they suggest that we should place an evaluation upon unresolved conflict which is diametrically opposite from our usual view. It may be that the groups which leave the most lasting impact are those which seem to drag on in conflict, never quite giving up, but never quite resolving basic disagreements among the members. It may be that the unresolved issues, the confrontations with differing outlooks and views, the feelings of outrage and dismay, puzzlement and challenge, last longer and are more of a force for learning than the warmth and comradeship and the feeling of completion and closure of a more 'successful' T-group experience. Such questions will, of course, have to be settled by further research and experience. It seems reasonable at least to suggest that the appropriate criteria for evaluating the learning impact of a T-group experience may *not* be the experience by staff and participants of feelings of completion, cohesion, and emotional satisfaction.

References

Baumgartel, H. (1961) 'Report on research: Human relations laboratory, session I, Bethel, Maine, summer 1960.' Unpublished manuscript. Washington, D.C.: National Training Laboratories.

Greening, T. C. and H. S. Coffey (1964) 'Working with an "impersonal" T-group.' Prepublication draft.

Harrison, R. (1962) 'The impact of the laboratory on perceptions of others by the experimental group.' Chapter II in C. Argyris, *Interpersonal Competence and Organisational Effectiveness*. Homewood, Ill.: Irwin-Dorsey.

Harrison, R. (1965) 'Cognitive models for interpersonal and group behaviour: A theoretical framework for research.' Explorations in Human Relations Training and Research (Whole No. 2). Washington, D.C.: National Training Laboratories.

Harvey, O. J., D. E. Hunt and H. M. Schroder (1961) *Conceptual Systems and Personality Organisation*. New York: John Wiley.

Kelly, G. A. (1955) *The Psychology of Personal Constructs*. New York: Norton.

Stock, Dorothy (Whitaker, D. S.) and J. Luft (1960) 'The t-e-t design.' Unpublished manuscript. Washington, D.C.: National Training Laboratories.

Witkin, H. A., R. B. Dyk, H. F. Paterson, D. R. Goodenough and S. A. Karp (1962) *Psychological Differentiation*. New York: John Wiley.

Personality and the 'Laboratory Style'

*Fred I. Steele**

Much laboratory training activity assumes that all individuals have adequate skills for learning from immediate experience. The following study is based on the alternate premise that this type of learning requires a scientific posture toward one's world, and that this posture may be much more difficult for some personality types than for others. The author investigated this premise using the Sensation–Intuition scale of the Myers–Briggs Type Indicator (1962), and assuming that the Intuitive (N) mode of perception would be more facilitative of operation in the 'Laboratory style' than the Sensation (S) mode. Using three laboratory populations, it was found that the S–N scale does predict tendencies toward laboratory interpersonal value orientations (as measured by the Managerial Behaviour Questionnaire) and ratings of effectiveness in a T-group. The scale was found less effective in predicting actual change. Several implications for laboratory selection and design are suggested.

Introduction

In recent years, there has been a steady growth in the use of the laboratory method for effecting organizational and individual change (Argyris, 1962; Bennis, 1962; Blake and Mouton, 1964; Bradford, Gibb and Benne, 1964; Buchanan, 1964; Schein and Bennis, 1965; Weschler and Schein, 1962). Accompanying this growth in use has been an increase in the amount of theoretical and research effort aimed at the development of a better understanding of the dynamics of laboratory training as a change process and as a social force. This report represents one facet of this continuing effort at better understanding.

For the purpose of this paper I shall define 'laboratory training' as any one of a number of change induction processes growing out of the explorations of the National Training Laboratories (Benne, 1964) that focus primarily on behavioural data internal to the change programme itself. The emphasis in these programmes is on using the actual experiences of the

* Fred I. Steele is assistant professor, Department of Industrial Administration, Yale University. The author acknowledges the financial support of the Richard D. Irwin Foundation for this research; the author thanks Edgar Schein, Warren Bennis, John Thomas, William McKelvey, Louis Barnes, Chris Argyris, Roger Harrison, and the NTL Institute for Applied Behavioural Science for all the other kinds of support so essential to the completion of this study. Published in the *Journal of Applied Behavioural Science*, 1968, **4** (1), 25–46.

participants themselves as the main inputs to learning. A major component in this process has usually been the T-group, or Training Group. Members of a T-group are encouraged to use their experiences with one another as examples of interaction and reaction, from which they can learn more about various phenomena including themselves, their impact on others, the impact of others on them, group functioning, leadership and its dynamics, and organization for a task.

Those who have worked as staff members at laboratory training sessions have at one time or another perceived some participants as learning from and/or functioning well at a given laboratory, while others have a relatively negative experience in terms of change or ability to understand what is happening. It was precisely this kind of perception on my own part which led me to the view that there is some real question as to what a laboratory training experience can be expected to accomplish for certain types of people.

The basic proposition that served as the foundation for the research reported here was very simple: It was the assumption that individuals who have certain relatively stable personality traits would tend to be more responsive than other types of individuals to the laboratory training process and also would tend to be more comfortable with the laboratory approach to organizational interpersonal relationships. Accordingly, the studies described in this paper attempted to determine whether scores on dimensions of 'laboratory interpersonal values' before and after a laboratory and also behaviour in a T-group could be predicted from prelaboratory scores on the Sensation–Intuition scale of the Myers–Briggs Type Indicator. This scale was chosen because it seemed particularly relevant to a major cognitive demand of the laboratory process, i.e., learning from the data of one's actual immediate experiences at the laboratory.

Background

From several previous research findings there was conclusive evidence that the basic assumption about the effects of personality on training outcomes was worth testing. In his study on the differential effects of personality on preference for participation in decision making on the job, Vroom (1960) found that, in the work groups he studied, participation was generally satisfying for those having a high need for independence and low authoritarianism scores; the reverse was true for those with scores low on need for independence and high on authoritarianism. Since one of the values assumed to be associated with the laboratory process is a sharing of control or influence, this finding would suggest that there may indeed be some limitations on the laboratory's effectiveness due to personality differences.*

In another type of study, Stern, Stein and Bloom (1956) found that personality types (stereopaths, preferring depersonalized and modified social relationships, rigid orderliness, and exhibiting pervasive acceptance of authority and denial of impulses) who were deviant in relation to the values of the college they were attending (which encouraged intellectual curiosity and exploration) did less well on tests, had lower grades, and a higher first-year dropout rate than nonstereopaths (Ch. 10). This finding highlights the possibility of mixed effects when different types' of people are placed in a culture which is oriented toward change in a specific direction.

Several studies have dealt with personality in relation to laboratory training; but I shall cite here only the two most relevant to the present discussion, since a more thorough review has already been provided by Stock (1964). Mathis (1955) found that laboratory participants characterized by intrapersonal conflict and tendencies toward free expression of fight and pairing were rated higher on changes in sensitivity, sophistication, and productivity than were those characterized by tendencies toward dependency, flight and immobilization.

The training study that is probably most important for our present purpose is one carried out by Miles (1960). He related three personality variables to change in performance on the job—which he took as one important measure of learning at the laboratory. 'Perhaps the most interesting finding was that none of our three personality variables (with the possible exception of flexibility) was directly related to gain at the end of the lab . . .. Rather, ego strength, flexibility, and need for affiliation played a clear role in the person's interaction with the lab, permitting him to un-freeze, become involved, and receive feedback. These process factors, in turn, were the major determinants of learning' (p. 306).

Several implications may be drawn from the studies discussed above. The Vroom and the Stern, Stein, and Bloom data would indicate that personality may indeed be an important factor limiting the effects of attempted changes toward more individual participation, be it in job decision making or in the learning process itself. Those who are most stereotyped, rigid, authoritarian, and so on appear to have a higher probability of becoming dissatisfied with and/or of dropping out of the programme.

From the studies of laboratory training itself, it appears that such

---

* Examined in another light, the present study may be considered as an attempt to go a step beyond Vroom's findings; that is, as an examination of the extent to which the limitations he found will still be in evidence for a more intensive change process aimed at specifically reducing the kinds of effects which he found.

characteristics as free expression, flexibility, and some sort of conflict or other motivation may be related to greater learning in the laboratory setting. Dorothy Stock (1964), in summarizing her review of the research on laboratory training, stated 'These findings converge on the idea that personality factors having to do with receptivity, involvement, lack of defensiveness, and a certain kind of energy or openness may be important facilitators of learning' (pp. 434–435).

Demands of laboratory process and its relationship to personality

Yet the results to date are not clear enough or complete enough to allow us to state with confidence either which personality variables, if any, relate to changes effected by a laboratory programme or how close we should expect this relationship to be. It was for this reason that I undertook further research on personality variables and the outcomes of laboratory training. From the mixed results obtained with the personality variables described above, from Stock's summary of possible 'facilitators of learning', and from my own observations of the training process and its complexity, I decided to reexamine a fundamental assumption of the laboratory training process; people learn best about behavioural concepts when they learn from their own immediate experience. This assumption seems to me to imply that all individuals tend to have an adequate ability to learn from the immediate data in the world around them, and I seriously question it. To me, the process of 'learning from the data' requires a number of skills: to think thematically; to deal with the reality of multiple causation of behaviour; to use analogies to clarify a process; to make connections and to see correspondences which may be quite appropriate but not one-to-one in their relationship to one another; and (tied in with the others) an ability to generate hypotheses and to understand the context in which the data occur.

It is the last of the skills on this list which are most important for our purposes. Basically, one cannot get useful, change-inducing information about the world and himself without being somewhat selective at certain times; and to be selective means to generate some set of rules or guidelines indicating what data are important for testing an idea as well as for generating the idea itself. In a T-group, we are asking people to become scientists in their day-to-day exchange with their environment. From the conduct of science we can, therefore, apply the principle that only by gathering selected data can the T-group process result in real learning; otherwise, the data can prove almost anything the actor wants them to prove, since they are usually determined by a number of conditions.

For example, when a T-group fails to make a decision within a time limit during an intergroup exercise, the literal-minded member may then say, 'My conclusion is that groups cannot reach decisions; that should be left to individuals. My experience has just proved this to me'. Others in the group may go farther, considering the possibilities that their poor performance was related to the lack of trust in the group, to the fact that they did not really want to make a decision then, or to the fact that they become so anxious about the time limit that they let their anxieties control them and block exploration. Going on to these kinds of alternatives instead of stopping at the first, most literal exploration of the data (which happens in many cases to fit preconceived notions of why things happen) requires a mode of thinking which can generate alternative explanations for the occurrence of a given set of events. Accordingly, I decided that a scale which attempts to measure exactly this dimension would be likely to differentiate those more and less responsive to and comfortable with the laboratory training process. This is the Sensation–Intuition (S–N)* scale of the Myers–Briggs Type Indicator (Myers, 1962). Conceived as a measure of preference for basic modes of perceiving or becoming aware of the world, the two ends which define the scale may be briefly described† as follows:

Sensation (S): This is the process of becoming aware of things directly through one of the five senses. The focus here is on factual stimuli in the environment. The type of individual who prefers this process focuses on facts, attention to detail, realism, practicality, and thoroughness.

Intuition (N): This is, by contrast, the process of indirect holistic perception, where the perceive adds to whatever is given (in the stimulus situation itself) through ideas and associations generated from within. The individual who prefers intuition cares as much about the multiple possibilities that occur to him as he does about the actualities. This type of person is characterized by insight, originality, ingenuity, grasp of the complicated, comfort with abstract thought, and a bent for experimentation.

Preference for one mode of perception (S or N) does not generally mean exclusion of the other. It merely means that one mode was more central during an individual's development and that he uses that mode when given a chance. 'Preference-type', then, represents the individual's habitual, purposeful ways of perceiving the world, chosen because he has found them to be good, interesting, and above all, trustworthy.

From this brief description of the S–N scale, we can make some fairly straightforward connections. For one, the Intuition end of the scale appears to be related to abstractness in Harvey, Hunt and Schroder's (1961) concrete–abstract dimension of cognitive complexity. Similarly, there

---

* Note that the symbol for Intuition is N, not I.

† The descriptions are a synthesis of Myers (1962), Ross (1962), and Saunders (1960).

7

would appear to be greater flexibility and tolerance for ambiguity associated with the Intuitive mode of perception. These are merely further
indications that the S–N scale could be quite central to the laboratory
process described earlier. Thus an Intuitive perceiver would appear much
more likely than a Senser to be able to operate in the 'scientific' manner that
the laboratory is trying to promote. He would be able to generate hypotheses, select among the data, and generalize across situations that are not
one-to-one in correspondence. This view is supported by the test developers'
findings that 93 per cent of a sample of 'creative men' (the majority were
scientists and architects) scored as Intuitives (Myers, 1962).

Accordingly, the general hypothesis was developed that those individuals
who scored higher (toward the Intuitive end) on the S–N scale would tend
to deal with their worlds in a more laboratory-oriented manner and would
be more effective in this setting and would learn more from a training
laboratory than would those individuals who scored lower (toward the
Senser end of the scale). The remainder of this paper describes the procedure and results of two studies designed to obtain information concerning
the validity of this hypothesis. Since somewhat different procedures were
used in each, the two projects are described separately.

Study A

In this study, two laboratory populations were used as subjects: participants in a two-week human relations summer laboratory sponsored by the
National Training laboratories, of whom 72 out of 84 provided usable data;
and 58 'middle managers' who went through a two-week 'Grid' laboratory
(Blake and Mouton, 1964) as part of a full academic year they were spending
at a graduate school of business administration, from whom 39 usable
responses were obtained.* The human relations participants were from a
wide variety of organizations and occupations, while the middle managers
were predominantly from business and industry.

Procedure

Which dependent variables to use as criteria of laboratory 'directions'
posed a familiar dilemma (Bergin, 1962; Miles, 1960). For both the human
relations and middle-manager laboratories it was decided that an appropriate criterion of change would be expressed 'organizational interpersonal
values'. These values are defined as personally held conceptions of how

* The fairly low response return in the middle-manager laboratory led to a check on
the distributions on the S–N scale (which was returned by 55 out of 58) for those who did
and did not provide complete data. There was no difference on the S–N dimension.

people should deal with others in organizational interpersonal situations. This criteria was chosen with the view that specific values, operating as standards of what is good or desirable in interpersonal work situations, are a focal force influencing behaviour in these situations; and further, that changes in values are an important outcome of laboratory training efforts.

These values are seen as solutions to basic problems (Kluckhohn and Strodtbeck, 1961) related to organizational interpersonal situations, and they may be characterized by what Buhler (1960) terms 'constructive intent'; that is, they are beliefs about what relationships should be like in an organization in order that it be effective or accomplish something.

An investigation of the literature on interpersonal and group behaviour (Argyris, 1962; Bales, 1950; Bennis, 1962; Benuis and Peabody, 1962; Fleishman, 1953; Leary, 1957; Lorr and McNair, 1963; Schutz, 1958) led to the formulation of four 'problems' which defined interpersonal value dimensions for this study. These dimensions were then simplified and assigned a 'laboratory' and 'nonlaboratory' end, as follows:

1. Control (C): How should control, power, influence, and so on be distributed in work relationships? The laboratory (high) end of the dimension was defined as 'Shared Control' and the nonlaboratory (low) end as 'Unshared Control'.

2. Trust (T): To what extent should parties to a work relationship strive to enhance their trust of one another? The laboratory end is 'High Trust', and the non-laboratory end is 'Low Trust'.

3. Feelings (F): To what extent are personal feelings relevant as elements of information to be shared and dealt with in a work relationship? The laboratory end is 'Feelings Relevant', and the nonlaboratory end is 'Feelings Irrelevant'.

4. Receptivity (R): To what extent should people in work relationships be open to receiving new information, points of view, or possibilities from others? The laboratory end is 'Openness', and the nonlaboratory end is 'Closedness'.*

5. Total: A fifth score—a 'total laboratory values' measure—was defined simply as the sum of the scores on the other four dimensions.

A new instrument, the Managerial Behaviour Questionnaire (MBQ), was developed to measure these four interpersonal values dimensions. The MBQ presents seven open-ended items, each in the form of a one-paragraph description of a conflict situation, the subject is asked to write two responses:

* This orientation would not, of course, be called 'closedness' in the individual's own words, but rather something like 'stability', 'perseverance', and so on. For an elaborate analysis of the dynamics of open and closed orientations to the world, see Rokeach (1960).

(A) what he feels he should do in the given situation, and (B) why he feels he should do this—what the personal guidelines are that are helpful to him in making his decision in each conflict situation. He is also asked to indicate on a 7-point scale how strongly or how 'sure' he feels about each answer.* Scores obtained empirically range from 65 (extreme nonlaboratory score) to about 140 (extreme laboratory score) on the individual dimensions, and from 320 to 550 on the 'Total' laboratory scores.

Each laboratory population received an orientation to the research project on the first afternoon of their respective sessions. The human relations participants and staff completed the Myers–Briggs Type Indicator (which contained the S–N scale) and the Managerial Behaviour Question-naire in their T-group rooms. The middle managers took the same instruments home and returned them at one of the following meetings. At the close of each laboratory, both samples again completed the MBQ. Human relations participants filled it out on the Thursday afternoon before the Friday closing of their session, and the middle managers completed and returned the MBQ within six days after their last class period. In addition, the human relations subjects were given the S–N scale a second time, at the close of their laboratory session.

All of the MBQs were coded blind by the author, except for a random sample of 30 questionnaires that were also coded by an associate in order to check the reliability of the scoring system.†

Hypotheses

From the conceptualization outlined earlier, several specific hypotheses were formulated on the assumptions that (a) values before the laboratory would reflect individual differences plus the effects of the culture back home, and (b) values at the laboratory would reflect both of these factors plus the impact of the laboratory culture. Specifically—

I. Before the laboratory, there would be a positive correlation between preference for Intuition (N) on the S–N scale and the laboratory ends of the interpersonal values (MBQ) dimensions.

II. After the laboratory, there would be a positive correlation between Intuition and the laboratory interpersonal values.

* See F. I. Steele (1965) for the text of the MBQ, a more complete description of its rationale, instructions for coding, and data on reliability and validity. The criteria used for developing the MBQ appear to be quite similar to the recommendations made by Smith (1963) for a values measure; it is specific, it presents actual choice situations, it obtains statements in the respondent's own words, and so on.

† Correlations (Pearson r) between individuals' scores for the two coders were: Control: 0·821; Trust: 0·827; Feelings: 0·868; Receptivity: 0·643; Total: 0·935.

III. The positive correlations described in I and II would be larger after the laboratory than before it.

Results

One preliminary indicator that our hypotheses were at least plausible is the way the staff members at the human relations laboratory scored on the S–N scale. All six scored as Intuitive types (above 100 on the scale), and as a group they had a mean score of 135, a score which indicates a strong preference for Intuition. These very limited data do not validly prove, but they do suggest at least that a preference for Intuition is likely to be associated with the activities required by staff work in laboratories. This tendency can be seen more clearly if we contrast the staff scores with those for the participant samples: human relations (n = 72) had a mean score of 117·6, and the middle managers (n = 39) had 98·7 as their mean score.

Another preliminary question concerned the Sensation–Intuition scale and its use as a relatively stable measure of preference for cognitive functioning. This was checked by comparing the human relations scores from the before-laboratory and after-laboratory administrations. This after-laboratory mean was 116·1, a difference of only −1·5 points from the before-laboratory mean, and this difference was not significant. The correlation between before- and after-scores was 0·864. These data suggest that the S–N scale is quite adequate as a measure of stable personality differences, at least in the situation being studied.

Advancing to a direct test of our hypotheses, we shall now consider the associations between the S–N scale and the laboratory interpersonal values dimensions. Tables 1 and 2 present correlations before and after the laboratories for each sample. An analysis of variance showed that it was reasonable to consider each laboratory (as opposed to each individual T-group) as a single treatment situation; however, since the results for the two laboratories were somewhat different, they have been reported separately rather than pooled as a sample of 111 subjects.

The first hypothesis stated that Intuition would be positively correlated with high laboratory values scores before the laboratory sessions. For the human relations group, this hypothesis was supported on the Trust, Feelings, and Total dimensions. For the middle managers, however, this prediction was not upheld; in fact, the correlations tend to be in a negative direction.

Hypothesis II predicted a positive correlation between Intuition and laboratory values after the laboratory session. This prediction was clearly upheld for all values dimensions in the human relations sample. In the

Table 1—*Product–moment correlations[a] between laboratory values and the sensation–intuition scale (Human Relations Laboratory, N = 72)*

	MBQ values dimension				
	Control	Trust	Feelings	Receptivity	Total
Before laboratory	0·162	0·311**	0·321**	0·108	0·292**
After laboratory	0·321**	0·251*	0·301**	0·292**	0·398**
Critical ration for change in correlation from before to after	1·289[b]	n.s.	n.s.	1·661*	n.s.

[a] A positive correlation indicates an association between Intuition and the Laboratory Interpersonal Value on each dimension.
[b] Trend significance, $p < 0.10$.
* $p < 0.05$.
** $p < 0.01$.
*** $p < 0.001$; all tests one-tailed.

Table 2—*Product–moment correlations between laboratory values and the sensation–intuition scale (Middle-Managers Laboratory, N = 39)*

	MBQ values dimension				
	Control	Trust	Feelings	Receptivity	Total
Before laboratory	−0·210	−0·276	−0·015	0·061	−0·170
After laboratory	0·058	−0·111	0·335*	0·059	0·135
Critical ration for change in correlation from before to after	1·574[a]	n.s.	2·612**	n.s.	2·107*

[a] Trend significance, $p < 0.07$.
* $p < 0.05$.
** $p < 0.01$; all tests one-tailed.

middle-manager data, it was upheld only on the Feelings dimension; however, only one negative correlation remained.

Hypothesis III stated that the after-laboratory correlations would be larger than those before the laboratory. For the human relations sample, this hypothesis was found true for the Control, Receptivity, and Total dimensions, although only Control and Receptivity showed statistically significant changes. For the middle managers, there were positive increases for Control, Trust, Feelings, and Total, with all but Trust reaching significance.

Thus Hypotheses I and II relating Intuition to laboratory values before and after the laboratory were generally upheld for the human relations sample but not for the middle managers. This difference in results may be explained in part by the different characteristics of the two samples. As indicated earlier, the human relations participants came from a variety of occupations and types of organizations and included a good number of people in the helping professions. Middle managers were a much more homogeneous group, since almost all were employed in business or industrial organizations—just those kinds of organizations that have been described by Argyris (1962) as placing a high value on the traditional, formal values of hierarchical authority, rationality, and nonemotionality. With this latter population, then, the effects of the participants' back-home cultures may have been particularly strong and—with relative uniformity—directed away from the laboratory interpersonal values under consideration.

The process would go something like this: The Intuitives, according to the preference-type theory behind this study, would be more likely than the Sensers to have tried to deal with phenomena in the 'laboratory' manner early in their organizational life (i.e., to deal with feelings, to keep questions open for more data, to establish collaborative rather than hierarchical relationships, and so on). To the extent that this style was felt by those already well integrated into the organization to be inappropriate, the Intuitives were also more likely to have had negative sanction applied to them for that behaviour. Therefore, we might expect them to draw back somewhat after having been 'burned'. This sequence, although only speculation, is supported by the before-laboratory negative correlations for the middle-manager group, and by the generally positive shift in these correlations as the laboratory experience served to 'loosen them up'.

Finally, on the overall results there seems to be a higher positive correlation on the Control, Feelings, and Total dimensions than for Trust and Receptivity. Data from other work with the MBQ (Steele, 1965) indicate that these results may in part be due to the MBQ's greater effectiveness at measuring values related to sharing Control and Dealing with Feelings. Another factor may be related to a greater disparity between the laboratory orientation and a traditional organizational orientation on these two dimensions, at least in terms of expressed values.

Study B

The subjects for this study were undergraduate and graduate students who were participants in four T-groups held as courses during the regular academic terms. Each group met for $1\frac{1}{2}$ to 2 hours twice a week for approximately 16 weeks. In two of the groups the author served as trainer; in the other two groups the trainer was a fellow faculty member engaged in numerous training activities.

Procedure

At the first meeting of each T-group, the members completed the Sensation–Intuition scale as part of the Myers–Briggs Type Indicator. No other measurements were taken until the end of the term. During the last session, the participants rated the members of their own T-group (excluding themselves) on ten dimensions related to effective behaviour and change in the group. These dimensions are shown in Table 3. In addition, the trainer

Table 3—*Pearson product–moment correlations between peer ratings of T-group behaviour and the S–N scale (Four Student Groups, N = 45)*

Peer rating questions	Correlation with intuition
1. Worked hard to influence others toward his point of view	0·480***
2. Has usually been willing to go along with what others want to do	−0·150
3. Has been willing to disagree with or criticize others' ideas or actions	0·394**
4. Warm and supportive toward other group members	0·210
5. Seemed interested and involved in the group's activities	0·438**
6. Tried out new ways of doing things	0·406**
7. Helped clarify and make more understandable to others the events and processes in the group	0·491***
8. His overall effectiveness as a member contributed significantly to the group's progress	0·491***
9. He seemed to understand and learn from the reactions of others to his ideas and actions in the group	0·236
10. His overall effectiveness as a group member has increased	0·212

** $p < 0.01$.
*** $p < 0.001$; one-tailed tests.

for one group rated (on a 5-point scale) the members of his group on the dimensions of Overall Effectiveness in Group, Change, and the four laboratory interpersonal values areas described earlier (see Table 4). These ratings were obtained at a point when the trainers had no knowledge of either the individuals' S–N scores or of their ratings by their peers in the T-groups.*

Hypothesis

The general working hypothesis for both peer and trainer ratings was that a preference for Intuition would tend to be associated with higher

* The possibility that the author was contaminating the results by guessing at the members' strengths of preference for Intuition was checked by comparing the data for his two groups with the data for the other trainer, who had almost no familiarity with the S–N scale and very little knowledge about the hypotheses being tested by the author. The results were very similar for each pair of groups.

ratings on understanding, activity, experimentation, and so on in the groups and with perceived change, as well as with higher ratings on the laboratory values, at the end of the laboratory.

Results

The correlations between the S–N scale (with Intuition as the positive end) and the ratings by peers and trainers are shown in Tables 3 and 4. In the ratings by peers, there is a significant tendency to describe Intuitives as active, willing to own up to their ideas, involved experimenting, clarifying and making events understandable for others, and as contributing to the group's progress. The correlations on warmth, learning, and increase in effectiveness are also in the predicted direction but are not significant.

Table 4—*Pearson product–moment correlations between trainer ratings of T-group members' behaviour and values and the S–N scale (four student groups, N = 45)*

Trainer rating	Correlation with Intuition
Overall effectiveness in group	0·384**
Change in the T-group	0·262*
Values shared control	0·378**
Values high trust	0·298
Values sharing relevant feelings	0·410**
Values receptivity to new information	0·320*

* $p < 0.05$.
** $p < 0.01$; one-tailed tests.

In Table 4 we see that all of the correlations are positive and statistically significant, with Overall Effectiveness, Values Sharing Relevant Feelings ranking highest. As with the peer ratings, Change has one of the lowest correlations.

These data provide fairly solid support for the premise that a preference for Intuition as a mode of perception tends to make an individual comfortable and effective in laboratory training situations; by extrapolation they also suggest that the Intuitive would be more effective than the Senser at operating in the 'laboratory' manner in other settings (e.g., work or family). The findings are much less impressive on the question of the association between Intuition and change at the laboratory. Although the trainer ratings were significant on this dimension, in general these data do not indicate much predictive power as to who learns or changes from participation in a laboratory. Rather, the peer data can be seen as indicating a possible association between Intuition and a rather general factor of 'effectiveness' in operating in a 'laboratory' style. Add to this the trainers' general ratings (by definition) as well as their ratings on laboratory interpersonal values— these ratings which were made largely on the basis of behaviour in the group. The pattern is quite similar to the results of Miles (1960) which were described earlier.

Discussion and action implications

Our original prediction that a preference for Intuition as a perceptual mode would be a major factor in specifically determining who changes at a laboratory did not receive much support in these studies, although the trend is clearly in the right direction. The positive result for trainer ratings of change can be explained by a general 'effectiveness' factor on which the trainers were rating and by Miles's (1960) factors of involvement and reception of feedback. Similarly, the shift on Feelings from no correlation to a positive one of 0·335 in the middle-manager laboratory could be explained as a loosening-up following an overreaction pattern, as discussed earlier. Several factors could have contributed to the generally low results on Change. For one, regression toward the mean would be working against our change hypothesis. For another, using personality-types to predict who changes may be expecting too long a chain of variables to fall into place. (Again see Miles, 1960). Finally, it seems quite likely that specific changes effected in the laboratory setting are influenced by many other factors, in addition to individual cognitive preferences: the composition of the group (Harrison, 1965), the style of the trainer, or the establishment of particular kinds of relationships within the group (Clark, 1963).

Relative to the positive association between Intuition tendencies toward the 'laboratory style' of operation, most of the data do confirm the general hypotheses, both in terms of rated behaviour in the T-group (student laboratory) and in terms of the expressed or rated interpersonal values after the laboratory (human relations laboratory, student laboratory). The hypothesis did not hold up for the middle managers, probably for two reasons. One mentioned earlier is that they were a homogeneous sample, they were lower on the S–N scale, and came from more traditionally bureaucratic settings with stronger sets to behave in nonlaboratory ways. Another reason may be the nature of the Grid laboratory in which the middle managers participated. It is, by design, a much more highly structured and more specific type of laboratory: one of its major goals is the learning of a relatively concrete, specific system for diagnosing leadership behaviour. As a result, we probably should not have expected the same results from the Grid sample, since the original hypotheses were based on a view of laboratory training which included demands on the individual to generalize from complex data to even more complex situations, to make rough analogies, and to generate hypotheses from within which can be tested in the laboratory situation. These demands are not totally absent in the Grid laboratory setting, but they are not nearly so central to the process as in the human relations and student laboratories used as samples.

Overall, the data point to a connection between stable preferences for Intuition and a rather general factor which we may call the 'laboratory style' of behaviour; this 'style' includes high activity, individuality, and collaboration; and a preference for helping, experimenting, dealing with feelings, becoming involved, and understanding processes and relating them to other situations. Many of these behaviours represent what I described at the beginning as a 'scientific' posture toward the world; we therefore have here some evidence that not all people are likely to be able or will choose to operate in this scientific manner. From this study also has come more knowledge about at least one dimension, the Sensation–Intuition dimension, which appears to relate to this 'scientific' (or laboratory) style.

Of the many possible action-implications deriving from these findings, only a representative few will be mentioned here. First, one expressed in negative terms: It may not be realistic to try to change all persons toward a single laboratory style of behaviour, and, therefore, subjects such as those who are strongly Sensation-oriented should be screened out in advance of a laboratory. A second is less pessimistic: We should design specific learning experiences in which the context of the data is clear, in which the key variables are highlighted through design of the experience, and in which Sensation-oriented individuals are specifically helped to generalize to situations that on the surface appear very different from the one in which they are immediately located. We might also generate a relatively concrete list of goals for laboratory training for Sensers (or similar types)—a list which would differ in some essentials from the more complex 'scientific-mode' goals which we now tend to establish for all laboratory participants.

A third suggestion is even more interesting. We might question whether the preference for Sensation or Intuition is really as stable as the data from the human relations group indicate. The lack of change in their case may have been due to the fact that the laboratory was not specifically designed to change people in this area. We might therefore design laboratory programmes which are specifically aimed at helping Sensation-oriented individuals to appreciate, develop, and use the Intuitive mode to a greater degree. This might be a very useful preliminary step toward the development of a more laboratory-oriented 'style'.

In the main, this study has shown that 'learning from the data' is just too simple a way of conceptualizing both what happens in laboratory training and the kind of day-to-day process which that training is trying to foster. The problem for the laboratory participant is to learn from the data and to learn things which are appropriate for the context in which the data are imbedded. This learning process makes some fairly specific demands on individual participants, including the ability to generate alternative hypotheses as to why an event occurred; to make connections on the basis of 'hunches', which are then tested with new data; and to draw analogies between situations which do not completely overlap or fit perfectly. The studies reported in this paper indicate that an individual's relatively stable preference for different modes of becoming aware of the world (as measured by the Sensation–Intuition scale of the Myers–Briggs Type Indicator) may be one useful dimension for predicting whether given individuals will be able to meet the demands of the 'laboratory style'. In addition, the results indicate that the basic conceptualization of the Sensation–Intuition dimensions may be utilized to suggest a wider range of training experience better suited to different types of individual participants.

References

Argyris, C. (1962) *Interpersonal Competence and Organisational Effectivness.* Homewood, Ill.: Irwin Dorsey.
Bales, R. F. (1950) *Interaction Process Analysis: A Method for the Study of Small Groups.* Cambridge, Mass.: Addison-Wesley.
Benne, K. D. (1964) 'History of the T-group in the laboratory setting.' In L. P. Bradford, J. R. Gibb and K. D. Benne (Eds.), *T-group Theory and Laboratory Method: Innovation in Re-education.* New York: John Wiley.
Bennis, W. G. (1962) 'Goals and meta-goals of laboratory training.' *Human Relat. Train. News,* 6 (5), 1–4.
Bennis, W. G. and D. Peabody (1962) 'The conceptualization of two personality orientations and sociometric choice.' *J. soc. Psychol.,* 57, 203–215.
Bergin, A. E. (1962) 'The effects of psychotherapy: Frontiers in the analysis of outcome.' Paper presented at Symp. on the Empirical Status and Future of Psychotherapy. *Amer. Psychol. Ass. Conv., St. Louis.*
Blake, R. R. and Jane S. Mouton (1964) *The Managerial Grid.* Houston: Gulf.
Bradford, L. P., J. R. Gibb and K. D. Benne (Eds.) (1964) *T-group Theory and Laboratory Method: Innovation in Re-Education..* New York: John Wiley.
Buchanan, P. (1964) 'Evaluating the effectiveness of laboratory training in industry.' Paper read at A.M.A. Seminar, New York, Feb. 24–26.
Buhler, C. (1962) *Values in Psychotherapy.* Glencoe, Ill.: Free Press.
Clark, J. V. and S. A. Culbert (1965) 'Mutually therapeutic perception and self-awareness in a T-group.' *J. appl. Behav. Sci.,* 1 (2), 180–194.
Fleishman, E. E. (1953) 'Leadership climate, human relations training, and super-visory behaviour.' *Personnel Psychol.,* 6, 205–222.

Harrison, R. (1965) 'Group composition models for laboratory design.' *J. appl. Behav. Sci.*, **1** (4), 409–432.

Harvey, O. J., D. E. Hunt and H. N. Schroder (1961) *Conceptual Systems and Personality Organisation*. New York: John Wiley.

Kluckhohn, F. and F. L. Strodtbeck (1961) *Variations in Value-orientations*. Evanston, Ill.: Row, Peterson.

Leary, T. (1957) *The Interpersonal Diagnosis of Personality*. New York: Ronald Press.

Lorr, M. and D. McNair (1963) 'An interpersonal behaviour circle.' *J. abnorm. Soc. Psychol.*, **67** (1), 68–75.

Mathis, A. G. (1955) 'Development and validation of a trainability index for laboratory training groups.' Unpublished doctoral dissertation, Univer. of Chicago.

Miles, M. B. (1960) 'Human relations training: Processes and outcomes.' *J. counsel. Psychol.*, **7**, 301–306.

Myers, J. B. (1962) 'Manual for the Myers–Briggs type indicator.' Princeton, N.J.: Educational Testing Service.

Rokeach, M. (1960) *The Open and Closed Mind*. New York: Basic Books.

Ross, J. (1962) 'Faster analysis and levels of measurement in psychology.' In S. Messick and J. Ross (Eds.), *Measurement in Personality and Cognition*. New York: John Wiley. Pp. 69–81.

Saunders, D. R. (1960) 'Evidence bearing on the existence of a rational correspondence between the personality typologies of Spranger and Jung.' Research Bulletin Rb-60-6. Princeton, N.J.: Educational Testing Service.

Schein, E. H. and W. G. Bennis (1965) *Personal and Organisational Change Through Group Methods: The Laboratory Approach*. New York: John Wiley.

Schutz, W. C. (1958) *FIRO: A Three-dimensional Theory of Interpersonal Behaviour*. New York: Holt, Rinehart & Winston.

Smith, M. B. (1963) 'Personal values in the study of lives.' In R. W. White (Ed.), *The Study of Lives*. New York: Prentice-Hall. Pp. 324–347.

Steele, F. I. (1965) 'The relationship of personality to changes in interpersonal values effected by laboratory training.' Unpublished doctoral dissertation, M.I.T.

Stern, G. G., M. I. Stein and B. Bloom (1956) *Methods in Personality Assessment*. Glencoe, Ill.: Free Press.

Stock, D. (1964) 'A survey of research on T-groups.' In L. P. Bradford, J. R. Gibb and K. D. Benne (Eds.), *T-group Theory and Laboratory Method: Innovation in Re-education*. New York: John Wiley. Pp. 395–441.

Vroom, V. (1960) *Some Personality Determinants of the Effects of Participation*. Englewood Cliffs, N.J.: Prentice-Hall.

Weschler, I. R. and E. H. Schein (1962) *Issues in Human Relations Training*. No. 5 in Selected Readings Series. Washington, D.C.: National Training Laboratories.

CHAPTER 6

Intra-Group Dynamics

Gibb (1964a) makes the point that much of the early T-group research was generated to test some of the issues of academic interest in social psychology. This is particularly true of sociometric theory, which was the preoccupation of many early researchers (Stock, 1964). Increasingly research is being conducted on issues prompted by essentially T-group concerns, but in order for this to happen at all, descriptive and speculative work had to be generated. There is, obviously, still a very great need for 'sound theory', but there is an even greater need for refinement of theories in such a way as to clarify the experimental manipulations necessary to make a test of them. The writers included in this section have very little to build on other than the insights and descriptions of trainers, yet their research is arguably amongst the most important for the development of the training method itself.

In a short paper, Lubin and Zuckerman (1970) focus on the level of emotion generated in T-groups. Whilst this would appear to be the only paper on this subject, it does seem unfortunate that the comparison is made between T-group training and 'sensory deprivation' studies. It is to be doubted that even the T-groups most adamant critics would readily accuse it of being more stress provoking than the enforced restriction of visual, auditory and tactile sensations. As the authors themselves point out stress is used in a relative rather than an absolute sense; the T-group is *less* stressful than sensory isolation, but perhaps more important questions remain. Is it more or less stressful than other training methods? How functional or dysfunctional is the stress, if there is any, for the individual and for the group? Is there an optimum level of stress for growth? The questions remain, though Lubin and Zuckerman have produced the experimental manipulation which is so necessary to further movement from theory to research in this area.

Another area of potential and acknowledged importance is that of the development of trust. Most theorists see the establishment of trust as a

189

critical issue in group development. McGregor (1968), for example, writes, 'The effective performance of a managerial team is in a basic fundamental sense a function of open communications and mutual trust between all the members, including the leader'. Probably the most active theorist and researcher in this field or sub-field is Gibb (1964b) and it is from his theories and researches that Friedlander, whose work is reproduced here, has derived his experimental manipulation.

Friedlander's conclusion that greater emphasis needs to be placed upon the formation of trust within a team, not only supports Gibb's theoretical model, it also neatly confirms McGregor's analysis of the dimension. Nevertheless, it produced one puzzling finding, that trust does not increase as the result of T-group training (Friedlander, 1967). According to Gibb's theory, the T-group provides the opportunity for the person to participate with others in creating a trusting climate, to become aware of the process of such creation and to learn how to generalize these learnings to other dyadic and group situations. Accordingly Friedlander's data on trust is very important, but he finds it to be a *prerequisite* of effective training not part of the training itself. It should be remembered, however, that Friedlander's groups were all ongoing organizational work groups and that the emphasis of the training was on problem-solving in a work-related context. It could be that the issues Gibb sees as critical are less likely to occur in non-stranger task groups such as the ones used by Friedlander.

Closely related to issues of trust are the studies currently being carried out by Clark and his associates at the Graduate School of Business Administration at the University of California, Los Angeles. Whilst not focusing directly upon trust, the emphasis in these studies is on what the authors term *mutually therapeutic perceptions* and it is interesting to note that the participants who shared the most 'awareness of self and other' behaviour were the ones who entered into interpersonal relationships in which the members perceive each other as 'high in level of regard, empathy, congruence and unconditionality of regard'. (See also Culbert (1968) in trainer behaviour chapter.)

Using a different theoretical model, one derived from Kelman's work on social influence, Smith and Pollack (1968) have also focused on the actual dynamics of the T-group.

Kelman's (1958) model of social influence, which, the authors argue, is readily applicable to learning in the T-group, distinguishes between influence based on compliance, identification, and internalization. Compliance occurs when an individual accepts influence because the influencer has the potential to reward or punish him. Identification occurs when an individual accepts influence from an agent because of the latter's attractiveness. Internalization occurs when influence is accepted because there is value-congruence between the agent and the individual being influenced. Smith and Pollack used measures of Kelman influence styles as predictor variables in a well-designed study covering two separate laboratories. Their general prediction was that those changes which persist after training will relate positively to internalization but not to identification or compliance. The prediction was upheld.

If it could finally be established that the nature of relationships established within the T-group are critical to the learning process, it would still be necessary to investigate what aspect of the relationship were important. One variable of theoretical importance here is the concept of 'feedback', and, as Gibb (1964) notes, a number of studies have been conducted in this area though most remain unpublished.

The work of Gibb (1952) himself is particularly interesting. Gibb's work tends either to be related to task-groups or to combine variations in role-playing as well as feedback, but nonetheless, it provides some useful data. In one study Gibb investigated the effect of role playing with and without feedback on self-insight, the capacity to conceptualize a new role, and the capacity to put a new role into practice (role flexibility). In the first area, self-insight, Gibb found that there was a significant difference between a group having a T-group experience and one without such training. The group which had role playing training as well as the T-group experience, however, showed 'a significant improvement' over all other groups.

Miles (1958) went further than Gibb and his associates by trying to identify the factors which influence the effectiveness of feedback. He argued that negative feedback would be more effective in inducing change than positive or mutual feedback. Obviously there is nothing startling about this idea since positive and neutral feedback may only confirm the subjects' presentations. Miles, however, was more interested in discerning the dynamics of change. Under what conditions is feedback accepted and acted upon? His study revealed, as predicted, that strong negative feedback was most effective in inducing change, but in some cases only when it was congruent with the subjects' motivational state. Strong negative feedback in the area of warm interpersonal relations to a person who regarded this area of behaviour as unimportant had little or no effect. A further finding was that the more threat-oriented an individual the less receptive he was to interpersonal feedback. Feedback about task accomplishment, however, was accepted much more readily even when motivation and orientation were not congruent with the direction of the feedback. It would appear to be more legitimate and easier to accept task-oriented feedback than to give and accept more person-centered feedback.

Conclusion

This section has focused on issues which are critical to the learning process. Again, we have been forced to conclude that the research results are more provocative than conclusive. There does, however, seem to be at least some support for (Clark and Culbert, 1965; Smith and Pollack, 1968) the notion that relationships established within the T-group are extremely important in predicting and understanding outcomes.

References

Clark, J. V. and S. A. Culbert (1965) 'Mutually therapeutic perception and self-awareness in a T-group.' *Journal of Applied Behavioural Science*, 1, 180–194.
Culbert, S. A. (1968) 'Trainer self-disclosure and member growth in two T-groups.' *Journal of Applied Behavioral Science*, 4, 47–74.
Friedlander, F. (1967) 'The impact of organizational training laboratories upon the effectiveness and interaction of on-going work groups.' *Personnel Psychology*, 20, 289–307.
Gibb, J. (1952) 'Effects of role playing upon (a) role flexibility and upon (b) ability to conceptualize a new role.' *American Psychologist*, 7.
Gibb, J. (1964a) 'The present status of T-group theory.' In L. P. Bradford and coworkers, *T-group Theory and Laboratory Method*. London: John Wiley.
Gibb, J. (1964b) 'Climate for trust formation.' In L. P. Bradford and coworkers, *T-group Theory and Laboratory Method*. New York: John Wiley.
Kelman, H. C. (1961) 'Processes of opinion change.' *Public Opinion Quarterly*, 25, 57–78.
Lubin, B. and M. Zuckerman (1970) 'Level of emotional arousal in laboratory training.' *Journal of Applied Behavioral Science*, in press.
McGregor, D. (1968) *The Professional Manager*. London: McGraw-Hill.
Miles, M. B. (1958) 'Factors influencing response to feedback in human relations training.' Unpublished manuscript, Teachers College, Columbia University.
Smith, P. B. and H. Pollack (1968) 'The participant's learning style as a correlate of T-group learning.' Paper delivered to International Congress of Applied Psychology, Amsterdam.
Stock, D. (1964) 'A survey of research on T-groups.' In L. P. Bradford and co-workers (Eds.), *T-group Theory and Laboratory Method*. New York: John Wiley.

The Primacy of Trust as a Facilitator of Further Group Accomplishment*

Frank Friedlander

Division of Organizational Sciences,
Case Institute of Technology,
Cleveland, Ohio

Organizational and laboratory training programmes are frequently difficult areas in which to explore and test the validity of a specific theory. Most research on such programmes tends to be empirical, evaluative of a specific programme, and thus less relevant to a broadly applicable theory of change. The study reported in this article focuses directly upon Jack Gibb's model in which the formation of trust is theorized to facilitate (and in part be a prerequisite to) further group accomplishment. In this longitudinal study, we explored the impact upon later group accomplishment of early high and low trust, in groups which participated and did not participate in organizational training laboratories. Results indicate the pre-laboratory trust is a key predictor of eventual group accomplishment, although trust itself did not increase as a result of training. Furthermore, the trainee's concept and meaning of trust merged with his concept of an effective group and an effective group meeting as a function of training.

The concept of trust is one which is interwoven throughout much of the philosophical and analytical literature on group dynamics and organizational change. The degree of trust can be a useful concept in describing the climate of *intergroup* relations, such as that between two groups which are competing or cooperating (Shepard, 1964). Trust is also highly relevant to the climate *within* any one group, particularly if the formation of trust is a prerequisite to the group moving forward as a unit toward further accomplishment.

Foremost among theories which are concerned with trust as a facilitator to subsequent group development is that suggested by Gibb (1964). In this article, we shall describe a study which bears directly upon Gibb's theory of group development as contingent upon trust formation.

The theory

The formation of trust and acceptance of self and others, the reduction of fear, and the consequent growth of confidence, are seen by Gibb as con-

* A draft of a paper Published in *Journal of Applied Behavioral Science*, **6**(4), (1970).

cerns which facilitate subsequent individual and group development. Since the person learns to grow through his increasing acceptance of himself and others, he must learn to create defence-reductive climates that will reduce his own fears and distrusts. He then makes change possible for himself in other dimensions. Gibb views the critical function of T-groups as one of augmenting this process of personal learning.

Gibb suggests a contingency hierarchy in which the development of each factor facilitates subsequent development in other factors. Subsequent to acceptance and trust formation are sequentially, the flow of feelings, goal formation, and the implementation control mechanisms and organization. Although growth occurs as a concurrent and interdependent development on each of these four dimensions, it is optimal when the sequential order is maintained. Thus growth in each dimension is contingent upon growth in each of the dimensions preceding it in the hierarchy (Gibb, 1964).

Purpose

The purpose of the current study was to explore a core segment of Gibb's theory, specifically the extent to which intragroup trust is a necessary prerequisite to further group accomplishment. Adequate research of this issue demands a longitudinal study of group trust and group accomplishment. This was achieved by studying groups, which, over a period of time, interacted in their usual organizational environment and groups which, in addition, participated in laboratory training. By comparing these two sets of groups at different points in time, we were able to focus on the differing impacts on later group accomplishment of groups high and low in trust, and also note the impact of laboratory training upon the relationship between group trust and other dimensions.

A previous study (Friedlander, 1967) indicated that groups participating in laboratory training did *not* increase significantly in the degree to which members trusted one another. In the current study, we are not interested pursuing the issue of increased trust as a result of training. Rather, we intend to explore the degree to which initial group trust is predictive of other kinds of accomplishment at a later point in time. Does a group which has higher trust at one point in time accomplish more at a later point in time than a group with lower initial trust? If so, is the facilitative role of high trust augmented in laboratory training groups as compared to groups not participating in training?

The groups

In their regular back-home work setting, the twelve work groups in this study were coherent units composed of from five to fifteen members. Each met (usually weekly or biweekly) and worked together regularly for a variety of purposes, including problem discussion and resolution, general coordination, information dissemination, decision making, policy formulation, future planning, etc. As such, the twelve groups represented task-oriented work units which use typical lateral and hierarchical interaction patterns toward their task accomplishment. Four of these groups eventually participated in organizational training laboratories and the eight others did not, thus providing the project with four training groups and eight comparison groups.

The training

Since each of the training laboratories was lead by a different trainer, the nature of the training quite naturally varied among the four groups. In general, however, the sessions were conducted away from the organizational location, and were attended by all members of the particular work group. The purposes of the sessions were generally to identify problems facing the work group system and the reasons for their existence; to invent possible solutions to the problems in the form of needed system changes, and to plan implementation of these solutions through regular and newly constructed channels. Within this problem-solving context, numerous interpersonal and intragroup processes were explored which directly influenced the total work system.

Development of criteria

Frequently, in studies dealing with the impact of laboratory training, criteria (what is 'supposed' to change) are specified by the researchers, as an outcome of his own personal or theoretical interests. In this study, we attempted to derive criteria which were of direct concern and relevance to group members. The method employed utilized open-end interviews, followed by questionnaires developed from the interviews, followed by statistical analysis of the questionnaire responses into a smaller number of factors.

A series of interviews with group members prior to training resulted in the collection of an extensive amount of material dealing with the problems and issues which members perceived in their work groups. These interview comments were rephrased into questions to form the main body of a questionnaire. Relevant group-descriptive dimensions, issues, and hypotheses recurrent in the professional literature provided an additional source of information. In addition to evaluation of the adequacy and effectiveness of the group and its meetings, the variables encompassed perceptions of the actual network of feelings, both in terms of the perceptions of one's own position in the network as a member and of the perceptions by members of relationships existing between other members of the group.

In an effort to reduce these items to a more comprehensive set of dimensions, a factor analysis was performed from which six underlying dimensions of group process and interaction evolved. Details of the factor analysis and of the factor definitions may be found in an earlier study (Friedlander, 1966).

Definition and measurement of trust

Although we did not purposely devise a specific measure of trust, it is interesting to note that this construct nevertheless did evolve from the (factor) analysis. The nature and number of factors derived from a factor analysis generally cannot be predetermined.

One of the six factors which evolved was concerned almost entirely with perceptions of trust *versus* competitiveness within one's work group. The five items in this factor and the direction in which they were scored were:

There is a destructive competitiveness among members of the group (−).
Others in the group are reluctant to sacrifice ideas so that the group may agree (−).
There are too many personal opinions raised at meetings, as opposed to the broader point of view (−).
There is trust and confidence in each other among members of the group (+).
Conflict within the group is submerged, rather than used constructively (−).

It should be clear that the factor represents a bipolar dimension, running from intragroup trust to intragroup competitiveness. A group high on this dimension is one in which the members hold trust and confidence in each other. A group scoring low can be characterized more as a collection of individuals who are reluctant to sacrifice their individual personal opinions and ideas for the sake of a working consensus. This reluctance occurs in an environment of destructive competition and one in which conflict is submerged.

Definition and measurement of other group dimensions

The remaining five factors which evolved from the factor analysis, and which were considered as additional measures of accomplishment were:

Group effectiveness in solving problems and in formulating policy through a creative, realistic team effort. Groups high on this dimension arrive at creative team solutions, sharing responsibilities and problems openly.

Leader approachability describes groups in which members feel that the leader is approachable and that they can establish a comfortable relationship with him. Groups low on this dimension withdraw from the leader, do not push their ideas, do not behave according to their feelings, and seem intent on catering to the leader at the possible sacrifice of group output.

Mutual influence describes groups in which members mutually influence each other and the leader, and assume responsibility for setting group goals.

Personal involvement and participation is descriptive of groups in which members, want, expect, and achieve active participation in group meetings. The combination of high expectations and actual participation implies a fulfilment which is reflected in the desire to continue group meetings.

Worth of group meetings is a generalized measure of the feelings about the meeting of one's group—as either good, valuable, strong, pleasant, etc., or as bad, worthless, weak, unpleasant, etc.

The questionnaire from which these data were obtained, the *Group Behaviour Inventory*, was administered twice to each of the twelve groups. For the four training groups, the second administration followed the training by six months. For the eight comparison groups, the second administration followed the first administration by six months.

Analytical method

Two methods were utilized to explore the extent to which a high degree of trust is a prerequisite to further group accomplishment. In the first of these, we explored the extent to which eventual (post-study) group accomplishment could be predicted from an earlier knowledge of the degree of trust within a group. In the second analysis, we were interested in the degree to which the trust dimensions converged or diverged from other dimensions of group accomplishment. In both analyses, group accomplishment was defined (from the factor analysis) as greater Group Effectiveness, Leader Approachability, Mutual Influence, Personal Involvement, and Worth of Meetings. And in both analyses, we took into account the fact that some of the groups had participated in laboratory training while others had not.

The primacy of trust

In exploring the degree to which early trust is a predictor of later group accomplishment, it was necessary to deal with two related questions: (1) is early trust a better predictor of specific group accomplishment than any other early measure among training groups, and (2) is early trust a better predictor of later group accomplishment if training has occurred in the intervening period than if not?

The data indicate a positive answer to our first query. Entering Table 1 from the left (pre-study) margin, and viewing only the correlations for training groups (in italics), early trust predicts eventual Group Effectiveness better ($r = 0.60$) than does any other dimension; it is even a better pre-dictor of eventual Group Effectiveness than early Group Effectiveness ($r = 0.55$). Similarly, early Group Trust is the best predictor of eventual Worth of Meetings ($r = 0.54$)—even better than predicted by the measure of Worth of Meetings ($r = 0.42$).

It should be noted that for training groups, better predictions *in general* can be made from a knowledge of early competence in that *same* dimension rather than from any other dimension (the coefficients in the diagonal cells are higher than any other coefficients in that same column or row). Thus, *Trust is the only group characteristic* that enables us to predict eventual Group Effectiveness and Worth of Meetings better than an early knowledge of these same two group dimensions.

We now return to our second query concerning the impact of laboratory training upon the importance of trust as a prerequisite to group accom-plishment. Note in Table 1 that greater predictability from one dimension to another is generally possible for comparison groups than for training groups (coefficients not in italics are generally higher than those in italics). There are two major exceptions to this general finding. Again entering Table 1 at the left margin for the Trust dimension, we find that from a knowledge of early Group Trust, eventual Group Effectiveness can be predicted better for trainees ($r = 0.60$) than for comparison groups ($r = 0.51$). Similarly, among trainees early Trust is a far better predictor of eventual Worth of Meetings ($r = 0.52$) than among comparison members ($r = 0.53$).

Unlike any of the other variables measured in this study, Group Trust, prior to any training, seems to be a significant factor in the eventual accomplishment which groups reach. Groups high in Trust prior to training tend to be those which, after training, are effective and have worthwhile meetings. Correspondingly, groups in which members are competitive with one another prior to training, are those which, after training, are less effective and have less worthwhile meetings.

In a previous section, we mentioned some relevant findings from an earlier analysis of the same groups and the same training. Of the six dimensions of group accomplishment measured in this study, only three

Table 1—*Before–after correlations between group trust and five other dimensions of group accomplishment*[a, b, c]

Earlier (Pre-study) Measure of	Later (Post-study) Measure of					
	Group Trust	Group Effectiveness	Leader Approachability	Mutual Influence	Personal Involvement	Worth of Meetings
Group Trust	*0·57* / 0·68	*0·60* / 0·51	*0·23* / 0·42	*−0·11* / 0·05	*0·06* / 0·34	*0·54* / 0·33
Group Effectiveness	*0·32* / 0·52	*0·55* / 0·80	*0·01* / 0·50	*0·09* / 0·13	*0·22* / 0·56	*0·37* / 0·57
Leader Approachability	*0·29* / 0·57	*0·30* / 0·49	*0·50* / 0·81	*0·06* / 0·33	*0·34* / 0·46	*0·31* / 0·24
Mutual Influence	*−0·02* / 0·31	*0·25* / 0·25	*0·19* / 0·33	*0·54* / 0·71	*0·36* / 0·45	*0·18* / 0·27
Personal Involvement	*−0·08* / 0·34	*0·11* / 0·53	*0·11* / 0·37	*0·28* / 0·37	*0·43* / 0·80	*0·05* / 0·43
Worth of Meetings	*0·23* / 0·31	*0·58* / 0·58	*−0·08* / 0·40	*0·13* / 0·23	*0·22* / 0·46	*0·42* / 0·64

[a] Before–after correlations for trainees are in italics and for comparison members in regular print.

[b] For predictive purposes the table should be entered from the left (pre-study) margin, and then across that row to the appropriate post-study dimension. For example, the correlation between early group trust and later worth of meetings is 0·54 for trainees and 0·33 for comparison members.

[c] N = 31 trainees, N = 60 comparison members.

improved significantly as a result of laboratory training (Friedlander, 1967). Group Trust was one of those which did *not* improve. Thus, although trust itself did not increase as a result of training, it did act as a catalyst in augmenting the impact of laboratory training upon two other kanor dimensions of group accomplishment.

The convergence of trust with other dimensions

Whereas the previous section was concerned with the degree to which high trust prior to laboratory experience is linked with group accomplishment after training, this section deals with the degree to which the trust dimension converges with or diverges from other dimensions as a function of training. We are concerned here with the relationship between trust and other dimensions prior to training compared with the relationship between trust and other dimensions after training. Differences between these two sets of relationships will be indicative of the changing meaning and conception of trust as a function of training and non-training experience.

Within each cell in Table 2, the coefficient in the 'pre' column indicates the correlation between two dimensions prior to the training period, while the coefficient in the 'post' column indicates the correlation after the training. The relationship, for example, between Group Effectiveness and Worth of Meetings decreased 0·11 (from 0·70 to 0·59) for trainees, but increased 0·16 (from 0·60 to 0·76) for comparison groups. This difference of 0·27 (which is significant beyond the 0·05 level after an r to z transformation) indicates that the concepts of Group Effectiveness and Worthwhile Meetings *moved further apart* as a function of training. Apparently, prior to training, perceptions of Group Effectiveness and Worthwhile Meetings overlap to a large degree. Laboratory experience, however, serves in such a way as to allow members to differentiate between these two concepts (or sets of feelings). An effective group now is less necessarily one which has good, pleasant, and valued meetings.

The remaining interdimensional changes which are significant all indicate a *convergence* in dimensional concepts as a result of training, and *all are concerned with the dimensions of Group Trust*. The most pronounced of these is the increase in relationship between Group Trust and Worthwhile Meetings from 0·28 prior to training to 0·78 after training, a difference which is significant beyond the 0·01 level when compared to comparison members. Evidently, after laboratory training there is a strong tendency for worthwhile meetings to be characteristic of groups in which members hold trust and confidence in each other rather than groups which act more as a collection of competitive individuals. Prior to training, no such (significant) relationship existed between worthwhile meetings and intragroup trust.

Table 2—Correlations among six group dimensions prior to training and after training for training and comparison groups[a, b, c]

	Group Effectiveness		Leader Approachability		Mutual Influence		Personal Involvement		Worth of Meetings	
	Pre	Post	Pre	Post	Pre	Post	Pre	Post	Pre	Post
Group Trust	*0·41* / 0·66	*0·60* / 0·54	*0·28* / 0·67	*0·38* / 0·41	*0·05* / 0·22	*0·00* / 0·17	*0·29* / 0·48	*0·20* / 0·23	*0·28* / 0·36	*0·78* / 0·43
Group Effectiveness			*0·52* / 0·57	*0·44* / 0·55	*0·28* / 0·27	*0·19* / 0·30	*0·32* / 0·68	*0·24* / 0·51	*0·70* / 0·60	*0·59* / 0·76
Leader Approachability					*0·31* / 0·31	*0·09* / 0·35	*0·28* / 0·44	*0·40* / 0·46	*0·38* / 0·34	*0·37* / 0·47
Mutual Influence							*0·49* / 0·42	*0·65* / 0·43	*0·30* / 0·27	*0·19* / 0·38
Personal Involvement									*0·28* / 0·55	*0·43* / 0·49

[a] Interdimensional correlations for trainees are in italics and for comparison members in regular print.
[b] Cells bounded by a heavy-lined box are those in which the change in correlation between two dimensions for trainees differs from the change in correlation for comparison members beyond the 0·05 level of significance. Tests of significance were computed after an r to z transformation.
[c] N = 31 trainees, N = 60 comparison members.

A second example of dimensional convergence occurs between the concept of intragroup trust and perceptions of Group Effectiveness in solving problems through team effort. After training, an effective group is seen as one in which members have trust and confidence in each other, whereas prior to training these sets of feelings are only moderately related.

A third example of convergence took place between Group Trust and Leader Approachability. Perceptions of groups in which members can establish an unconstrained and comfortable relationship with their leader are only moderately related to intragroup trust prior to training. Six months after laboratory experience, however, leader approachability within a group and trust within that group are seen as closely related.

It is important to note that all three instances in which concepts of dimensions *converged* as a function of laboratory experience involved the trust and confidence dimension. Prior to training, group effectiveness, leader approachability, and worthwhile meetings were relatively unassociated with feelings of trust and confidence among members. Subsequent to training, however, the concept of trust became significantly more associated with these three dimensions of group accomplishment. Thus, it can be said that subsequent to training, but not prior to it, as trust and confidence vary so do group effectiveness, leader approachability, and worthwhile group meetings.

Summary

1. Work groups in which members have high trust in one another *prior* to laboratory training reach greater degrees of group effectiveness and have more worthwhile meetings *after* laboratory training; conversely, groups in which members feel competitive with each other prior to training are less effective and have less worthwhile meetings after training.

2. The degree to which eventual (post-study) group effectiveness and worth of meetings is contingent upon already established feelings of trust is significantly greater in training groups than in comparison groups. Thus, trust acts as a catalyst in combination with laboratory training to foster group competence, but does not act in this way in groups which have not participated in training.

3. Although high trust seems to augment the impact of training, it does not seem to have increased significantly itself as a function of training.

4. Trust (prior to training) is the group characteristic which best predicts or accounts for post-training effectiveness and worthwhile meetings.

5. When the relationships among the several group characteristics before training are compared to those relationships six months after

laboratory training, the only significant convergent movements are those between group trust and group effectiveness, between group trust and leader approachability, and between group trust and worth of meetings. Thus, feelings of trust vary far more directly with group effectiveness, leader approachability, and worth of meetings subsequent to laboratory training than they do prior to training or without training. No other convergent movements were noted among the six dimensions.

Discussion

This study yields direct empirical data concerning Gibb's theory of the primacy of trust formation. It suggests that far more emphasis needs to be placed upon the formation of trust within a work group if that group is to go forward toward further accomplishment through laboratory methods. Greater efforts should be focused upon building this trust *prior* to laboratory training or at least very early in the training if durable increases in the group's effectiveness are to be gained.

Acceptance, confidence, and trust in each other may be a particularly relevant issue for members of an ongoing organizational work group which is striving to become an effective task-team through laboratory training. The natural history of such groups, *prior* to training, may have been one in which the responsibility for problem solving and group maintenance was vested in the formal leader rather than shared by the membership, in which formal rules rather than informality and intimate social action was the accepted norm, in which interaction was kept on an impersonal basis for fear that 'familiarity breeds contempt', in which procedural specifications rather than spontaneous self-initiated patterns were the mode of attempted progress, and in which persuasion, influence, and control were exerted under the assumption that members cannot be trusted to make decisions for themselves. These patterns, based upon fear and distrust, may have become an integral and accepted process by which the group 'knows' it can operate. The ongoing work group must learn, either prior to or early in the laboratory experience, that alternative modes of group operation based upon acceptance and trust of individual members and of the total group are equally feasible and potentially more effective.

Corollary to the effect of the group's natural history prior to the laboratory are members' realizations that the group will be returning to an organizational environment in which pressures will be exerted toward prior modes of operation. A relevant question in the minds of members might then be: 'Can I trust group members, the leader, myself, and my laboratory experience sufficiently so that I can experiment and innovate in my own behaviour patterns *during* the laboratory without the fear of negative repercussions *when I return to my back-home organizational environment?'* Groups attempting to move forward toward increased learning and accomplishment will be hindered to the extent that these fears and distrusts remain unexplored and unresolved. The major issue then becomes how to create a climate in which these fears and distrusts can be displaced by feelings of confidence and acceptance of oneself and of group members.

References

Friedlander, F. (1966) 'Performance and interactional dimensions of organisational work groups'. *Journal of Applied Psychology*, **50**, 257–265.

Friedlander, F. (1967) 'The impact of organisational training laboratories upon the effectiveness and interaction of ongoing work groups.' *Personnel Psychology*, **20** (in press).

Gibb, J. R. (1964) 'Climate for trust formation.' In L. P. Bradford, J. R. Gibb and K. D. Benne (Eds.), *T-group Theory and Laboratory Method.* New York: John Wiley. Pp. 279–309.

Shepard, H. A. (1964) 'Responses to situations of competition and conflict.' In R. L. Kahn and E. Boulding (Eds.), *Power and Conflict in Organisations.* New York: Basic Books. Pp. 127–135.

Level of Emotional Arousal in Laboratory Training

Bernard Lubin

Mental Health Centre at Kansas City, Kansas City, Mo.

*Marvin Zuckerman**

Albert Einstein School of Medicine, Philadelphia, Pa.

In order to study the level of emotional arousal produced by laboratory training, data from the highest level of a four T-group laboratory were tested against the following stress conditions from perceptual isolation investigations: six hours, eight hours, and 24 hours. Data were collected on a self-administering adjective check list which provided scores on anxiety, depression, and hostility. Analyses of covariance were conducted using pre-stress scores as covariates to provide statistical control in the absence of experimental matching of subjects.

Laboratory training mean scores on anxiety, depression, and hostility for the four T-groups at the highest level (stress condition) were significantly lower than the mean scores from the stress condition of three perceptual isolation studies. Comparison of the post-stress frequency distributions for the four samples indicates that no scores occur for laboratory training at or beyond the point traditionally accepted as deviant (T score of 70 on the standardization sample for the instrument), whereas the stress condition of each of the three perceptual isolation studies produced scores at or beyond this point.

The use of laboratory training (sensitivity training, group process training, T-group training) as an educational method has continued to increase since its development 20 years ago (Bradford, L. P., Gibb, J. R. and Benne, K. D., 1964). Argyris (*Business Week*, 1963) estimated that in the first 16 years of its use approximately 10,000 persons had participated in laboratory training conducted by the National Training Laboratories (now 'the Institute for Applied Behavioural Science'), the organization principally concerned with developing laboratory training as an educational method. During the past

* We wish to express our thanks to Harry Brittain and Alice W. Lubin for their assistance, and our special gratitude to James A. Norton. Partial support for this investigation was provided by Public Health Research Grant FR 00162-02. Originally published in the *Journal of Applied Behavioral Science*, 1969, **5**, 483–490.

five years, several thousand additional people have participated in training laboratories.

Two recent reports criticize laboratory training because of the alleged high level of stress to which participants are subjected (*Business Week*, 1963, Gottschack, 1966). The critical statements assert that the level of emotional arousal induced by laboratory training is extraordinarily high and is likely to be psychologically damaging to participants. In these critical statements, however, no objective evidence has been presented.

Whether laboratory training produces exceptionally high levels of stress should not be left for polemics; it is a question to be answered with empirical methods. The purpose of this paper is to provide some exploratory findings in regard to the question.

Method

This report involves a comparison of the combined mean scores from four T-groups on a measure of anxiety, depression, and hostility taken at the peak session (session six) of a one week laboratory training conference against mean scores on the same instrument from the stress condition of three situations in which known stress producing procedures were employed.

Forty-three male, managerial level Ss who were divided into four T-groups completed the Multiple Affect Adjective Check List (MAACL) (Zuckerman, M. and Lubin, B., 1965) just before the laboratory training conference began and at the end of each of the eight T-group sessions. (The MAACL consists of three experimentally validated scales: anxiety, depression and hostility.) Analyses of variance showed significant session differences on the three scales over the nine testing occasions. Means on the three scales increased steadily over the sessions, peaked at session six, and declined in the last two sessions. The highest scores on anxiety, depression and hostility scales occurred for all four T-groups session six (peak session). Therefore, session six, just after the midpoint of the conference, was the session in which the highest level of stress occurred.

Comparison data were collected in three independent studies. The MAACL was administered to normal male Ss in three perceptual isolation experiments (total N = 61).

In the perceptual isolation studies, measurements were made prior to the beginning of the experiments, and at the following post confinement points: six hours, eight hours, and 24 hours.

Results

Analyses of variance of anxiety, depression and hostility mean scores under pre-stress conditions for the laboratory training conference and the three perceptual isolation groups revealed significant differences, with laboratory training producing the lowest mean scores. In order to control for initial differences among groups, analyses of covariance were conducted, using pre-stress mean scores as covariates. (Analysis of covariance is a well known and accepted method of adjusting experimental data for initial differences on the same or closely related measures.)

The analyses of covariance resulted in significant F ratios for the three scales (anxiety, depression, and hostility). The significance levels were: anxiety = 0·001, $p < 0·005$, depression = $p < 0·025$, and hostility = $p < 0·0005$.

Table 1—*Stress session means*

Group	N	Anxiety Un-adjusted	Anxiety Adjusted	Depression Un-adjusted	Depression Adjusted	Hostility Un-adjusted	Hostility Adjusted
Laboratory training (session 6)	43	7·93	8·21	15·77	15·97	8·19	9·20
Perceptual isolation (6 hours)	19	10·63	10·55	19·84	20·01	14·47	14·15
Perceptual isolation (8 hours)	29	10·52	10·41	18·79	18·72	13·93	13·26
Perceptual isolation (24 hours)	13	10·85	10·30	19·77	19·02	14·31	12·92

Table 1 presents both unadjusted means and means adjusted for pre-stress scores on anxiety, depression and hostility for the four groups.

The results of the *t* tests among the adjusted means are shown in Table 2.

As we are only interested in testing the hypothesis that the laboratory training combined means for session six are significantly *lower* than the post-stress means from each of the perceptual isolation studies on all three variables, the *t* tests are one-tailed tests.

Table 2—*t tests among adjusted means* (d.f. = 99)

Comparisons	Anxiety	Depression	Hostility
Perceptual isolation (6 hours) *vs.* laboratory training (session 6)	2·48*	2·65**	4·67**
Perceptual isolation (8 hours) *vs.* laboratory training (session 6)	2·64**	2·07*	4·17**
Perceptual isolation (24 hours) *vs.* laboratory training (session 6)	1·86*	1·71*	2·85**

* = $p < 0·05$.
** = $p < 0·01$.

8

All *t* values are significant and in every instance the combined mean (the four T-groups) for laboratory training at session six is lower.

In order to compare the frequency distributions of the three variables from the four studies, 5 × 4 tables were constructed for each variable. Raw scores were converted to their corresponding *t* scores (M. Zuckerman and B. Lubin, 1965, p. 7). Chi square tests for the three variables indicated a significant relationship between experimental condition and distribution of scores on the anxiety and hostility measures for both pre-stress and stress conditions. No relationship was found for the depression variables (Pre-stress: anxiety $= 0.01 > p > 0.001$; depression $= 0.70 > p > 0.80$;

Table 3—*Frequency distribution of anxiety scores from stress conditions (frequencies converted to percentages)*

				t score			
Group	N	0–39	40–49	50–59	60–69	70 and +	Total
Laboratory training (session 6)	43	00	21	74	05	00	100
Perceptual isolation (6 hours)	19	00	11	36	21	32	100
Perceptual isolation (8 hours)	29	03	07	49	17	24	100
Perceptual isolation (24 hours)	13	00	08	38	23	31	100
		03	47	197	66	87	400/400

Table 4—*Frequency distribution of anxiety scores from stress conditions (frequencies converted to percentages)*

				t score			
Group	N	0–39	40–49	50–59	60–69	70 and +	Total
Laboratory training (session 6)	49	05	19	72	04	00	100
Perceptual isolation (6 hours)	19	05	05	47	37	06	100
Perceptual isolation (8 hours)	29	00	14	52	24	10	100
Perceptual isolation (24 hours)	13	00	08	61	23	08	100
		10	46	232	88	24	400/400

Table 5—*Frequency distribution of anxiety scores from stress conditions (frequencies converted to percentages)*

Group	N	0–39	40–49	50–59	60–69	70 and +	Total
				t score			
Laboratory training (Session 6)	43	19	16	51	14	00	100
Perceptual isolation (6 hours)	19	00	05	05	53	37	100
Perceptual isolation (8 hours)	29	00	10	24	28	38	100
Perceptual isolation (24 hours)	13	00	00	08	62	30	100
		19	31	88	157	105	400/400

hostility $= p < 0.001$. Post-stress: anxiety $= 0.01 > p > 0.001$; depression $= 0.10 > p > 0.05$; hostility $= p < 0.001$).

Tables 3, 4 and 5 present a summary of the frequency distributions for the four groups on the three variables under stress conditions. For ease of viewing, frequencies were converted to percentages.

A *t* score of 70 is generally accepted as the point beyond which scores on a psychometric instrument are considered to be unusually high, as that point represents a score that is higher than that achieved by 98 per cent of the standardization sample. Inspection of Tables 3, 4 and 5 reveals that under the highest stress level produced by laboratory training, *no* scores occur at or above the level of $t = 70$, whereas the stress condition of each of the perceptual isolation studies produced scores above this point.

Discussion

There is no generally agreed upon criterion of stress (E. E. Levitt, 1967), therefore, we have used a relative rather than an absolute definition, i.e., peak session scores in the laboratory training conference (session six) tested against scores on the same instrument from known stress producing situations.

Perceptual isolation experiments consist of confining the subject and restricting his visual, auditory and tactile sensations during this period. Previous studies utilizing the MAACL show a statistically significant increase over control conditions on anxiety and depression scores after six or more hours of perceptual isolation (M. Zuckerman and B. Lubin, 1965, p. 8).

We found that laboratory training at its most stressful point produces significantly lower mean scores on anxiety, depression and hostility than the stress conditions of three perceptual isolation studies. In addition, for laboratory training, no scores on the three variables (anxiety, depression or hostility, occurred at or above the point conventionally accepted as deviant for the standardization sample of the measuring instrument, whereas each of the stress conditions of the three perceptual isolation studies produced scores beyond the deviant point.

The findings may be generalized to other human relations laboratory training conferences which employ designs including, for example, T-groups, theory sessions, special interest seminars, and skill training exercises.

Laboratory training consists of experience-based learning and emphasizes, among other things, the analysis of current interpersonal transactions and group level phenomena in order to unfreeze behavioral–attitudinal–emotional patterns. From the outset, the identification, sharing and exploration of feelings is legitimized and encouraged. A wide range of feelings are evoked and shared: warmth, support, concern, affection, and helpfulness in addition to those feelings, such as anxiety and anger, which arise from a state of tension. The latter feelings are the ones emphasized by the small number of critics, some of whom have participated in laboratory training and some of whom have not.

As indicated by the title of this report, this study was conducted for the purpose of providing some objective data regarding the question of stress during laboratory training. Ideally, the design of this study should have been based upon the employment of the same subjects in all conditions in an appropriate crossover design.

Additional investigations might be oriented toward the selection process of participants for laboratory training. Other investigations could compare peak session data from laboratory training with a broad range of stress producing situations, and might contrast affective data from laboratories differing in design and focus such as: personal growth, community development, inter-group relations, conflict management, and organizational development.

References

Bradford, L. P., J. R. Gibb and K. D. Benne (1964) *T-group Theory and Laboratory Method*. New York: John Wiley.

Burke, H. L. and W. G. Bennis (1961) 'Changes in perception of self and others during human relations training.' *Hum. Rel.*, **14**, 165–182.

Business Week (1963) 'Yourself as others see you.' March 16, 160.

Gottschalk, L. A. (1966) 'Psychoanalytic notes on T-groups at the Human Relations Laboratory, Bethel, Maine.' *Compr. Psychiatry*, **7**, 472–487.

Levitt, E. E. (1967) *The Psychology of Anxiety*. Indianapolis: Bobbs Merrill.
Lubin, B. and M. Zuckerman (1967) 'Affective and perceptual-cognitive patterns in sensitivity training groups.' *Psychol. Rep.*, **21**, 365–376.
Zuckerman, M. and B. Lubin (1965) *Multiple Affect Adjective Check Lists: Manual*. San Diego, California: Educational and Industrial Testing Service.

CHAPTER 7

Course of Development in the T-group

It is not surprising that one of the central areas of T-group research is concerned with the identification of predictable phases or sequences within and across groups, since the identification of such developmental trends is of importance to the establishment of theory, research, and sound training design.

Tuckman (1965) has suggested that most of the theories can be synthesized to fit one model, the four developmental stages which he labels forming, storming, norming, and performing. Some theories, notably those of Bion (1961), Schutz (1958), and Hampden-Turner (1966) do not fit easily into this successive phase model, indeed they emphasize the recurrent cycle model which holds that the group will never fully resolve issues.

Not only are there conflicting theories of development, but also conflicting evidence. Lubin and Zuckerman (1967) introduce a distinction between *group development* which they note has sometimes been used to refer to significant differences among sessions in a single group and to refer to significant differences among phases in a single session, and *developmental trends* which is used to refer to events which appear at similar points in time in various groups. 'Group development' is used, hereafter, when we are referring to a single group over a period of time, and 'developmental trends' when we are referring to similarities over time and across groups. While there is little conflicting evidence with regard to group development, there is a great deal with regard to developmental trends.

There are a number of studies of group development and while many are anecdotal some notably those of Barron and Krules (1948), Stock and Ben-Zeev (1958), Hill (1955), and Mills (1964) employ highly reliable observational and rating techniques. Since the studies by Barron and Krulee, Hill and Stock and Ben-Zeev have been more than adequately summarized by Stock (1964), we shall only look briefly at Mills' findings before covering in

213

more detail the more recent studies expressly concerned with developmental trends.

Mills devised a rating system—Sign Process Analysis—to study the interaction of one human relations training course over the period of an academic year, some 68 sessions in all. He identified five principal periods: (1) the encounter; (2) testing boundaries and modelling roles; (3) negotiating an indigenous normative system; (4) production, and (5) separation. For each phase he identified the central issues, the predominant activity and the group properties which emerge. For example, the fourth stage, that of production, is marked by concern shown over whether or not the group can create something of lasting value, while for the member the issues are: can I communicate ideas that are both relevant and in such a form that they can be tested against reality? In the realm of activities the members apply what they know about the processes of observation, emotional expression, interpretation, formulation and testing. The emergent properties are marked by task redefinition, lowering of the level of group aspiration, and relaxation of norms governing what should or should not be expressed.

Mills adds to Tuckman's classification with his fifth stage, though his other stages could be forced, if somewhat inappropriately, into Tuckman's forming, storming, norming, and performing categories. Accounts of the terminal phase of the group are relatively rare and Mills' analysis which lays emphasis on the group as striving to convince itself that it has produced something of enduring value, serves to highlight the re-entry problem familiar to many T-group trainers.

It would seem that the evidence to support the notion of group development is clear, if largely subjective and anecdotal, whereas the evidence with regard to developmental trends is conflicting and ambiguous though for the most part largely empiric and non-anecdotal. Studies by Reisel (1959), Lakin and Carson (1964), and Lubin and Zuckerman (1967) do not unequivocally confirm the hypothesis of developmental trends, yet those by Mann (1967) and Dunphy (1968) do.

Reisel's work is interesting since not only does it span the two emphases in dealing as it does with both group development and developmental trends, but it also presents evidence which both supports and denies ideas about the latter. For Reisel the initial problem was that of finding if regularities existed in T-groups progressing through time and to describe the similarities that might be found. In order to do this he isolated three dimensions for describing phases in T-group behaviour; involvement, degree of emotionality, and satisfaction. Working from diaries kept by members of three groups over a thirty session period, Reisel rated participants on these three dimensions. Initially he pooled the data for all three groups and was able to conclude: (1) the general impact of training produces systematic patterns of reaction in its participants; (2) the greater the trainee involvement, the greater the emotional reaction (somewhat less firmly); (3) there is a strong suggestion that the greater the emotional reaction, the more the trainees experience dissatisfaction.

Moving from the macroscopic level, Reisel focused on reaction to training within groups. His major findings here were that: (1) group 1 showed cyclical behaviour on all dimensions; (2) group 2 had well-defined patterns (non-random sequences) including one cyclical pattern; (3) group 3 revealed the greatest diversity of behaviour, having sequences along the involvement and emotionality dimensions, but demonstrating a random flow of satisfaction. All Reisel could conclude is that 'each group develops an individualized personality, patterning or identity, coupled with generally meaningful regularities of development'.

Finally it was asked 'Along what, if any, of the patterned dimensions do the groups show similarity?' Early results suggested that when all individual members are studied as a unit ($N = 69$) convincing similarities emerged. However, when the groups were studied as separate entities considerable variation was noted. Reisel sought to understand this by making a comparison among all and between parts of groups in a search for possible similarities or differences. All groups seem to maintain the pattern of involvement, though only group 1 showed this significantly; to a lesser degree, satisfaction patterns tend to be the same, relatively high at the outset, swinging downwards as training progressed, and showing similar fluctuations for all groups. The major area of difference lay in the sphere of emotionality, no relationship across groups was revealed in this area.

Reisel concluded that if the study is taken in its entirety, the results provide empirical support for the theoretical views which hold that the T-group develops in a systematic rather than a haphazard fashion. Unfortunately, parts of his study indicate almost the opposite or, at very best, they can be seen as supporting the unique character of each group's emotional patterning.

Lakin and Carson (1964) also touch upon issues relevant to developmental trends in small groups. The authors investigated the extent to which participants in a sensitivity training group perceived changes in the group process. They collected data from participants in four T-groups at a two-week residential training laboratory conducted by a state mental health agency. The participants were required to provide ratings of the intensity of group concern for each of 11 variables for each of their 16 T-group meetings. Lakin and Carson discovered that there were significant variations in

the ratings across the 16 meetings and that the four groups varied considerably in regard to the point at which particular variables gained and lost
ascendency in the pattern of meetings. The groups differed maximally on
the 'group atmosphere' variable; some groups emphasized this earlier than
others by several meetings. 'Competitiveness' declined and 'cooperation'
showed an increase, but none of the other variables showed a discernible
trend. Like Reisel, the authors are forced to conclude that each T-group
experience is more unique than it is standard.

The study by Lubin and Zuckerman (reprinted here) concludes similarly
that there is low consistency of trends from one group to another, although
their data supports the hypothesis of some similarity of group trends over
sessions. On the other hand, both Mann (1966, 1967) and Dunphy provide
studies which more firmly support hypotheses of developmental trends.
Mann's (1966) study has already been reviewed in an earlier chapter, so we
shall conclude this section with an examination of Dunphy's (1968) work.

His investigation was concerned specifically with two sections of a
Harvard undergraduate course, 'Social Relations 120: Analysis of Interpersonal Behaviour' (these classes must be the most researched in the world:
Bales, Slater, Mills, Mann, Dunphy). The primary focus of the investigation was changes as reflected in the content of weekly reports written by
individual group members. Dunphy lists the advantages of this approach as
being (1) reduction of verbal data to be processed, (2) enforced contribution from all, (3) study must focus on aspects of the group which members
themselves regard as important. He appears to be unconcerned that these
'strengths' could also be regarded as weaknesses. In order to test for the
existence, extent and nature of common phases movements, the entire text
of the written reports was subjected to a computer system of content analysis
called the General Inquirer (Dunphy, Stone and Smith, 1965). Dunphy
predicted that:

(1) The content of the written reports from the two self-analytic groups
will show similar quantitative and qualitative changes over time, i.e.
common 'phase movements'.

(2) These phase movements will explain more variance in the data than
will differences between the two groups.

(3) The characteristics of consecutive phase movements will reflect an
emerging group unity and an increasing emotional involvement on the part
of the group members.

Dunphy concludes the first part of his report by claiming developmental
trends which support his hypotheses. He distinguishes an early period
(phases 1–3) where relationships are largely negative and counterpersonal.

The first phase being an attempt to import external normative standards, the second and third characterized more by rivalry and aggression. The fourth phase is essentially negative but realizes a new concern for absenteeism and communications. The last two phases, on the other hand, are qualitatively different, with emotional concerns well to the fore.

Like Mann (1967) who uses sub-group formation as his explanatory device, Dunphy attempts to explain the generation and dissolution of his phases, though he uses the notion of 'role differentiation' to unlock the mystery. He concludes that groups have common role specialists and that these people serve as important reference points for members as group culture develops.

As Dunphy acknowledges we have no way of knowing how representative these two groups are: composition, for example, was not controlled; at its most basic level, age and sex could also influence developmental trends.

Nonetheless, the Mann and Dunphy studies represent a step in the right direction in that they not only seek to discover trends, but also to account for them in terms of the role behaviour of individuals or sub-groups.

Conclusion

The identification of predictable phases or sequences may be of importance to trainers but the very individual measures utilized often make it difficult to generalize from the findings. A great deal more work needs to be done in this area before results can be fully utilized in designing or monitoring training activities.

References

Barron, M. and G. K. Krulee (1948) 'Case study of a basic skill training group.' *Journal of Social Issues*, **4**.

Bion, W. R. (1961) *Experiences in Groups*. London: Tavistock.

Dunphy, D. (1968) 'Phases, roles and myths in self-analytic groups.' *Journal of Applied Behavioral Science*, **4**, 195–225.

Dunphy, D., P. Stone, M. Smith and D. Ogilvie (1965) *The General Inquirer: A Computer Approach to Content Analysis*. M.I.T. Press.

Hampden-Turner, C. M. (1966) 'An existential "learning theory" and the integration of T-group research.' *Journal of Applied Behavioral Science*, **2**, 367–386.

Hill, W. F. (1955) 'The influence of subgroups on participation in human relations training groups.' Unpublished Ph.D. thesis, University of Chicago.

Lakin, M. and R. C. Carson (1964) 'Participant perception of group process group sensitivity training.' *International Journal of Group Psychotherapy*, **14**, 116–122.

Lubin, B. and M. Zuckerman (1967) 'Affective and perceptual cognitive patterns in sensitivity training groups.' *Psychological Reports*, **21**, 365–376.

Mann, R. D. (1966) 'The development of the member-trainer relations in self-analytic groups.' *Human Relations*, **19**, 84–117.

Mann, R. D. (1967) *Interpersonal Styles and Group Development*. New York: John Wiley.

Mills, T. M. (1964) *Group Transformation*. Englewood Cliffs, New Jersey: Prentice Hall.

Reisel, J. (1959) 'A search for behavioral patterns in sensitivity training groups.' Unpublished Ph.D. thesis, University of California, Los Angeles.

Schutz, W. C. (1958) *FIRO: A Theory of Interpersonal Relations*. New York: Rinehart.

Stock, D. (1964) 'A survey of research on T-groups.' In L. P. Bradford and co-workers, *T-group Theory and Laboratory Method*. New York: John Wiley.

Stock, D. and Ben-Zeev (1958) 'Changes in work and emotionality during group growth.' In D. Stock and H. Thelen (Eds.), *Emotional Dynamics and Group Culture*. Washington, D.C.: NTL-N.E.A.

Tuckman, B. (1965) 'Development sequence in small groups.' *Psychological Bulletin*, 63.

Affective and Perceptual Cognitive Patterns in Sensitivity Training Groups*

Bernard Lubin

Indiana Department of Mental Health

Marvin Zuckerman

Albert Einstein Medical Centre

The identification of predictable phases or sequences in small groups is important for the development of theory, research, and training methodology. For the trainer, the establishment of reliable knowledge concerning group development would permit the design of more efficient training procedures and would permit him to devote more of his attention to novel group developments.

Conflicting evidence has appeared, however, concerning the occurrence of developmental trends in small groups. The work of Bales and Strodtbeck (1951) and Philip and Dunphy (1959) tends to confirm the hypothesis of developmental trends, while studies by Reisel (1959) and Lakin and Carson (1964) yielded negative evidence.

The phrase 'group development' has sometimes been used to refer to significant differences among sessions in a single group (Hill, 1955; Stock and Ben-Zeev, 1958) and significant differences among segments of a single session (Bales and Strodtbeck, 1951). For the sake of clarity, we wish to indicate that we are using the phrase 'developmental trends' to refer to predictable sequences of events which appear at similar points in time in

* Originally Published in *Psychological Reports*, 1967, **21**, 365–376. © Southern University Press 1967.

We wish to express our thanks to Harry Brittain, Alice W. Lubin, and Morton Lieberman for their assistance, and our special gratitude to James A. Norton. Partial support for this investigation was provided by The Association For The Advancement of Mental Health Research and Education, Inc. and Public Health Research Grant FR 00162-02.

The training staff consisted of William Dyer, Daniel Hopson, Bernard Lubin, Alexander C. Rosen and Charles N. Seashore. Special appreciation is extended to Charles N. Seashore who facilitated the collection of data, and we are indebted to the other members of the staff for their cooperation.

various groups. In this definition, the emphasis is upon consistency or similarity of trends across groups.

This investigation attempts to extend the inquiry concerning developmental trends in small groups and to determine some of the affective and perceptual-cognitive patterns during a 1-wk. sensitivity group conference. The approach is from the perspective of the participants.

Method

Forty-five administrative level Ss participated in the conference.* They ranged in age from 32 yr. to 67 yr. (M = 47·3, SD = 7·9). The minimum educational attainment for any of the participants was 2 yr. of college work, and the mean was 3·4 yr. of college work. They were divided into four approximately equal groups in such a way as to maximize heterogeneity within each group in terms of geographical location, size of site of residence, age, and education.

The Multiple Affect Adjective Check List (MAACL) was administered to Ss 1 hr. prior to the beginning of the conference and at the end of each of eight training group (T-group) sessions. The development and validation of the MAACL is described elsewhere (Zuckerman and Lubin, 1965). It is an experimentally validated self-administering adjective check list consisting of 132 items from which three scores are derived: Anxiety, Depression, and Hostility.

At the end of each of eight T-group sessions, in addition to the MAACL, participants completed the following nine-point scale-questions. (Only the extreme cues are presented.)

		1	9
Q1.	I felt that this session was	Not worthwhile	Very worthwhile
Q2.	In regard to my participation in this session I was	Very inactive	Very active
Q3.	In this session, there was	Very little open sharing of feelings	Much open sharing of feelings
Q4.	The level of conflict in this session was	Very low	Very high
Q5.	In this session, the discussions	Had very little relevance to issues within the group	Were very relevant to issues within the group

* The data for this study were collected in an Institute of the National Council of Juvenile Court Judges. Analyses are based upon 43 of the 45 Ss for whom complete data were available.

Results and discussion

Representatives of sample

Thirty-nine of the Ss were individually matched for age, education, and sex with counterparts from the normative sample of the MAACL (Zuckerman and Lubin, 1965). The t tests between pre-conference Anxiety and Depression scores and those of matched normals were not significant, indicating that participants in this conference can be considered to have been drawn from the general population in reference to these two variables. The t test for Hostility was significantly lower than that for the normative sample ($t = 2 \cdot 4$, $p < 0 \cdot 05$). The non-significant t tests for Anxiety and Depression and the significant t test for Hostility, with a higher mean in the normative sample, support the hypothesis that conference participants were not more 'emotional' than the general population.

Emotional involvement in the conference

Each S's pre-conference scores were contrasted with the mean of his scores for eight sessions on Anxiety, Depression, and Hostility. The paired-observation t tests were significant at the $0 \cdot 01$ level for Anxiety, Depression, and Hostility, with conference means higher than pre-conference scores on the three variables, thus demonstrating 'emotional involvement' in the conference.

Analyses of group, session, and interaction effects

Although an attempt was made to maximize the heterogeneity of Ss when groups were initially composed, the analyses of variance indicated that the four groups differed significantly on the three affect variables at the pre-conference testing. Therefore, analysis of covariance was used in order to test for between-group differences during training sessions with difference in pre-conference of first-session scores partialled out. For the five-scale questions, first-session scores were employed as the covariate, with the sum of scores of the remaining seven sessions used as the dependent variables. For the three affect variables (Anxiety, Depression, and Hostility), pre-conference scores were used as the covariate, with the sum of scores for the remaining eight sessions as the dependent variables. No covariance adjustment was necessary, however, in the tests for session differences and group by session interactions since these are both 'within-subjects' effects (Winer, 1962, p. 607).

Group differences

The results of the analyses of covariance for between-group differences averaged over sessions are presented in Table 1. It is obvious that group differences are significant for four of the eight variables even after the initial group differences were controlled. Thus, we can say that groups differed significantly in their experience of Anxiety, Hostility, feeling that sessions were worthwhile (Q1), and perception of the level of activity (Q2). Groups did not differ significantly in terms of the perceived degree of openness and sharing of feelings (Q3), perceived level of conflict within the group (Q4), relevance of discussions to issues within the group (Q5), and Depression.

Session differences

Table 2 presents the summary of the analyses of variance for session differences for the four groups on the eight variables. Session differences were significant for all eight variables.

Analyses of trends

Table 2 also reveals that session by group interactions were significant for six of the eight variables. These interactions can be seen in Fig. 1 which presents the session by session changes for the four groups on the eight variables. In the case of the three affect variables, pre-conference means are included. In each case, the session by group interaction tests whether the trends over sessions for the four groups depart significantly from parallelism with one another. It is this level of analysis which tests for similarity of developmental trends among groups.

Q1. (Worthwhileness of session)—The session by group interaction is significant. Inspection of the figure shows that this is probably due to group 3's having a large drop at Session 3 and Group 1 remaining high at Sessions 7 and 8 while the other three groups drop.

Q2. (Degree of activity during session)—The session by group interaction is not significant at the 0·05 level. This is interpreted to mean that the four trends do not depart significantly from parallel with one another. However, Group 1 rises from Session 6 to Sessions 7 and 8 while the other three groups fall, as in the case of Q1.

Q3. (Degree of open sharing of feelings)—The interaction is significant at the 0·05 level. It appears largely due to the changes from Sessions 4 to 5 to 6 of Groups 1 and 4 as contrasted with Groups 2 and 3. Again, the curve of Group 1 rises after Session 6 while the other three groups fall. This is a consistent pattern for Group 1 on Q1, Q2, and Q3.

Table 1—*Tests of adjusted between group differences averaged over sessions: analyses of covariance*

Variable		Groups	Ss within groups
Q1	d.f.	3	38
	MS[a]	298·7424	45·3005
	F	6·5947	
	p	$0·001 < p < 0·005$	
Q2	d.f.	3	38
	MS	165·7421	40·7146
	F	4·0708	
	p	$0·01 < p < 0·025$	
Q3	d.f.	3	38
	MS	139·5003	54·0234
	F	2·5822	
	p	$0·05 < p < 0·10$	
Q4	d.f.	3	38
	MS	223·0556	84·8387
	F	2·6292	
	p	$0·05 < p < 0·10$	
Q5	d.f.	3	38
	MS	63·5849	64·1351
	F	0·9914	
	p	$0·25 < p < 0·50$	
Anxiety	d.f.	3	38
	MS	472·8767	142·4472
	F	3·3197	
	p	$0·025 < p < 0·05$	
Depression	d.f.	3	38
	MS	863·0939	346·2423
	F	2·4927	
	p	$0·05 < p < 0·10$	
Hostility	d.f.	3	38
	MS	1686·1319	183·3310
	F	9·1972	
	p	$< 0·0005$	

[a] All Mean Squares shown are adjusted for the appropriate covariate in each case. Please see text.

*Q*4. (*Level of conflict*)—The interaction is significant. This appears to be primarily due to the contrast between the changes of Groups 1 and 3 from Sessions 3 to 4 and the change of Group 3 as contrasted with all other groups from Sessions 7 to 8.

*Q*5. (*Relevance of discussion to issues within the group*)—The interaction is significant and the trend comparison resemble those for Q1.

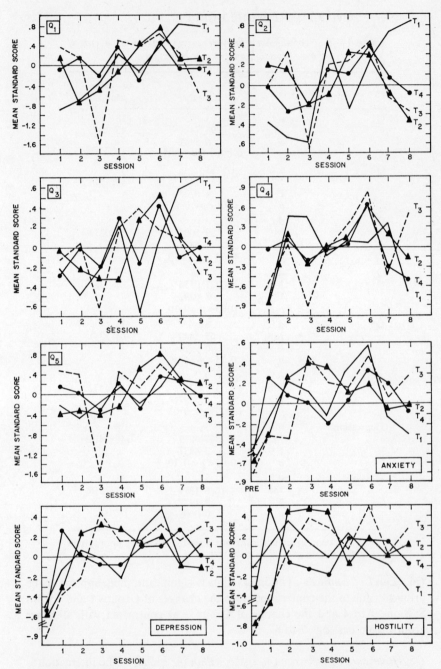

Fig. 1. Session-by-session changes on the eight dependent variables for each of the four T-groups. Please see text for definition of the variables. Points plotted are means of standard scores, with SD obtained from the pooled estimate of variance of all sessions.

Anxiety—The interaction is significant at the 0·05 level. Groups 2 and 3 appear to show similar trends and so do Groups 1 and 4 but the latter two differ markedly from the first two, especially at Sessions 3 and 4.

Depression—The interaction is not significant.

Hostility—The interaction is significant, and trend comparisons are very similar to those for Anxiety, except that Group 1 does not show the peak at Session 6.

Table 2—*Analyses of variance for session differences*

Variable		Sessions	Session × group	Session × subjects within groups
Q1	d.f.	7	21	273
	MS	22·497	9·204	2·155
	F	10·439	4·271	
	p	<0·0005	<0·0005	
Q2	d.f.	7	21	273
	MS	8·159	3·789	2·481
	F	3·289	1·527	
	p	0·001<*p*<0·005	0·05<*p*<0·10	
Q3	d.f.	7	21	273
	MS	7·056	4·002	2·209
	F	3·194	1·812	
	p	0·001<*p*<0·005	0·01<*p*<0·025	
Q4	d.f.	7	21	273
	MS	23·171	8·059	2·871
	F	8·071	2·807	
	p	<0·0005	<0·0005	
Q5	d.f.	7	21	273
	MS	18·983	7·939	2·351
	F	8·074	3·377	
	p	<0·0005	<0·0005	
Anxiety	d.f.	8	24	312
	MS	25·689	4·474	2·863
	F	8·973	1·563	
	p	<0·0005	0·025<*p*<0·05	
Depression	d.f.	8	24	312
	MS	101·200	11·072	8·476
	F	11·940	1·306	
	p	<0·0005	0·10<*p*<0·25	
Hostility	d.f.	8	24	312
	MS	45·285	10·526	3·860
	F	11·732	2·727	
	p	<0·0005	<0·0005	

Recapitulation

Groups differed significantly on four of the eight variables, significant session effects were found on all eight variables, and significant interactions were found on six of the eight variables. For the two variables for which the interaction was not significant, in the case of Q2 the F ratio fell between the 5 and 10 per cent significance levels and the pattern in Fig. 1 appears similar to those of Q1, Q3, and Q5. In the case of Depression the F ratio falls between the 10 and 25 per cent levels of significance and the

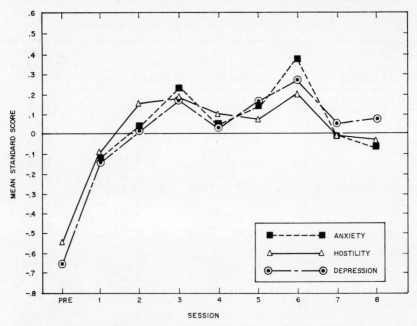

Fig. 2. Session-by-session on the three affect variables. Composite of the three T-groups. Points plotted are means of standard scores, with standard variation pooled over all sessions.

pattern appears similar to that on Anxiety. Thus the evidence indicates significant differences among sessions, implying some degree of similarity of group trends over sessions, but no consistent trends common to all groups. These findings confirm those of Reisel (1959) and Lakin and Carson (1964).

Despite the findings that groups differ significantly on four of the eight dependent variables, it seems to be instructive to present the composite trends for the four groups on all eight variables. These are presented in Figs. 2 and 3. Peaking seems to occur definitely at Session 6 for all variables.

No generalizable significance is attributed to Session 6 as such, as there is considerable variation in the number.

To the extent that participants feel that sessions are worthwhile, they report less anxiety, depression, and hostility. The relationship is certainly more complex than this statement alone would indicate. In this connection, the following additional findings should be considered.

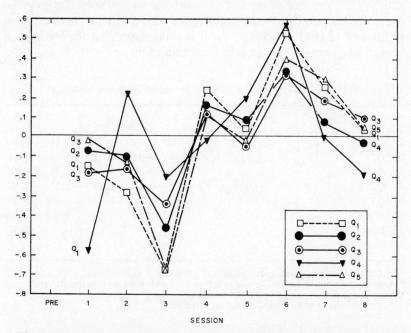

Fig. 3. Session-by-session changes on the five perceptual cognitive variables: composite of the four T-groups. Points plotted are means of standard scores, with standard deviation obtained from the pooled estimate of variance over all sessions.

There is a significant negative relationship between the effect variables and the degree to which feelings are openly shared in the group. As feelings are shared more openly, participants report experiencing less anxiety, depression, and hostility. These findings support a basic tenet of small group training philosophy that the open sharing of feelings tends to have a releasing effect upon group process and the behaviour of individual Ss.

By means of theory sessions, written materials, and the modelling behaviour of trainers, sensitivity training conferences stress the importance of keeping discussions focused upon interactions and processes that occur within the group. It is interesting to find that there is a significant negative relationship between Q5 (Relevance of discussions to issues within the group) and the affect variables. Overall, as discussions focus more upon issues within the group, Ss report experiencing less disturbing affect.

Although it is hazardous to rest any interpretation on non-significant correlations, it is worth noting that the correlations between level of activity (Q2) and level of conflict (Q4) with the three affect scales go in the negative direction, though to a small degree. This might have been expected in the case of level of activity, but it is somewhat surprising for level of conflict and may indicate an area for future study.

Table 3—*Intercorrelations among the eight dependent variables*[a]

Variable[b]	1	2	3	4	5	6	7	8
1. Q1		0·58[c]	0·85[c]	0·42[c]	0·76[c]	−0·46[c]	−0·44[c]	−0·41[c]
2. Q2			0·65[c]	0·48[c]	0·67[c]	−0·12	−0·06	−0·11
3. Q3				0·47[c]	0·82[c]	−0·45	−0·40	−0·44[c]
4. Q4					0·41[c]	−0·21	−0·22	−0·08
5. Q5						−0·43[c]	−0·41[c]	−0·39[c]
6. Anxiety							0·92[c]	0·86[c]
7. Depression								0·81[c]
8. Hostility								

[a] Correlations are based upon the sum of scores over eight sessions in the case of the five-scale-questions and upon the sum of scores over eight sessions plus the pre-conference testing in the case of the three effect variables.

[b] For definition of variables, please see page 220.

[c] $p = 0\cdot01$.

A more parsimonious interpretation of the correlation matrix results if we observe that the correlations cluster into two groups: (1) the affect variables (Anxiety, Depression, and Hostility) and (2) the perceptual–cognitive variables (Q1, 2, 3, 4 and 5). Of the latter, the three that seem most directly related to satisfaction with group sessions (Q1, 3 and 5) have a relationship to the affect cluster.

The high intercorrelations among the affect variables (Anxiety, Depression, and Hostility) and among the perceptual–cognitive variables, respectively, reflect the common variance within each of these sets of measures. The intercorrelations among the scales of the MAACL are reported in Zuckerman and Lubin (1965), and the common variance among scale-questions of the type employed in this investigation has been reported by Blake, Mouton and Fruchter (in press).

Overview and implications

The statements by Bennis and Shepard (1956) and Bion (1961) which discussed the phasic development of small groups were heuristic in nature and were intended to stimulate research and further theory development. Such statements necessarily present the case in broad terms and under ideal conditions, and they usually leave unspecified such crucial variables as trainer behaviour, group composition, intercurrent events in the group, specific elements of the training design, etc.

In order to understand the empirical evidence concerning developmental trends in small groups, it is necessary to consider the nature of the groups employed in the investigations and the methods by which observations have been made.

In both the studies by Bales and Strodtbeck (1951) and Philip and Dunphy (1959) in which confirmatory evidence for developmental trends were found, the parameters of authority and group goal were clearly defined. Authority was represented by the experimenter who selected as, assigned them to groups, and specified the nature of the task. In addition, time pressure for group decision was imposed. Non-participant observers coded behavioural acts according to a classification scheme devised for problem-solving groups. Observed behaviour was recorded as it occurred during the group sessions.

In this investigation and in the ones by Lakin and Carson (1964) and by Reisel (1959), T-groups rather than problem-solving groups were employed. In T-groups, authority is a complex concept and the trainer's role usually remains ambiguous well into the life of the group. Although the training conference has definite objectives, e.g., learning about oneself in interaction with others, learning about the functioning of groups and organizations, no goal or specific task under time pressure is assigned to the group. The problem for the group in each session is to discover, out of the many interests and needs of participants, those which are salient in each session and to devise the most effective means for moving towards these goals. In the report by Lakin and Carson (1964) and in this investigation, rating scales and checklists were completed by participants at the end of each session concerning their perceptions and feelings about group process. Participants in Reisel's study (1959) noted their impressions in diaries from which quantitative indices were later derived by means of content analyses.

Due to the important differences between this study and the ones by Bales and Strodtbeck (1951) and Philip and Dunphy (1959), the present investigation should not be considered to be a test of Bales hypotheses.

Another potentially meaningful area for research, which was touched upon in this investigation, concerns the phenomenology of the participant in small group training (Lakin and Carson, 1964; Weschler and Reisel, 1959). We found that participants experience less negative affect in those sessions: which they feel worthwhile, wherein there is more open sharing of feelings and wherein discussions are more relevant to issues within the group. There is some suggestion also that participants experience less negative affect in those sessions in which they have been more active and in which there has been conflict within the group. The last statement refers to the possibility that confrontation and conflict, within the levels occurring in training groups, may be experienced by participants as stimulating rather than disturbing. Indirect support for this finding is provided by Harrison (1965), who reports more learning in groups composed so that heterogeneity of member characteristics is maximized. If it is assumed that heterogeneity may increase the probability of conflict, then heterogeneity seems to be associated with less negative effect.

The key role played by emotional factors in the process of attitudinal and behavioural change has been recognized (Bull, 1951; Rosenberg *et al.*, 1960) and the vividness of the emotional component of the T-group experience is indicated by the many informal staff and participant references to the subject. However, there are only a few references in the training literature to the subject of affect, mood, or emotion.

Further investigations of developmental trends in training groups should include both observations made by non-participant observers and systematic reports of perceptions and feelings by participants about group process. The former should be derived from appropriate theory about small group training and the latter should involve comparable variables. Discrepancies between objective and subjective observations then might open additional areas for research. In such studies, trainer behaviour and group composition should be controlled, as these factors are important determiners of group process (Stock, 1964; Harrison and Lubin, 1965).

References

Bales, R. F. and F. L. Strodtbeck (1951) 'Phases in group problem solving.' *J. Abnorm. soc. Psychol.*, **46**, 485–495.

Bennis, W. G. and H. A. Shepard (1956) 'A theory of group development.' *Hum. Rel.*, **9**, 415–457.

Bion, W. E. (1961) *Experiences in Groups*. New York: Basic Books.

Blake, B. R., J. S. Mouton and B. Frutcher (1970) A factor analysis of training group behaviour. *J. soc. Psychol.*, in press.

Bull, N. (1951) 'The attitude theory of emotion.' New York: Coolidge Foundation (*Nerv. ment. Dis. Monogr.*, No. 81).

Harrison, R. L. (1965) 'Group composition models for laboratory design.' *J. appl. behav. Sci.*, **1**, 409–432.

Harrison, R. L. and B. Lubin (1965) 'Personal style, group composition, and learning.' *J. Appl. behav. Sci.*, 1, 286–301.

Hill, W. G. (1955) 'The influence of subgroups on participation in human relations training groups.' Unpublished doctoral dissertation, Univ. of Chicago.

Laking, M. and R. C. Carson (1964) 'Participant perception of group process in group sensitivity training.' *Int. J. Gp. Psychother.*, 14, 116–122.

Philip, H. and D. Dunphy (1959) 'Developmental trends in small groups.' *Sociometry*, 22, 162–174.

Reisel, J. (1959a) 'A search for behaviour patterns in sensitivity training groups.' Unpublished dissertation, Univer. of California, Los Angeles.

Reisel, J. (1959b) 'The trainer role in human relations training.' Paper presented at meetings of the Western Psychological Association, San Diego, Calif., April.

Rosenberg, M. J., C. I. Hovland, W. J. McGuire, R. P. Abelson and J. W. Brehm (1960) 'Attitude organisation and change: an analysis of consistency among attitude components.' Yale studies in attitude and communication. Vol. III. New Haven, Conn.: Yale Univer. Press.

Stock, D. (1964) 'A survey of research on T-groups.' In L. P. Bradford, J. R. Gibb and K. D. Benne (Eds.), *T-group Theory and Laboratory Method: Innovation in Re-education*. New York: John Wiley. Pp. 395–441.

Stock, D. and S. Ben-Zeev (1958) 'Changes in work and emotionality during group growth.' In D. Stock and H. A. Theler (Eds.), *Emotional Dynamics and Group Culture*. New York: New York Univer. Press. Pp. 192–206.

Weschler, I. R. and J. Reisel (1959) 'Inside a sensitivity training group.' Los Angeles: Institute of Industrial Relations, Univer. of Calif. (Indus. Relat. Monogr. No. 4.)

Winer, B. J. (1962) *Statistical Principles in Experimental Design*. New York: McGraw-Hill.

Zuckerman, M. and B. Lubin (1965) 'Multiple affect adjective checklists manual.' San Diego: Educational and Industrial Testing Service.

The Development of the Member–Trainer Relationship in Self-Analytic Groups[*]

Richard D. Mann

Harvard University

The goal of this paper is to bring together and build upon two traditions in the study of small groups: (1) the clinical study of long-term, self-analytic groups, such as therapy, training, and class room discussion groups; and (2) the systematic observation of group interaction by means of act-by-act scoring of individual behaviour. The nature and development of the relationship between the members of self-analytic groups and the group's therapist, trainer, or instructor constitute the particular focus of this study.

The primary impetus for this work was a dilemma often expressed by those students of group phenomena, the present author included, who function both as researchers and as clinicians, as scholars and as trainers. We may sense a painful discrepancy between what we are equipped to study with acceptable precision as researchers and what we find either in the clinical work of such men as Bion (1961), Bach (1954), and Frank *et al.* (1952) or in our own experiences in training groups. The clinical and theoretical literature abounds with insights, subtleties, and depth which are seldom mirrored in our research operations. Thus, one side of the dilemma is that the researcher yearns to pursue the intricate but suggestive propositions found in a body of literature developed largely outside the traditional modes of research in social science.

The other side of the dilemmas derives from the experience of the clinician or trainer, often the same person as the researcher, but operating

[*] This work has been supported by grants from the National Institute of Mental Health and the Social Science Research Council. The I.B.M. costs were defrayed in part by a grant to the Harvard Computing Center by the National Science Foundation, and the programming was skilfully executed by William Jonghin. My colleagues and fellow trainers have offered many useful suggestions in the course of this study, and I wish to express my appreciation to Robert F. Bales, Maxine Bernstein, Dexter Dunphy, Theodore Mills, David Shapiro, Philip Slater, Charles Whitlock, and Norman Zinberg.

Originally published in *Human Relations*, 1966, **19**, pp. 84–117; this article is an abbreviated form of what can be found in Mann's book *Interpersonal Styles and Group Development*, John Wiley, 1967.

in another domain of his life. Somehow, in that domain things may not seem as clear. The vivid details of a particular group obscure one's view of the enduring truths. Events stream by, memory fails us, and we may imagine that the researcher could assist us in capturing or codifying the experience. Perhaps even more acute may be the sense that our residual impressions derive from only the most dramatic moments or unforgettable group members. Even beyond the kind of documentation that researchers can provide, the clinician may search for additional means of developing and testing explanatory propositions which will make the concrete experiences more sensible to himself and to others. The present study represents one response to this dilemma.

A number of writers (Bach, 1954; Bennis and Shepard, 1956; Coffey *et al.*, 1950; Kaplan and Roman, 1964; Mann, 1953; Mills, 1964; Psathas, 1960; Thelen and Dickerman, 1949) have attempted to outline the development of self-analytic groups by describing the group processes and members' feelings active at various points in time. They suggest several regularities in group development across a variety of groups. There is wide agreement that the issue of dependency upon the trainer is particularly important at the beginning of the group, and some authors also note an initial anxiety and/or resistance aroused by the new situation. Some of the developmental models imply that a crisis point in the member–trainer relationship is likely to be activated by a mounting frustration experienced by group members (Thelen, 1950) and by a wave of hostile and counter-dependent feelings (Bach, 1954; Bennis and Shepard, 1956; Mills, 1964). The period following this crisis is variously described, but many authors point to a work phase, in which the earlier preoccupation with member-trainer relationship is eclipsed by 'group-centered' activity and the ascendant issues of intimacy among members. Whereas some authors' descriptions seem to imply that the group ends during the phase of work, integration, or mutual synthesis, Mills (1964) extends his group development scheme to include a stage of separation. One issue to be raised in the present study is whether the member–trainer relationship, often described as salient for the group only in the early stages, develops meaningfully over the entire life of the group.

In recent years there have been a number of attempts to reduce much, if not all, social interaction to a limited set of underlying factors or dimensions. Schutz's (1958) postulation of three basic needs, which he labels inclusion, control, and affection, is reflected both in Bennis's (1957) scheme of oral, anal, and phallic stages in group life and in Kaplan and Roman's (1963) examination of dependency, power, and intimacy themes. Several factor-analytic studies of individual differences in group behaviour (Borgatta *et al.*, 1958; Carter, 1954; Couch, 1960; Mann, 1961) have isolated factors whose content is highly congruent with Schutz's three-dimensional model. The inclusion, control, and affection issues and their effect upon the member–trainer relationship serve as useful points of departure in this study.

Throughout the discussions in the literature (Bach, 1954; Bennis and Shepard, 1956; Bion, 1961; Coffey *et al.*, 1950; Ezriel, 1952; Foulkes and Anthony, 1957), the content and intensity of a group member's feelings toward the trainer are often seen as being at least partially determined by the transference of old relations and modes of relating to authority figures onto the new situation. As a result, many clinical interpretations of the member–trainer relationship have been cast in the rich and evocative imagery of the family scene.

Not only do a member's earlier experiences influence the member–trainer relationship, but this relationship, endowed as it may be with a number of over-determined or parataxic qualities, contributes to the quality of the ties between a group member and all other aspects of group life. The writings of Bion (1961) and Ezriel (1952) emphasize the ways in which a group member may both express and disguise his feelings toward the trainer through his dealings with other group members or through his comments on events and persons external to the group. These processes, including the mechanisms of displacement and projection, are demonstrated well in the studies of Bennis (1961), Mills (1964), Slater (1961a), and Thelen (1950).

One deficiency in the work on member–trainer relations to date is the absence of adequate interweaving between the clinical observations and theoretical formulations, on the one hand, and a set of observation techniques and results on the other. One approach might be to rely on retrospective reports and ratings by group members, as in the work of Stock and Thelen (1958) or Wechsler and Reisel (1959). A second approach, the analysis of transcripts and tape recordings, offers several advantages since the behaviour under study is closer in time to the arousal situation, more likely to be unguarded, spontaneous, and even inconsistent in revealing ways. More importantly, the member's overt behaviour in the group can be expressive in so many indirect and disguised ways that the observer has more opportunity to recognize the complexity of a member's feelings.

The observation schemes that have been applied to the study of self-analytic groups, Bales's (1950) interaction process analysis and Mills's (1964) sign process analysis, seem quite removed from the dynamic processes and feelings which clinicians tend to describe or perceive. The empirical studies of Mills (1964), Psathas (1960), and Talland (1955) suggest both the potential gains and the inherent limitations of these scoring systems. Interaction process analysis, with its partial emphasis on task categories such as giving opinion and giving orientation, was not designed to assess individual motives or feelings, but to record the effects of behaviour on the small group as a social system. Sign process analysis examines the application of culturally, or subculturally, shared standards of valuation to a set of objects, within and beyond the interacting group. Although Mills's use of his data to illuminate the developmental process in a self-analytic group is highly relevant to this study, his technique is asking questions of quite a different nature than those embedded in the present inquiry. In short, these more sociological observation systems should be supplemented by a scoring system more congruent with the psychological study of individual dynamics.

In contrast to previous work, this study attempts: (1) to examine the member–trainer relationship throughout the entire development of the group; and (2) to carry out this examination by means of act-by-act observations of members' feelings, using concepts which have been employed profitably in the clinical and theoretical literature. The remaining sections of this paper present the scoring system developed for this purpose, the data for two self-analytic groups, a developmental scheme for analyzing the member–trainer relationship, and a discussion of the two groups under study.

The member-to-trainer scoring system

The member-to-trainer scoring system is designed to assess and record the implications of each act initiated by a group member for the state of his feelings toward the trainer. Although any act may also have meaning for the member's relations with other group members or express his feelings toward objects outside the group, in this scheme only those meanings of the act which are relevant for the member–trainer relationship are scored. Essentially, the question asked is: 'If this act is expressive of, or, more conservatively, congruent with, the member's feelings toward the trainer, what is the best estimate of what those feelings might be?'

The problem of inference

The kinds of data from which the scorer infers that an act is relevant to the trainer vary considerably, from the most direct and deliberate expressions of feelings toward the trainer to indirect, disguised, or inadvertent expressions of feelings. For this reason, a member's act is examined first to determine the kind of inferences which are needed to connect it with a feeling relevant to the trainer. Each act is examined with respect to a series of possibilities:

1. Does the act express the member's feelings toward, or in relation to the trainer (–T)? If no such expression is inferred, the act is not scored.

2. If the act is expressive of the member's feelings toward the trainer (–T), are these feelings expressed directly to the trainer or with explicit reference to him (–T), or are they expressed indirectly, symbolically, or inadvertently (–T')?

3. If the feelings are expressed indirectly or symbolically (–T'), are they expressed toward some object (e.g. person, fictional character, or institution) which symbolizes the trainer for the member because of the similarity between that object and the trainer (–T'), or are they expressed toward some object which, for the member, is different from the trainer in some way, enabling the member to express his feelings toward the trainer by way of contrast and comparison (–$\overline{T}'$)?

4. If the feelings are expressed indirectly or symbolically (–T' or –$\overline{T}'$), are they expressed toward an object inside the group, such as the group as a whole or some other group member (–T_i') or –$\overline{T}_i'$), or are they expressed toward an object outside the group, such as the Church, a political figure, or the Mona Lisa (–T_o' or $\overline{T}_o'$)?

5. If the act is expressive of the member's feelings toward the trainer (–T or –T'), does the member identify himself as the possessor of these feelings (M–T, M–T'), or does he express his own feelings by attributing those feelings to someone else, such as another group member or a person outside the group (M'–T or M'–T')?

6. If the member does not explicitly identify himself as the agent who is expressing or possessing the feelings (M'–T or M'–T'), are the feelings expressed his own, as in the case of projected hostility or anxiety (M'–T or M'–T), or are the feelings different from his own and is the member attempting to differentiate himself from the other agent who is expressing the feelings ($\overline{M}'$–T or $\overline{M}'$–T')?

This series of questions generates a set of fifteen types of scorable act, where each type represents a different kind of inference from the observed act to the inferred feelings. For our purpose in scoring, the fifteen types were collapsed into a set of four levels:

Level One: Acts which make direct reference to the trainer and in which the member either expresses the feelings as his own or attempts to differentiate himself from some other agent (M–T and $\overline{M}'$–T).

Level Two: Acts which express feelings toward objects inside the group and in which the member either expresses the feelings as his own or attempts to differentiate himself from some other agent ($M-T_i'$, $M-\overline{T}_i'$, $M'-\overline{T}_i'$, $\overline{M}'-T_i'$, and $\overline{M}'-\overline{T}_i'$).

Level Three: Acts which express feelings toward objects outside the group and in which the member either expresses the feelings as his own or attempts to differentiate himself from some other agent ($M-T_o'$, $M-\overline{T}_o'$, $M'-\overline{T}_o'$, $\overline{M}'-T_o'$, and $\overline{M}'-\overline{T}_o'$).

Level Four: Acts which express feelings toward the trainer or some symbolic equivalent for the trainer by attributing similar feelings to another agent ($M'-T$, $M'-T_i'$, and $M'-T_o'$).

The first task, then, in scoring an act is to determine what, if any, links exist (a) between the member and the agent to whom the feelings are attributed and (b) between the trainer and the object toward which or in relation to which the feelings are expressed. The process of setting up such equations, except in the case of direct M–T acts, is a complex one. Certainly key phrases or modifying adjectives may indicate that the member has made a symbolic equation between an object and the trainer, the surrounding context may illuminate the meaning of a displaced feeling, or the tone of voice may indicate whether the member is identifying with or differentiating himself from the agent to whom the feelings are attributed. For example, if member A attacks member B for being too secretive, it may be that member A resents the trainer for withholding his feelings from the group, but not necessarily. In its context, the attack may represent an attempt, by contrast, to reward the trainer for a recent expression of feelings, or it may be an attempt by member A to bid for the trainer's approval by demonstrating that he is open and frank even if member B is not. In the ordinary flow of human interaction the set of equations which connect the manifest content of an act with its meanings and implications for the set of here-and-now relationships is seldom fully explicit. The scorer's task is to reconstruct a plausible and predictive set of such equations. It sometimes happens in training groups that the member reveals what he feels his equations are or have been, and sometimes the trainer or other members seek to clarify what the member has meant. But most of the time the scorer is left to figure it out on the basis of fragmentary evidence.

The problem of categorizing

Once the issue of whether an act is expressive of a member's feelings toward the trainer is settled, and the inferences necessary to make the connection are determined, the next problem is how best to conceptualize, describe, and record the feeling expressed. The member-to-trainer scoring system examines three main areas of a member's feelings: impulse, authority relations, and ego state. Within the impulse area, which is subdivided into hostility and affection, are eight categories which describe the state of the member's aggressive and libidinal ties with the trainer at the moment of the act being scored. Within the authority-relations area are three categories which describe those feelings relevant to the power and dependency issues between a member and the trainer. Within the ego-state area are five categories describing the member's feelings toward himself in the context of the relationship with the trainer. The three areas are not mutually exclusive, and they may be viewed as three separate scoring systems applied to a single act.

The particular set of sixteen categories chosen owes much to the prior work of Bales (1950), especially for distinctions made within the impulse area, to Bennis and Shepard (1956), for distinctions drawn within the authority-relations area, and to Bibring (1953), for his differentiation of the various ego states. In addition, Melanie Klein's (1957) concept of reparation was helpful in untangling the important modes of expressing affection. A description of each category is presented below, with a set of the most frequent examples and its theoretical rationale.

Member-to-trainer categories

Impulse area

Hostility

1. Moving Against—expressing dislike, mistrust, or anger; attacking, rejecting, ridiculing, insulting. The focus in this category is the expression of hostile feelings against the trainer as a person rather than against the trainer's contributions or surface behaviour. The target of hostility tends to be the trainer's motives, personality, or general competence.

2. Resisting—disagreeing, arguing, blocking or parrying the trainer's suggestions or interpretations. The hostility falling in this category is responsive or reactive, either to an actual initiation by the trainer or to the implicit pressures of the whole training situation. The target of this relatively impersonal hostility tends to be the role performance of the trainer or 'the whole system' which the trainer is seen as representing.

3. Withdrawing—ignoring the trainer, leaving the room or engaging in 'out-of-field' behaviour; expressing boredom, lack of involvement, or indifference. The hostility expressed through withdrawing is more passive and indirect than in the other three hostility categories. In this category are

9

found the various ways in which the member–trainer relationship is broken, or its importance denied.

4. Guilt-inducing—blaming, complaining, accusing, feelings misunderstood or abused, shaming. The crucial element that differentiates this category from the preceding three is the addition of a moral context for the hostility. By invoking a presumably shared value and comparing the trainer's behaviour unfavourably to it, the member is expressing a kind of moral indignation through which he allies himself with a set of superordinate values against the trainer.

Affection

5. Making Reparation—forgiving, apologizing, denying hostility, blaming self rather than trainer, 'making up' for prior hostility of self or other. This category attempts to capture those expressions of affection which depend on their proximity to hostility for their full meaning. Making Reparation may precede a hostile remark, as if to neutralize the hostility before the fact, or it may follow hostility, of any kind, as if to undo and atone for the damage.

6. Identifying—playing the trainer's role in relation to another group member, copying the trainer, incorporating the trainer's ideas as one's own, expressing a wish to be like the trainer. A member's positive feelings toward the trainer, or the degree to which he accepts what the trainer has said, may be expressed through the member's dealings with other group members. The inference made from the manifest content of such acts is that the member is attempting to differentiate himself from some other group member who, he implies, is not sufficiently identified with or accepting of the trainer.

7. Accepting—agreeing, yielding, conforming, expressing satisfaction with the trainer's role performance. The relatively impersonal affection recorded in this category is responsive or reactive to the trainer's role performance.

8. Moving Toward—expressing liking, trust or warmth; caring, admiring, praising. This category focuses on the expression of affection in personal terms, with a clear implication that the relationship is important and meaningful to the member.

Authority-relations area

9. Showing Dependency—expressing a need for approval, direction, structure, or control; attempting to please the trainer. The expression of dependency needs in the member–trainer relationship tends to imply: (a) that the member feels less sure of what to do, less able to carry out what he

wishes to do, or less confident that what he is doing or has done is satisfactory than he would like to feel; and (b) that the member expects or hopes that the trainer can provide the necessary direction, assistance, or approval. This expectation is often based on the member's belief in an enduring power structure within which the trainer's role is to provide support and control when needed. While this conception of the trainer's role may facilitate the expression of dependency, acts may be scored in this category which rest on far more limited notions of the trainer's power and responsibility.

10. Showing Independence—relating to the trainer as a peer, stating one's own standards and/or judging one's own behaviour by them, emphasizing the mutuality of giving and receiving in the member–trainer relationship, deciding on action on one's own grounds. Bennis and Shepard (1956) stress the importance of unconflicted or non-compulsive orientation toward the trainer in independent group members. In the act-by-act analysis of feelings, such a conception is mirrored best by evidence that the member feels able to accept or reject the trainer and his contributions without reference to an implicit power structure which must be created, maintained, or destroyed. In addition, acts of independence express a member's capacity to act and/or reflect on his own behaviour using his own set of standards without making sure that they are the same as, or different from, the trainer's standards.

11. Showing Counter-dependence—asserting a lack of need for direction, assistance, or support from the trainer; opposing trainer's power, rebelling against rules or norms, ridiculing dependency in others. This category is scored only when opposition to the trainer appears to be based on an assumption that the trainer is or intends to be more powerful than the group members. It represents a response from within an authority structure and can be understood best as an aversion to being in a weak, needy, or constricted position.

Ego-state area

Anxiety (categories 12 and 13)

12. Expressing Anxiety—showing embarrassment, tension, or uncertainty; feeling criticized, judged, or threatened; fearing angry or punitive response from trainer. The member's feeling of being in danger, threatened, or vulnerable may be expressed by an attempt to assess and describe either (a) in what way the trainer seems threatening or (b) the inner consequences of the threat for him.

13. Denying Anxiety—denying feeling tense, worried, or concerned about trainer; joking about what others see as threatening in trainer's

behaviour or status, covering up tension by giddy or silly behaviour, re-assuring self or others regarding trainer's intentions or evaluations. Demonstrating the simultaneous activation of both anxiety and defences against it is not a simple matter. It rests on evidence that an important component in the act is an attempt at self-reassurance through disparaging the potential danger, insisting that one is calm and not upset, or professing invulnerability in the face of apparent danger.

14. Showing Self-esteem—feeling satisfied with self, capable of being open and honest, proud, at ease, 'headed in the right direction'. Many of the acts scored in this category could, in other contexts, be seen as denials of either anxiety or depression. The crucial differentiating features are that acts of self-esteem are not primarily reactions to increasingly uncomfortable ego states, but rather are primarily expressive of what Bibring (1953) calls 'the secure and self-assured ego'.

Depression

15. Expressing Depression—feeling guilty, sad, helpless, powerless; expressing a sense of being worthless or a sense of 'sliding downhill'. Acts scored in this category reflect the member's state of lowered self-esteem and lowered sense of potency in the context of the member–trainer relationship.

16. Denying Depression—resisting an implied criticism, bragging and asserting own potency, showing elation following another member's expression of sadness, refusing to see any power differentiation between members and trainer, blaming trainer rather than self, showing manic denial of implied guilt or responsibility for having harmed others. Not all excitement or exhilaration is scored as denying depression: the fundamental question involves the antecedents and context of the act. This category focuses upon the attempt to restore self-esteem and decrease depression through the mechanisms of denial, suppression, and reaction formation.

Several scoring conventions might be mentioned here. The scoring unit, or act, is defined as an uninterrupted set of phrases or sentences within which one scoring is possible. If the feelings expressed change within one speech, a new act is scored; if the member is interrupted by another member or the trainer, his next initiation is scored as a new act, even if it is scored identically with his previous act. An act may be multiple-scored, except that only one category may be scored within any sub-area (i.e. hostility, affection, authority relations, anxiety, and depression).

The trainer's contributions to the group are scored in terms of the feelings he attributes, explicitly or implicitly, to a group member or to the group as a whole. Either by interpreting and reflecting certain feelings or by responding *as if* the members had certain feelings toward him, the trainer conveys his assessment of the member–trainer relationship. This assessment is scored into the same sixteen content categories used for the members. In addition, the scorer notes whether the trainer (i) disapproves or is critical of the feeling he perceives in the member; (ii) merely notices and calls attention to the feeling; or (iii) approves of or rewards the feeling. Though the results of this scoring of trainer behaviour will be used to compare trainers, the trainers' acts are not pooled with the members' acts under study in this paper.

Two case studies

Description of the groups

Two self-analytic groups in an academic setting were chosen for intensive study, and, while they contain many unique features, they satisfy at least the minimal criteria of generating high personal involvement and extensive examination of the group's own process.

The two groups were composed of persons enrolled in a course entitled 'Case Analysis: The Interpretation of Interpersonal Behaviour', during the 1961 and 1962 sessions of the Harvard Summer School. The groups met for sessions of fifty minutes, five times a week, for a total of thirty-two sessions.

Discussions were concerned primarily with the process and structure of the group and with the analysis of individual differences in behaviour and feelings. The groups were given human relations cases for discussion and were assigned relevant readings in individual and group psychology. Approximately two-thirds of the group discussions were focused inside the group. Grades were based on term papers due in the fourth and fifth weeks and on final examination which tested the student's ability to integrate the group experiences, the case material, and the readings.

Two or three times the number of people who could be admitted applied to each group. The twenty-five persons selected for each group were chosen partly because their application showed evidence of interest and partly because they permitted a heterogeneous distribution of age, sex, and background. Each group was approximately half males and half females. The ages ranged from eighteen to forty-five, with the median age around twenty-three. The 1961 group (hereafter referred to as S1) contained fewer persons who were already employed than did the 1962 group (hereafter referred to as S2). Some of the group members were taking one other course, or more rarely, two others, in summer school, but many were enrolled only in this course.

Group S2 had three non-participating observers present throughout: one male observer, one female observer (who later scored the member–trainer interaction), and one male teaching fellow who assisted in the grading of papers and examinations. The other major structural difference between the groups was that S2 regularly began with a summary of the previous session by a member assigned the task for that day.

More difficult to summarize objectively and succinctly are the differences and similarities between the two trainers. The trainer for S1 was in his late twenties and was less experienced in the trainer role than the one in S2, who was in his late thirties. Both were psychologists with research interests in small groups. Both trainers tended to be non-directive, especially at first. They tended to focus their later comments on processes in the group and to offer interpretations and raise questions for the group regarding the group situation and the feelings aroused by it.

By referring to the scoring of the trainers' interventions it is possible to compare the two trainers on their tendency to interpret or reflect members' feelings in idiosyncratic ways. The trainer in S1 initiated 7 per cent of the total number of acts for members and trainer combined, as compared with 6 per cent for the trainer in S2, a slight but statistically significant difference. No differences of substance were found in comparing the trainers' tendencies to criticize or reward members for their expressions of feelings. Roughly 70 per cent of each trainer' interventions were neutral or non-evaluative. Certain differences between the trainers were evident from the transcripts and tapes. The trainer in S1 was somewhat more volatile and likely to express impatience or irritation. The trainer in S2 was more distant in his dealings with group members. His interventions were often in the form of questions to the group as a whole, and a number of direct requests addressed to him were turned back to the group for discussion.

The trainers were quite similar in terms of the kinds of feeling they tended to notice and call attention to. The statistically significant differences are that the S1 trainer interpreted and mirrored to the group more Withdrawing, the S2 trainer more Accepting, Showing Dependency, and Denying Anxiety. All four of these differences are in line with actual differences between the groups, but there is no way of assessing from these data the circular relationship between members' feelings and the trainer's interventions, and the extent to which the trainer reflects those feelings he wishes to encourage remains an unanswered but tantalizing question.

In summary, the two groups were quite similar in setting, size, and composition. Certain routines, such as the report on the previous session, were different, but the cases, assigned reading, and general orientation of the groups were much the same. The trainers differed less in their conceptions of the trainer role than in their personal styles within the role. The range of personal feelings expressed by the S1 trainer was greater, and the psychological distance between him and the group was correspondingly less than for the S2 trainer.

Scoring procedures

Group S1 was scored from verbatim transcripts over a year after the group was run; group S2 was scored from the tape recordings as it went along, and the scoring was completed within a month of the final session. Unfortunately, the tape recordings of two sessions in each group were unusable because of failures in the recording apparatus. The first session of each group, a brief orientation meeting, was not scored. This left a total of twenty-nine scored sessions for each group.

The scorer's for group S1 were the group's trainer and a graduate research assistant who had been a member of S1 and who also served as observer and scorer for group S2 the following summer. The proportion of all acts examined by the scorers which were scored as relevant to the member–trainer relationship varied from 50 per cent in some sessions to 98 per cent in other sessions. Two studies were made of the reliability of the scoring, one comparing the results for two scorers and another comparing the results for a single scorer across a time interval of six months. In both studies there was over 85 per cent agreement on the definition of a scorable act, and agreement on the distribution of acts into the sixteen categories of the scoring system was significantly different from chance at the 0·001 level. The difference between the total number of acts for group S1 and the total number for group S2 is accounted for largely by (i) a decision not to score the often lengthy report on the previous session in S2 and (ii) the greater ease in scoring S1 from a verbatim transcript.

Results

One technique for analysing the development of the group over time is to disregard the absolute level of a category and to examine the changes within each category, noting those sessions in which the category is high or low relative to its own average level over all sessions. In this study the definition of a run was broadened to include the possibility of disregarding one session which was discrepant from the preceding and subsequent session.

Session-by-session trends

The results of this run analysis are presented in *Figs. 1* and *2*. In order to assemble the data in this form: (i) the raw frequency distribution across the sixteen categories for each session was converted into percentage form, using the total number of acts in the session as the base; (ii) the percentages in each category, over all levels, for the twenty-nine sessions scored were split at the median; and (iii) runs of high sessions or runs of low sessions were determined by noting those sets of at least three (or five out of six) consecutive sessions which were (a) at or above the median or (b) below the median. The runs of high or low sessions are indicated in the figures; the blank spaces for a category, then, indicate sessions in which the oscillation around the median was so rapid that no sustained burst of that particular feeling was evident in the group.

Within group S1, several trends emerge in this analysis. There were two major surges of hostility which occurred near the middle and end of the group. After the first few sessions, affection was high; it decreased during the first surge of hostility and then increased again until the second surge of hostility. In the authority-relations area, an initial period in which Dependency and Counter-dependency were high was followed by a period, coinciding with the first wave of hostility, in which Counter-dependency was high, and in the last half of the group Independence reached its maximum. Anxiety was high in the early sessions, and again toward the end of the group; Self-esteem was high in the middle sessions, and Depression was high in the later session.

The development of group S2 proceeded in a somewhat different fashion. Hostility was high, as in S1, toward the middle and at the end. Most of the affection, however, was concentrated in the early sessions, with the notable exception of Making Reparation which was high only at the end. The early sessions were high in all three authority-relations categories, and, as in S1, there were subsequent bursts of Counter-dependency and then Independence. Showing Dependency returned to a high level toward the end of the group. In the ego-state area, the development was from a period in which Self-esteem was at its maximum, to a period of high Anxiety, and finally to one in which Depression was high.

Analysis by phases

It is evident from the two figures describing the group development that each group moved through phases or sets of sessions within which much the same patterns of feelings were observed. As a means of estimating the boundaries of these phases, tetrachoric correlations between adjacent sessions were computed, using the data described above, i.e. the median splits on each category. The result of these computations was, for each group, a string of correlations, describing the resemblance of neighbouring

Category	Session																												
---	02	03	04	05	06	07	08	09	10	11	12	13	14	16	17	19	20	21	22	23	24	25	26,27	28	29	30	31	32
Hostility																												
Moving Against	+	+		−	−	−	−	−	−	+	+	+	+	+					+	+	+	+	+	+			−	−
Resisting	−		−	−	−	−		−	+	+	+						+	+	+	+	+	+	+		+	+	+	+
Withdrawing							+	+	+	+	+	+				+	+	+	+				+	+	+	+	+	+
Guilt-inducing				−	−	+	+	+	+	+	+	+	−	−	−	−	−	−					+					
Affection																												
Reparation				−	−	−	−	−	+	+	+	+	+	+			+	+	+	+	+	+	−	+	−	−	−	−
Identifying		−	−			−	−	−	−	−	−	−	−				+	+	+	+	+	+	+	+	+	+	+	+
Accepting				+	+	+	+	+	+	+	+	+			+	+	+	+	+									
Moving Toward								−	+	+	+	−	−		+		+											
Authority Relations																												
Dependency	+	+	+	+	+	−	−								+	−		+	+	+	+	+	+	+	+	+	+	+
Independence	+	+		−	−				+	+	+	+	+					−	−	−	−			−	−	−	−	−
Counter-dependency									+	+	+	+	+															
Ego State																												
Expressing Anxiety	+	+	+	+	+	+	+	+	+	+	−	−	−	−	−	−	−	−	−	+	+	+	+	+	+	−	−	−
Denying Anxiety	−					−	−	−	+	−	−	−	−	−	−	−	−	−	−	−	−	−	−	−	−	−	−	−
Self-esteem							+		+								+	+		+								
Expressing Depression				+	+	+	+	−	−	−	−	−	−	−	−	−	−							+				+
Denying Depression							−	−															+	+	+	+	+	+

Fig. 1. Trend analysis by category for group S1

\+ Burst of high sessions where burst = at least 3/3 or 5/6 above or below median.
− Burst of low sessions.

Category	Session																												
	02	04	05	07	08	09	10	11	12	13	14	15	16	17	18	19	20	21	22	23	24	25	26	27	28	29	30	31	32
Hostility																													
Moving Against					–	–	+	+	+	+	+	+	+	+	–	–	–	–			–	–	–	+	+	+	+	+	+
Resisting		–	–	+	+	+	+	+	+	+	+	+	+	–	–	–	–	–			–	–	–	–	–	+	+	+	+
Withdrawing		–	+	+	+	+	+	+	+	+	+	+	+	+	+	+	+	+			–	–	–	–	–	–	–	–	+
Guilt-inducing	+	+		+			+	+	+	+	+	–	–	+	–	–	–	–			–	–	+	+	+	+	+	+	+
Affection																													
Reparation	+ +	+ +	+ +	+ +	+ +	+ +	+ +										+	+	+	+		+	+	+	+	+	+	+	+
Identifying		+ + +	+ + +	+ + +	+ + +	+ +	+ +					–	–	–	–	–	+	–	–	–	–	–	–	–	–	–	–	–	–
Accepting								–	–	–	–	–	–															–	–
Moving Toward								+	+	+	+	+		+			+						+		+	+			
Authority Relations																													
Dependency		+	+	+	+	+	+	+				–	–									–	+	+	+	+	+	+	+
Independence																+	+	+	+	+	+								
Counter-dependency														+	+	+								–	–	–			
Ego State																													
Expressing Anxiety					–	–	–	+	+	+	+	+	+	+	+	+	+	+	+	+	+	+	+	+	+	+	+	+	+
Denying Anxiety					–	–	–	–	–	–	–			–	+	+	+	+	+	+	+	+	+	+	+	+			
Self-esteem	+	+	+	+	+	+	+	+	+	+	+	+	+	+		+	+	+	+	+	+	+	+	+	+	+			
Expressing Depression										+	+	+	+	–	–	–	+	+	+	+	+	+	+	+	+	+	+	+	+
Denying Depression																+	+	+	+	+	+						+	+	+

+ Burst of high sessions where burst = at least 3/3 or 5/6 above or below median.
− Burst of low sessions.

Fig. 2. Trend analysis by category for group S2

pairs of sessions. Long runs of essentially similar activity within a group would result in positive correlations between the adjacent sessions; any substantial shift in the group's activity would produce a negative correlation at the turning-point. The boundaries of the phases to be discussed in some detail are defined by the presence of a negative correlation between the last session in one phase and the first session of the next phase. Where the phases are long and one session-to-session correlation within the phase is positive but quite low, the phases are divided into sub-phases for more careful analysis.

The percentage profiles for each phase or sub-phase in the two groups are presented in *Tables 1* and *2*. The statistical tests referred to in the tables compare with the percentage in a category for each phase with the percentage in that category for all other phases combined. The significance of the difference between percentages in adjacent phases was also assessed, and these results will be discussed in the text.

In the presentation of each phase or sub-phase, comments on the category rates as shown in the tables are supplemented by a brief descriptive account of the developing member–trainer relationships. The analyses presented in the tables are based on data for all scoring levels combined. However, where it seems useful to mention the degree to which the inferred feelings were expressed directly, the separate scoring levels will be discussed.

Group S1. For group S1, the first phase was the only one in which the majority of acts on the manifest level were expressions of feeling toward figures in the assigned cases, as reflected in a high proportion of acts scored on level three. However, the categories which were significantly high in these phases, Showing Dependency, Showing Counter-dependency, and Denying Anxiety, were high for all other levels as well. Identifying and Accepting were low in this phase. The major themes in the discussion were the proper behaviour for a new member of a group, weak males, the tendency of parents to make things worse by insensitive meddling, and various modes of handling parents. The two most salient issues for the group at this juncture appear to have been (i) whether members should express, or attempt to counter, dependency feelings toward the rather ambiguous trainer and (ii) how to assess the potential danger inherent in this new situation.

The acts in the second phase were scored mainly on level two, i.e. acts directed within the group but not explicitly toward the trainer. The sessions revolved around the issues of how much personal exposure was appropriate in this situation, what perils might follow from removing one's social mask, and how to achieve 'intimate interpersonal relations' with friends and, more

Table 1—Percentage profiles of member–trainer categories for group S1 by phase

Category	Phases and Sessions									
	1 2-4	2 5-7	3A 8-11	3B 12-13	4 14-17	5 19-21	6 21-26	7A 27-29	7B 30-32	Total
Hostility										
Moving Against	6·6	4·7	6·3	8·8**	4·5	3·9	6·9*	4·5	2·3**	5·5
Resisting	7·5	8·4	10·8*	6·9	10·0	11·1*	9·7	6·2*	7·5	9·0
Withdrawing	6·2	7·4	5·2	9·0*	4·5*	5·5	6·1	6·9	8·7**	6·4
Guilt-inducing	6·0	4·1*	8·0**	7·9	4·9	5·0	4·8	8·5**	4·5	6·0
Affection										
Making Reparation	5·7	4·2**	7·7	8·8*	10·5**	5·0	6·2	5·1	3·2**	6·4
Identifying	5·7**	7·8*	7·4**	6·5*	9·0	17·4**	11·4	11·4	13·4**	9·9
Accepting	5·1	9·1*	8·2	4·8*	6·3	7·2	6·2	5·7	7·9	6·9
Moving Toward	6·6	9·3**	5·2	5·4	5·4	6·0	4·4*	6·2	6·3	5·9
Authority Relations										
Showing Dependency	12·5**	7·6	8·7	9·6	6·8	5·8*	5·8**	8·0	7·9	7·9
Showing Independence	3·2	3·1	3·2	3·8	7·1**	4·9	2·4**	3·9	6·5**	4·1
Counter-dependency	6·0**	4·1	2·9	2·9	3·5	2·4	3·4	0·5**	1·7*	3·1
Ego State										
Expressing Anxiety	7·3	12·6**	7·8	7·3	7·7	6·8	9·8	10·5*	5·1**	8·4
Denying Anxiety	4·4*	4·3	3·8	1·5*	2·4	4·2	4·0	1·2**	0·8**	3·2
Self-esteem	2·1	2·0	1·9	2·7	4·0**	3·1*	1·0**	0·6	1·7	2·0
Expressing Depression	7·5	6·2*	7·8	7·5	5·3**	5·7*	9·2	12·7**	13·3**	8·3
Denying Depression	6·9	5·1**	5·1**	6·7	7·9	6·0	8·8*	8·2	9·2**	7·1
Base Numbers	722	740	1182	522	819	637	1216	648	709	7195

Note: Significance tests applied to the difference between each phase and all other phases combined.
* Significant at 0·05 level.
** Significant at 0·01 level.

importantly, with one's mother. There was a significant decrease in Showing Dependency, whereas Accepting, Moving Toward, and Expressing Anxiety were high in this phase. Perhaps the best summary of the phase would be that the group was concerned with the intimacy issues *vis-à-vis* the trainer. The group appears to have been polarized between those who expressed trusting and accepting feelings toward the trainer and those whose major feelings were ones of anxiety and apprehension.

From the second to the third phase the tone of the members' feelings shifted from positive to negative, with first Guilt-inducing and Resisting being high and then Moving Against and Withdrawing. The proportion of acts on level one, referring directly to the trainer, reached its highest level thus far in the group. In the first part of the phase the major focus of the hostility was on 'shoulds' laid down by authority and on the trainer's role and his expectations of the group. In contrast, the second part of the phase contained a more personal attack on the trainer both for 'betraying' the group, i.e. intervening via interpretations rather than leaving the group alone, and for exposing the group to a potentially damaging situation. In addition, one central group member who had alternated between a 'cool' rebellious stance and a position as the trainer's lieutenant and ally was bitterly attacked for being crude, insensitive, and unresponsive.

The group came as close is it ever would come to rejecting or expelling the trainer in the assertion to him, midway in the third phase, that 'You're all washed up', to which no members took exception. The attack on the trainer, and on the group member most identified with him in the minds of the group members, reflected a fusion of many issues. There was anger at the ambiguity in the trainer's role, which sometimes seemed permissive and even abdicating, but at other times controlling, critical, and generally unfair. In addition, the anger seemed to derive from a frustration of needs not for control, but for affection and sensitivity, both of which some members felt were in very short supply.

The fourth phase represented quite an abrupt shift in the group's relationship with the trainer. Three categories were higher in this phase than in any previous or subsequent phase: Making Reparation, Showing Independence, and Expressing Self-esteem. While Resisting increased, the other three hostility categories showed significant decreases from phase three to phase four. The most important development in the group during this phase was a debate over whether a rather impulsive act by the trainer implied that he was a 'schemer' or 'human', the issue being resolved, for most members, by a decision that he was human. The particular kind of human being the group had in mind was indicated by one suggestion that he was like the Mona Lisa. The preponderance of hostility in the previous phase was replaced by a preponderance of affection, especially Making Reparation. It appears that the dual issues of authority and intimacy, as they related to the trainer, were resolved by a compromise. The earlier equation of the trainer with the traditional male authority, suggesting power and threat derived from rules, judgments, and the capacity to punish, was modified by the inclusion of images more appropriate to one form of female authority, a distant but benevolent figure whose power and threat derive from the manipulation of love and attention. Both images remained with the group, some members preferring one, some the other, but the increases in Showing Independence and in Expressing Self-esteem suggest that this new resolution of member–trainer relations had a salutary effect on at least many of the group members.

The fifth phase was characterized by high levels of Resisting, Identifying, and Self-esteem. The major activity of the phase was a sequence of two splits within the group, where most of the group attempted to interpret the behaviour or modify the feelings of first one and then another group member who were particularly high on Resisting. Very little of the activity was directed toward the trainer explicitly, but there was considerable evidence that the trainer's views or approach had been heard and assimilated. This was the phase with the greatest preponderance of positive over negative feelings, but the reparation characteristic of the preceding phase was replaced by expressions of affection through the more indirect mode of identification with the trainer.

One new theme and several old ones dominated the sixth phase. The new issue was the end of the group, and in this phase both Expressing Depression and Denying Depression showed significant increases over the previous phase. The old issues were the question of the trainer's evaluations of group members, now made salient by the required papers and examinations, and the question of the trainer's insensitivity and capacity to hurt. Moving Against and Expressing Anxiety were significantly higher, and Identifying and Showing Independence were significantly lower than in the previous phase. This sixth phase was characterized by a mixture of sadness over the impending death of the group and apprehensive, resentful concern with the trainer's demands.

In the seventh and last phase, the discussions dealt mainly with evaluating the group and its effect on individual members, with death and immortality, and with the increasingly depressed tone of the group. The anxiety expressed in the sixth phase remained high for the first half of the seventh phase, but then declined sharply. The mode of expressing hostility shifted from the Moving Against of the sixth phase to Guilt-inducing and then to Withdrawing. Showing Independence increased at the end of the group. However, by far the most salient characteristic of the seventh phase was the high level of depression, a heavy, mourning quality which was broken by several wild interludes fantasying the rebirth and immortality of the group. The proportion of acts on level one was at its highest point in the final sub-phase, and the content referring to the trainer continued to be a mixture of such images as judge, doctor, and exploiter, with quite different images relating to bisexuality, feeding, and hunger.

Group S2. The development of the member–trainer relationship in group S2 began with the only phase for the group in which affection predominated over hostility. Identifying and Accepting were high throughout the first phase, with Moving Toward significantly high in the second half of the phase. An initially high level of Showing Counter-dependence was replaced in the second part of the phase by high levels of Showing Dependence and Showing Independence. In addition, Anxiety and Depression were low in the first phase.

A number of features characterized the discussion in the first part of phase one: (i) the older members, many of whom were teachers by profession, very quickly adopted the 'teacher role'; (ii) the younger members expressed their complaints about various overbearing or insensitive authority figures; and (iii) though some members seemed uncertain about whether the trainer's silence implied weakness, most members appeared to feel that the trainer and the course stood for worthwhile human values. The generally positive tone of the second half of phase one was fostered by the group's decision to have a party and by various attempts, particularly by the females, to obtain both the trainer's approval for the party and his promise to attend it. The other major issues of this sub-phase, which were connected directly with the decision to have a party, were: (i) whether group therapy was the appropriate model for the group, which involved the issues of how personal people should be; and (ii) how one can be spontaneous while under observation by oneself and by others.

Phase two began with the session following the party, which neither the trainer nor any of the observers attended. The phase was characterized by significantly high levels of Guilt-inducing, Expressing Anxiety, and Denying Anxiety. In addition, there were significant increases over phase one in Moving Against and Expressing Depression. All five categories which had been significantly high in the previous sub-phase (Identifying, Accepting, Moving Toward, Showing Dependency, and Showing Independence) decreased considerably.

In the session following the party, one group member arrived before the trainer and sat in the trainer's usual place. After the trainer had

Table 2—Percentage profiles of member–trainer categories for group S1 by phase

	Phases and Sessions									
Category	1A 2–5	1B 7–9	2 10–12	3 13–15	4 16–17	5 18–21	6 22–25	7A 26–29	7B 30–32	Total
Hostility										
Moving Against	9·8	4·0**	10·4	8·1	18·5**	6·7	5·5**	9·2**	10·1	8·5
Resisting	9·4	9·4	8·8	9·4	7·2	4·6*	8·9	5·8*	7·9	8·0
Withdrawing	2·2	3·4	3·7	2·6	4·0	3·8	1·7	2·0	2·2	2·8
Guilt-inducing	7·3*	3·7	8·0**	4·9	2·8	3·8	3·8	5·0	5·7	5·1
Affection										
Making Reparation	3·9	2·9*	4·7	2·6	6·4	3·1	3·6	6·6*	8·1**	4·5
Identifying	13·4**	7·1**	2·2**	2·3*	2·4	3·3	3·4	2·4**	2·2*	4·7
Accepting	10·0*	12·1**	7·8	6·5	6·4	4·6*	8·0	4·8**	6·6	7·8
Moving Toward	3·5	6·0**	1·0*	2·9	0·8*	2·3	1·1*	2·2	2·9	2·7
Authority Relations										
Showing Dependency	14·1	17·3**	10·4	10·4	8·0*	10·0	11·2	12·4	16·2*	12·7
Showing Independence	3·1	5·3**	1·8	1·6	3·6	1·5	3·2	0·0**	2·2	2·6
Counter-dependency	5·9**	3·2	2·4	4·2	1·6	3·8	3·4	2·0	1·5*	3·2
Ego State										
Expressing Anxiety	4·5**	9·0	13·3**	9·7	13·3	16·2**	11·2	14·1**	5·4**	10·6
Denying Anxiety	2·9**	6·6	10·6**	7·1	14·5**	9·7	9·7*	5·0	5·4	7·6
Self-esteem	1·2	1·1	0·2	0·0	0·4	0·0	1·7	0·4	0·5	0·7
Expressing Depression	5·9**	5·0**	9·6*	19·2**	6·8**	18·5	16·0	20·3*	16·0	12·7
Denying Depression	3·1**	3·9*	5·1	8·4	3·2*	7·9	7·4	8·0*	7·1	6·0
Base Numbers	491	620	490	308	249	390	526	502	407	3983

Note: Significance tests applied to the difference between each phase and all other phases combined.
* Significant at 0·05 level.
** Significant at 0·01 level.

successfully reclaimed his seat, the group spent much of the session either in accusing the trainer of deserting the group or in discussing the theme of guilt. Prohibitions against being too personal in the group gained strength in this phase, and concern was widely expressed regarding the role of women and the silent group members. The immediate effect of the party was to raise two possibilities regarding the trainer, both of which the group had trouble in accepting or rejecting. One possibility was that the party amounted to an attack, of unknown impact, on the trainer, as a result of which the trainer was either wounded or silently furious. The other possibility was that the trainer's failure to attend the party proved his lack of feeling for the group and general untrustworthiness.

Phase three was quite similar in content to phase two, with one major exception. The predominant ego-state category shifted from Expressing Anxiety in phase two to Expressing Depression. The imagery surrounding the trainer shifted correspondingly, from an emphasis on the trainer as an untrustworthy and threatening object to the trainer as a powerful leader, potentially all good or all evil, who could control or toy with the group at will. In addition, many of the feelings toward the trainer were being displaced onto one group member whose championing of Freud and therapy had aroused much debate in the group.

In phase four, Moving Against and Denying Anxiety, on both direct and symbolic levels, reached their maximum point. Expressions of Depression declined abruptly from their high level in the previous phase. One group member and, indirectly, the trainer were attacked one day for being authoritarian and 'crude', i.e. seeing 'the sexual side of things', and then, the next day, another group member and, more directly, the trainer were attacked for having a bad influence, for misleading the group and inciting it to be aggressive. It is interesting to note that, in phase two, one technique used by the group members in their attempt to make the trainer feel guilty for not having attended the party was to claim, jokingly, that they had lost control during the party, and that there had been much drinking and sexual promiscuity. In phase four, the trainer and one member strongly linked with the trainer were accused of being too preoccupied with sexual matters. All of this suggests that phase four was a brief, if temporary, respite from the group's depressed reaction after the party. The sexual and aggressive feelings which were both a reason for and a consequence of the party were, in this phase, projected onto the trainer, creating an image of a malignant seducer.

In phase five, Expressing Anxiety and Expressing Depression were high. The discussion centered on guilt, responsibility, and fears of being either 'swallowed up' by overprotective mothers or unattended by people who are

10

detached and unresponsive. Both in relation to the trainer and in relation to a number of group members, especially the silent ones, a dilemma had arisen: strong desires on the part of many members to atone for some unspecified guilt and to involve the trainer and the silent members in a close, trusting relationship were counterbalanced by fears that if they *were* less detached, they would be either unbearably critical or overwhelming. These fears were made more intense by the fact that, in addition to desires for closeness, there were feelings of anger and rejection toward the trainer, which made the situation appear all the more hopeless.

In the first session of phase six, the presence of unexpected guests in the room precipitated a new development. The debate over guests and the eventual decision not to expel them were followed by a series of discussions, the major theme of which was responsibility for one's fate. An emphasis on free will and the originality of youth was accompanied by a modification in the image of the trainer. He was seen as somehow older and wiser, the possessor of knowledge which all members wanted but some still feared and resisted. The more impersonal tone of the member–trainer relationship was mirrored in the fact that Moving Against and Moving Toward were significantly low, while Resisting and Accepting increased significantly over the previous phase. Expressing Anxiety was lower and Expressing Self-esteem was higher than in the previous phase, and Denying Anxiety was significantly high.

The seventh and final phase is divided into two sub-phases. Only Making Reparation, which was high, and Identifying, which was low, were sustained across both sub-phases. The impersonal tone characteristic of the previous phase was not maintained. Moving Against increased, while Resisting and Accepting decreased from phase six to phase seven. Expressing Anxiety, Expressing Depression, and Denying Depression were high only in the first part of phase seven, and Showing Independence was particularly low. In the second part of the phase seven Expressing Anxiety decreased sharply and was significantly low. Showing Counter-dependency reached its lowest point in the group, and Showing Dependence was high.

The discussion in the first half of phase seven was concerned primarily with an individual's responsibility. There was general consensus that the burden of guilt for the destruction caused by Hitler, atom bombs, and capital punishment fell on everyone. The covert meanings of these discussions seemed to be delicately balanced between (1) making reparation by relieving the trainer of full responsibility for the group's development and (2) expressing resentment that the trainer had failed to control the members of the group. Both the attempt at reparation and the resentment were more explicit in the final few sessions, as were the feelings of dependency. In a way, some group members seemed to be trying to start the group all over again. They were prepared to take responsibility and to forgive the trainer for what they had seen as his failures in the area of control, if not for failures in the area of affection. Notably absent from the discussion were the issues of intimacy. In the final session, one member invited the group to a party and was refused in sepulchral tones.

Comparison of S1 and S2

Before comparing the development of groups S1 and S2, a comparison of the percentage profiles over all sessions might set the developmental differences in a useful perspective. The analysis of high and low categories in runs of sessions and the phase analysis emphasized the within-group changes in each category, relative to the total over all sessions for that group, but the groups did not have the same over-all amounts of the various categories.

Table 3 presents the percentage profiles, by group, for all sessions combined. Although there were several exceptions worth noting, S1 was higher in the impulse-area categories and lower in the authority-relations and ego-state areas. Furthermore, the percentage of all impulse-area acts scored in the affection sub-area for group S1 was 52·0 per cent as compared with 44·7 in S2.

When these overall differences are integrated with the developmental sequences in each group a fuller picture of the two groups emerges. For example, despite the fact that S2 was significantly higher, over all sessions, on Moving Against, the changes over time within each group were quite similar with one burst of direct hostility just before the midpoint and another near the end of the group. In addition, there was a tendency in both groups for the first wave of direct hostility to be preceded by an increase in Guilt-inducing. Whereas Withdrawing was high in group S1 during the first attack and toward the end, the rate was quite constant throughout S2, and all phases in S2 were lower than the lowest phase in S1.

In the affection area, the contrast in developmental sequences was mirrored by contrasts in overall levels. For the group S2 the early sessions were the highest on Identifying, Accepting, and Moving Toward. Not only was there a relative decline in Identifying and Moving Toward, but the group as a whole was considerably lower on these categories than S1. In contrast to S2, Identifying in group S1 was low in the beginning and high in the middle end of the group. Making Reparation emerged in the middle of S1, shortly after the first wave of hostility, and before the rise in Identifying, whereas the phases high in Reparation for group S2 were at the very end of the group.

Changes in Showing Dependency for the two groups were fairly similar, with high early phases being followed by low phases in the middle. However, S2 was characterized by a terminal increase of dependency, and the level of Showing Dependency throughout the group was much higher than in S1. Showing Independence was high in the early and middle sessions of S2 and high in the middle and final sessions of S1, and, over all sessions, S1 was higher on Showing Independence than S2. The overall percentages of Showing Counter-dependence were nearly the same in the two groups. For both groups, the highest sessions were the earliest ones, and there were moderately high sessions toward the middle of both groups' development.

Table 3—Percentage profiles over all sessions for groups S1 and S2

	Group		
Category	S1	S2	*p*
Hostility			
Moving Against	5·5	8·5	0·01
Resisting	9·0	8·0	n.s.
Withdrawing	6·4	2·8	0·01
Guilt-inducing	6·0	5·1	0·05
Affection			
Making Reparation	6·4	4·5	0·01
Identifying	9·9	4·7	0·01
Accepting	6·9	7·8	n.s.
Moving Toward	5·9	2·7	0·01
Authority Relations			
Showing Dependency	7·9	12·7	0·01
Showing Independence	4·1	2·6	0·01
Counter Dependence	3·1	3·2	n.s.
Ego State			
Expressing Anxiety	8·4	10·6	0·01
Denying Anxiety	3·2	7·6	0·01
Self-esteem	2·0	0·7	0·01
Expressing Depression	8·3	12·7	0·01
Denying Depression	7·1	6·0	0·05
Total	7195	3983	

The amount of anxiety, both expressed and denied, was higher for group S2. While expressions of anxiety emerged in the early sessions and returned toward the end of S1, they emerged somewhat later in S2 and were high throughout most of the middle and late phases, declining only in the last three sessions. Expressing Self-esteem, which was high over all sessions for group S1, tended to reach its high point in one of the middle phases for both groups. Group S2 was higher on Expressing Depression; Group S1 was higher on Denying Depression. In both groups depression was higher in the late sessions, but the period of little depression for S1 was in the middle and for S2 was at the beginning of the group. In both groups there was some tendency for Denying Anxiety to be high just before Expressing Anxiety 'was high, and a similar tendency for Denying Depression to be high just before Expressing Depression was high.

The development of the member–trainer relationship

A useful schematic outline of the stages of development in member–trainer relations should be capable of handling the similarities and differences between the two groups under study. It should also be congruent, it is hoped, with prior and future observations.

The major focus of the scheme to be presented here is on the trainer as a psychological object for group members, an object which is apprehended at times as primarily external to the members and at times as primarily internal to the members. The developmental sequence contains five steps: Appraisal, Confrontation, Re-evaluation, Internalization, and Separation. The presentation of the scheme in serial order is not intended to imply some inexorable progression from one to the next without the possibility of re-cycling through a stage more than once. Rather, the scheme suggests a set of analytically distinguishable moments in the total member–trainer relationship. After presenting the total scheme, the histories of the member–trainer relationship in the two groups will be recast in terms of this paradigm.

Stage one: Appraisal

In the early session of a group, feelings toward the trainer derive from four main processes active in the group:

1. The trainer is the focus for much of the anxiety aroused in members by the new situation. By virtue of having, or appearing to have, the greatest familiarity with groups of this kind, the trainer is held responsible for the tension experienced by the members.

2. Members tend to perceive and use the trainer as an ally both in reducing their anxiety and in controlling their impulses. In many ways, a member's feelings toward the trainer are an externalization of his characteristic internal mode of relating to superego demands and prohibitions. The projection of superego functions onto the trainer may produce acquiescence and dependency, it may arouse rebellion and counter-

dependency, or it may result only in heightened anxiety and fear of censure.

3. Members tend to project their ego-ideal onto the trainer, partly as a means of allaying anxiety, but also as a means of setting up a relationship that will be satisfying. As a result, the early sessions of a group may have the quality of a 'honeymoon period' in which most of the inferences about the trainer's motives of personality are expressions of how members wish he would be.

4. The trainer's behaviour is a source of frustration for group members. Dependency needs go unmet; rebellion is not curbed through counter-measures; affection is not reciprocated; withdrawal and indifference are challenged by the rather personal tone of the interventions; and the anxiety remains high.

All in all, the early sessions contain quite a range of feelings, but one common denominator of them is that the trainer is external to the member, that he is an object to be reckoned with in whatever habitual ways the member brings to the group. The first stage is one in which the accumulated set of expectations derived from parents, teachers, and others is tried out for size, perhaps as much in hope that it will not fit as in hope that it will.

Stage two: Confrontation

At some point early in the group's development there tends to be an abrupt shift in the member–trainer relationship. Though one of the more prominent features of the stage tends to be the eruption of hostility, the issues involved are more complex than can be expressed by such terms as revolt or attack. Some of the major functions of the confrontation seem to be the following:

1. The expression of hostile or counter-dependent feelings serves both to challenge the authority of the trainer and to test the limits of his permissiveness. It is not uncommon for the accusation that the trainer is too controlling to be fused, as if there were no contradiction, with other accusations that he is not controlling enough. The sum total of all the complaints and insistencies that the trainer adjust his behaviour usually reflects both sides of members' simultaneous wishes for autonomy and security.

2. The increased hostility characteristic of the confrontation stage has its roots not only in the issue of control but in the issues of affection and intimacy. The content of the hostility in the two groups under study reveals the members' exasperation with the trainer's failure to reciprocate affection and esteem. Feelings of being abused, ignored, or rejected, feelings barely

stifled in the early sessions, find expression in this stage. In part the hostility contains an accusation that the trainer is unfair, and in part the hostility is the members' revenge and retaliation for the trainer's indifference. However, if ambivalence characterizes the members' feelings about the issue of control, it characterizes their feelings in the intimacy area as well. The confrontation includes not only the most direct hostility but some of the most direct appeals to the trainer to move closer to the group. While some voices are raised to suggest that the trainer leave, others tend to suggest that on his return he move his seat and be one of the group, that he get on a first-name basis with the group, or that he be more human. The seductiveness beneath the hostility suggests that the full meaning of the confrontation must take account of the persistent phantasies of closeness with the trainer as well as the desire to punish and reject him for his failure to gratify those wishes.

3. An important function of the hostility generated in this stage is to test the durability of the trainer, to assess his capacity to absorb an attack without either collapsing or retaliating in kind.

4. Finally, the confrontation serves the purpose of 'naming the devil' of crystallizing in the trainer the various vaguely apprehended dangers and uncertainties inherent in a new group. The ambiguous, half-in and half-out position of the trainer increases the likelihood that for most members the trainer is the most salient deviant, in the sense used by Stock, Whitman and Lieberman (1958). Not all members will agree that his deviance consists in being too personal, too reserved, too involved, or too independent, but many feel his deviance is a threat to the group. The confrontation is an attempt, in part, to control the trainer's deviant behaviour by appropriate punitive action.

Stage three: Re-evaluation

Following the confrontation, or, more properly, following each successive confrontation, the group has at its disposal a vast amount of new and relevant data to sift out and interpret. Various feelings have been expressed for the first time, to which the trainer has made some response, even if the response was silence. The hostility, and the particular forms it took, have aroused a number of internal responses in each member, and these must be sorted out for their meaning. The re-evaluation stage is one in which the previous images of the trainer are tested for their continuing usefulness, and one important means of re-evaluating an image occurs when the members compare the ego state appropriate to the image with how they feel at the moment. Several important processes which are likely to occur at this point may be outlined:

1. The members test out the appropriateness of their initial anxiety level and the accuracy of certain images of the trainer which expressed their anxiety. The fear of retaliation or punishment which arises after the confrontation stage is tested against the reality of the trainer's response. The confrontation stands as an admittedly severe provocation to the trainer, and much depends on his reaction to it, or at least on how the members interpret his reaction. The members are gathering crucial data on the trainer's self-control and his underlying malignance, both of which are highly relevant to their anxiety level.

2. At the same time, a rather new issue arises in the group, stemming from the confrontation, namely the issue of depression. The dual questions of the impact of the hostility on the trainer and the implication of the attack for the members' capacity to control their own aggression are raised. The increase in guilt and shame over being openly hostile interacts with the perceived effect of the hostility on the trainer. If the effect has been too great, the trainer too hurt, the guilt becomes a serious factor in the group. On the other hand, if the effect seems to have been negligible, and the trainer seems completely unmoved by the hostility, the members tend to experience his lack of response as rejection by an indifferent figure, and mistrust and anxiety will probably increase. Within some unspecifiable limits, however, the members may take the trainer's response to indicate both his durability and his continuing involvement, all of which bears on the members' fears of being uncontrollably dangerous and destructive. The second process that stems from the rise in guilt is the attempt to make reparation. In part the reparation is an attempt to deny the full implication of the anger expressed, but in part it reveals the other side of the ambivalent feelings aroused by the trainer. Reparation serves to maintain a desired relationship and to reassure the member that his capacity for hostility is counterbalanced and partially controlled by his capacity for affection.

3. The confrontation exposes, for all to see, how intensely involved with the trainer the members actually were, how vulnerable and dependent they had been. One aspect of the re-evaluation, then, tends to be a series of attempts to clarify the members' own standards and private sources of self-esteem. Although this process serves members' own needs of the moment, it has an interesting relevance to the trainer beyond the need to develop some independence from him. In the usual training group, it turns out that the most effective gift to the trainer, the one most likely to be received in silence, but gratefully, is the gift of a member's independent, self-accepting clarification of his own needs and values. Thus, while much of the re-evaluation is done without explicit reference to the trainer, it may often

have relevance to the process of reparation simply by virtue of being carried out in the presence of the trainer.

Stage four: Internalization

In this stage the relations with the trainer shift for some members, if not all, to relations with the trainer as an internal object. Much depends upon the particular history of the group up to this point, and the two major characteristics of this stage, identification and 'work', will take quite different forms as a function of earlier resolutions of the member–trainer relationship. In some groups this phase may be by far the longest; in others it may be ephemeral and recurrent for only brief periods.

1. The process of identification is an intricate matter in most training groups. Though it is convenient to refer to identification as a coherent and single process, in reality quite different mechanisms underlie the various kinds of identification observed in groups. Slater's (1961b) distinction between personal and positional identification is useful here. Personal identification, in the self-analytic group, would refer to a member's internalization of the trainer's perceptions, values, or style because the member feels affection or respect for the trainer as a person. It is this process that characterizes the internalization stage, rather than positional identification in which the member's envy and fear of the trainer's power impel him to destroy and supplant him. One might expect that positional identification would be reflected by a combination of identification with anxiety and/or hostility, whereas personal identification would be reflected by a combination of identification and affection.

Drawing upon the nature of earlier stages, it appears that internalization is mediated by a set of facilitating pre-conditions, probably not all of which are essential: (a) that the negative feelings toward the trainer and desires for autonomy be expressed by the members and absorbed by the trainer (Arsenian, Semrad and Shapiro, 1962); (b) that the feelings of anxiety and mistrust be reduced by realistic re-evaluation of the trainer's behaviour; (c) that the sense of guilt over expressing hostility be assuaged by realistic appraisal that the trainer remains intact and involved; and (d) that reparation in the form of positive feelings expressed and independent clarification of members' needs and values be accomplished.

From this set of notions it follows that a number of factors may conspire to block or disrupt the identification process. Particularly if the image of the trainer remains too malignant and threatening, or if the consequences of hostile feelings are thought to be too devastating, personal identification will tend to be difficult, shallow, or fragile.

Increases in anxiety reflect growing doubts about the trustworthiness and benevolence of the trainer, which lead to a growing unwillingness to permit the trainer to serve as an internalized adjunct to the member's more enduring personality structure. On the other hand, increases in depression reflect the member's sense of helplessness to maintain a positive relationship with the trainer, either because the member feels unable to control his hostility or because he disparages his capacity to work independently or well, as a form of continuing reparation to the trainer. As either anxiety or depression mounts beyond a certain point, internalization decreases, and the trainer tends to be seen again as an external object with whom the members must contend.

2. The capacity to work, to perform the expressive and analytic tasks of a training group, is put to a continuous and demanding test in this stage. The trainer's relevance is primarily as one source of internal standards of judgment, but not the only one, and as one model for performance, but not the only one. Many of the members' concerns expressed in the work phase revolve around other group members or the group's formal task, if any. Members may find that they have internalized different aspects of the trainer, and these aspects may or may not be mutually compatible. Some may identify with the value of openness he professes, others with the role of observer he seems to fill. And there is, throughout this stage, the continual need and tendency to determine what parts of the trainer's views or skills are relevant to either the members or the work at hand.

Even more central to this work phase is the challenge of developing satisfactory answers to a set of questions that plague the group: (a) What is work in this group, and what are laziness and avoidance of the task? (b) What constitutes success or productive effort? (c) How much of the group's time must be spent in productive effort, or even in attempting to work? The extent to which the trainer is directly relevant to this process derives from his having already provided, however, subtly, his views on work and failure by his interventions all during the group's development. In this stage it is not uncommon for a trainer's views to be expressed by a member as his own, not that their eventual acceptance by the group is a necessary consequence of this internalization. However, one of the most frequent outbursts in the group at this stage is the expression of irritation at the trainer for having deviously planted his views in the group, leaving no possible room for the members to make independent innovations.

Stage five: Separation

As the group comes to a close, several changes in the member–trainer relationship become evident. Some of the most important processes associated with the issue of separation may be suggested briefly:

1. To the extent that important bonds of affection and involvement with the trainer have developed, the end of the group arouses a genuine anticipation of loss and sadness. In addition to expressions of depression and anticipatory mourning, various attempts may be made to deny the full impact of the separation. The euphoric tone, the insistence that the group cannot really end because each person will carry the group away inside him, the promises to have a reunion, all these developments serve to emphasize the meaningfulness of the internalization process which has already taken place. But they serve also to conceal the unfinished business, the residue of negative or unpleasant feelings which could not be resolved.

2. Some of the stifled feelings of frustration, insecurity, or anger may emerge shortly before the end of the group. Part of this phenomenon can be attributed to a final broadside from the members whose negative feelings had gone unexpressed or unheeded throughout the group's history. But another part of the phenomenon derives from a more general attempt to undo the internalization process prior to separation, to reconstitute the trainer as an altogether external object. In this light, much, but not all, of the resurgent anxiety and hostility serves as a distancing device preparatory to separation.

3. The themes of failure become important in the final stage of the group, as reflected in the chagrin that all the hopes aroused in the group have a dwindling chance of being realized. It is not uncommon for one of these hopes, the phantasied relationship of intimacy with the trainer, to be acted on with some vigor. The pressure for the trainer to affirm the extraordinary quality of the group and to give it his benediction is but one of the many ways in which the trainer is asked to make a final break with his role in the group. It is as if the members were saying that only the most heartless and inhuman of creatures could deny the group its final request for total absolution and love. Pleas that the trainer should now, at last, reveal all his secrets are of the same general order.

Discussion of the case studies

To return to groups S1 and S2, some of the major similarities and differences in the nature of the member–trainer relationships can be highlighted and interpreted with reference to the developmental model. On the one hand, there were some general similarities between the groups, particularly in the initial stage of appraisal and the final stage of separation. On the other hand, the substantial differences between the groups in the nature and extent of the internalization process may be traced to equally divergent processes in the re-evaluation stage which followed the confrontation.

One facet of the re-evaluation stage is that members review and possibly modify the operative images which express their feelings toward the trainer. In group S1 the earlier images suggesting a controlling, insensitive, and dangerous object were joined, if not replaced, by more benign images, such as the reference to the Mona Lisa. The re-evaluation stage in group S1 was further characterized by active attempts to undo and control the aggression of the previous period. Reparative processes, which had actually increased before the hostility had fully subsided, were sustained over a number of sessions, and signs of distress in the ego-state area were relatively infrequent.

The period after the confrontation in group S2 was filled with signs of distress. The attack on the trainer seems to heighten the sense of danger, while arousing new concerns about members' incapacity to control their hostility. In a very real sense, most of the sessions following the confrontation were spent working on the dilemmas crystallized in the re-evaluation stage, and no sustained period of internalization followed the re-evaluation stage. Particularly striking was the delay in reparative processes until the terminal phase, when rather successful attempts were made to undo the attack on the trainer for perceived failures in the control area. However, review of the later phases of the groups will be deferred until after an examination of the possible antecedents of the differences between the two stages of re-evaluation.

The confrontation stages in the two groups were quite similar in many respects, but two differences stand out as possibly relevant to the divergent consequences of the hostility. First, the hostility expressed toward the trainer in S2 was more directly connected to the issue of intimacy than in S1, although both control and intimacy issues were salient in each group. The first wave of negative feelings in S2 followed the party and the trainer's failure to attend it. The disappointment and anger were expressed initially through members' attempts to make the trainer feel guilty for abandoning the group, then through attempts to transfer the responsibility for sexual and aggressive motives from group members to the trainer. Thus, one difference between the two groups arises from the fact that in S2 the expressions of hostility, stemming in part from frustrations in the affection area, intensified, rather than relieved, the members' feelings of mistrust, their sense of being rejected, and their feelings of helplessness.

A second difference between the confrontation stages of the two groups lies in the control area. While both groups contained a number of members whose initial response was to adopt either dependent or counter-dependent orientations to the trainer, group S2 contained a sizeable minority who worked hard to bypass the issue of appraising the trainer. These older members, most of whom were teachers themselves, demonstrated their conception of the group and their appropriate role in it by propelling the group into a highly task-oriented mood in the first few sessions. The relevance of this difference between the groups may rest in the fact that the confrontation in S2 represented, for the older members particularly, the collapse of a rather premature attempt at positional identification and work. The anger, the salience of the affection issue, even the focus on the trainer, all ran counter to the hopes of those who attempted to avoid any direct personal involvement with the trainer. In some ways, then, the source of S2's development was affected by the fact that the most independent members were active before, rather than after, the confrontation. They remained relatively inactive until the final phases, during which they were instrumental in suggesting some ways out of the dependent position that was characteristic of this group throughout its development.

Turning now to the consequences of the re-evaluation stage for the two groups, it appears that for S1 the immediate consequence of a decrease in anxiety and an increase in reparative processes was a period of internalization. The period was short-lived, however. Increases in anxiety and direct hostility signalled a disruption of the work phase, although the rate of identifying remained higher than before the first evaluation period. For group S2 it is difficult to isolate any period of sustained internalization, although phase six was characterized by the kind of image modification which often precedes identification. Much of the group's discussion following the confrontation period consisted of attempts to manage the unresolved issues of anxiety and depression which surrounded both the control and affection areas. In both groups, then, it is clear that feelings of being threatened and feelings of mistrust, on the one hand, and the sense of failure and ineffectiveness, on the other, operated to block or disrupt the process of internalization. Recurrent waves of hostility, continuing until the end of both groups, suggest a much-needed antidote to any simple notions of orderly progression through stages of development. Residual frustrations and changes in the nature of the trainer as a stimulus object combined to provoke further confrontations and further re-evaluations.

From the evidence gathered on these two groups at least, the process of separation appears to be a combination of two rather dissimilar dynamics. In one sense, there was a recapitulation of the groups' prior history, prompted by an intensification of unresolved issues. In another sense, the separation process involved attempts to deny any and all failures, as if the members and trainer as well were struggling to make the experience 'suitable for framing'.

For group S1, the unresolved issues that returned with some force were those of mistrust, now crystallized around grades and examinations, and the related issue of accomplishment. Much of the depression that dominated the final sessions was an expression of the members' feeling that it was useless to attempt any more work, or that the total experience had not been very productive. There were voices raised, some euphoric and others more dispassionate, to suggest that the sense of failure ignored the revised definition of work and success arrived at in the group. For group S2, the unresolved issues were the question of dependency, now intensified by the impending grades, and the chronic problems of apprehension and guilt. The authority and control area was reviewed, and rather direct and effective reparative processes were begun. The affection area was barely touched, although the continuing ramifications of frustration in that area were evident in the particular form taken by the terminal depression.

The major techniques by which group members in S1 attempted to seal off and terminate the group experience, including their involvements with the trainer, were withdrawal, mourning, and manic denial. These efforts at reaching closure were mixed with continuing evidence of identification, but the separation process was increasingly predominant over the internalization process. Although much of the discussion toward the end of S2 was directed toward re-evaluating the control issue, the final session was devoted to separation in a particularly interesting manner. Each member announced, in turn, and without comment from other members, what benefits he had derived from the group, his gratitude, and his final appraisal of the group. This mechanism expressed neatly the members' need to separate themselves from the trainer and other group members, permitting a smooth transition from the status of group member to the status of solitary alumnus.

Conclusion

This study isolates the member–trainer relationship in self-analytic groups from what is obviously a far more complex set of relationships and processes. The assumption that group members may be expressing their feelings toward the trainer when they discuss events or individuals inside and outside the group is fundamental to this assessment of the member–trainer relationship. However, one could assume with equal profit that the reverse is true, that feelings toward the trainer reflect the state of the member-to-member relationships or a member's relationship with someone outside the group. This study neglects, rather than disparages, the importance of other aspects of group development.

The effort to assess the member–trainer relationship, on the basis of not only direct references but indirect and symbolic acts, seems to have yielded meaningful results. Though much is overlooked in the member-to-trainer scoring system, especially the non-verbal behaviour, this method provides a fairly reliable and appropriate description of the members' feelings. The haunting problem of incomparable descriptions of two groups, or of two sessions within a group, may be partially solved by using this or some similar scoring system.

The developmental model constructed to analyse the member–trainer relationship outlines five stages: appraisal, confrontation, re-evaluation, internalization, and separation. It is clear from the two cases examined that the model is not a statement of the inevitable course of the member–trainer relationship. What it did provide for future research, is a framework against which the particular developments in a group may be examined. It suggests a series of interpersonal processes whose outcome will influence the members' future relationships with the trainer.

Where this study diverges from some previous discussion of group development is in casting what most authors conceive of as one goal of such groups, the process of group-centered work, in terms of the member–trainer relationship. Not only is the work phase closely related to the process of identification with the trainer, but it is both produced by and threatened by changes in the member–trainer relationship.

The periods of work which are characterized by independent efforts to perform the expressive and analytic tasks of the group may reflect the quite different processes of positional and personal identification. Where positional identification implies an effort to elbow the trainer out of his threatening or frustrating position, personal identification implies the trust and affection that underlie the internalization stage.

The influence of the member–trainer relationship on the members' capacity to work is further suggested by attending to which processes facilitate and which processes disrupt or block the members' efforts to internalize the trainer. Reality-testing, reparation, and various mechanisms of defense operate to control the disruptive consequences of hostility, anxiety, and depression. However, the two case studies suggest how difficult it is to attain or sustain this control in the face of intense feelings on the part of the members and continuing or increased pressure from the trainer.

The developmental model implies that the members of a self-analytic group are likely to experience the same feelings toward the trainer at the same time. This is only partially true. Nearly unanimous expressions of one feeling or another do occur, and Bion's (1961) notion of unconscious collusion fits some of the data. More often, however, any summary statistic for all members reflects one or more polarities within the group. Sometimes both polar positions can be subsumed within a stage of the developmental model, as when the expression and denial of anxiety are simultaneously high in the appraisal stage. At other times, however, the stage is named after the dominant mood or feeling, such as when a set of sessions is called the internalization stage despite evidence that resistance was high for a number of members. In calling attention to the feelings that are common to most of the members, the model fails to make explicit the obvious fact that some members may be expressing quite divergent feelings.

It remains to be seen what modifications of these methods and concepts will follow from the study of additional groups. Variations in what the members bring to the group by way of expectations, personal conflicts, or characteristic behavioural styles can be assumed to affect the outcome of the group, as can variations in the trainer's conception of the group and his personal style. What this study may offer is a way to investigate such problems and the beginning of a conceptual framework for their analysis.

References

Arsenian, J., E. V. Semrad and D. Shapiro (1962) 'An analysis of integral functions in small groups.' *Int. J. Group Psychother.*, **12**, 421–434.

Bach, G. R. (1954) *Intensive Group Psychotherapy.* New York: Ronald.

Bales, R. D. (1950) *Interaction Process Analysis.* Cambridge, Mass.: Addison-Wesley.

Bennis, W. (1957) 'A genetic theory of group development.' Unpublished manuscript, Massachusetts Institute of Technology.

Bennis, W. G. (1961) 'Defences against "depressive anxiety" in groups: the case of the absent leader.' *Merrill-Palmer Quart. Behav. Develpm.*, **7**, 3–30.

Bennis, W. G. and H. A. Shepard (1956) 'A theory of group development.' *Hum. Relat.*, **9**, 415–437.

Bibring, E. (1953) 'The mechanisms of depression.' In P. Greenacre (Ed.), *Affective Disorders.* New York: International Universities Press. Pp. 13–48.

Bion, W. R. (1961) *Experiences in Groups.* New York: Basic Books.

Borgetta, E. F., L. S. Cottrell and J. H. Mann (1958) 'The spectrum of individual interaction characteristics: an inter-dimensional analysis.' *Psychol. Rep.*, **4**, 279–319.

Carter, L. F. (1954) 'Recording and evaluating the performance of individuals as members of small groups.' *Personnel Psychol.*, **7**, 477–484.

Coffey, H. S., M. Freedman, T. Leary and A. Orsorio (1950) 'Community service and social research.' *J. soc. Issues*, **6**, No. 1, 25–64.

Couch, A. S. (1960) 'Psychological determinants of interpersonal behaviour.' Unpublished doctoral dissertation, Harvard University.

Ezriel, H. (1952) 'Notes on psychoanalytical group therapy: II. Interpretation and research.' *Psychiatry*, **15**, 119–126.

Foulkes, S. H. and E. J. Anthony (1957) *Group Psychotherapy.* Harmondsworth, Middx.: Penguin Books.

Frank, J. D., J. Margolis, H. T. Nash, A. R. Stone, E. E. Varon and E. Ascher (1952) 'The behaviour patterns in therapeutic groups and their apparent motivation.' *Hum. Relat.*, **5**, 289–317.

Kaplan, S. and M. Roman (1963) 'Phases of development in an adult therapy group.' *Int. J. Group Psychother.*, **13**, 10–26.

Klein, M. (1957) *Envy and Gratitude*. New York: Basic Books.

Mann, J. (1953) 'Group therapy with adults.' *Amer. J. Orthopsychiat.*, **23**, 332–337.

Mann, R. D. (1961) 'Dimensions of individual performance in small groups under task and social-emotional conditions.' *J. Abnorm. soc. Psychol.*, **62**, 674–682.

Mills, T. M. (1964) *Group Transformation: an Analysis of a Learning Group*. Englewood Cliffs, N.J.: Prentice-Hall.

Psathas, G. (1960) 'Phase movement and equilibrium tendencies in interaction process analysis in psychotherapy groups.' *Sociometry*, **23**, 177–194.

Schutz, W. C. (1958) *FIRO: A Three-dimensional Theory of Interpersonal Behaviour*. New York: Holt, Rinehart and Winston.

Shepard, H. A. and W. G. Bennis (1956) 'A theory of training by group methods.' *Hum. Relat.*, **9**, 403–414.

Slater, P. E. (1961a) 'Displacement in groups.' In W. G. Bennis, K. D. Benne and R. Chin (Eds.), *The Planning of Change*. New York: Holt, Rinehart & Winston.

Slater, P. E. (1961b) 'Toward a dualistic theory of identification.' *Merrill-Palmer Quart. Behav. Developm.*, **7**, 113–126.

Stock, D., R. M. Whitman and M. A. Lieberman (1958) 'The deviant member in therapy groups.' *Hum. Relat.*, **11**, 341–372.

Stock, D. and H. A. Thelen (1958) *Emotional Dynamics and Group Culture*. New York: New York University.

Talland, G. A. (1955) 'Task and interaction process: some characteristics of the therapeutic group discussion.' *J. abnorm. soc. Psychol.*, **50**, 105–109.

Thelen, H. (1950) 'Emotional dynamics: theory and research.' *J. soc. Issues*, **6**, No. 2.

Thelen, H. and W. Dickerman (1949) 'Stereotypes and the growth of groups.' *Educ. Leadership*, **6**, 309–316.

Wechsler, I. R. and J. Reisel (1959) *Inside a Sensitivity Training Group*. Los Angeles: University of California.

Recent Publications

Cooper, C. L. (1970) 'T-group training and self-actualisation.' Unpublished manuscript, University of Southampton.

Crawshaw, R. (1969) 'How sensitive is Sensitivity Training.' *American Journal of Psychiatry*, **126** (6), 870–873.

Fiebert, M. S. (1968) 'Sensitivity training: an analysis of trainer intervention and group process.' *Psychological Reports*, **22**, 829–838.

Gertz, B. (1969) 'Peer Group Evaluation in Sensitivity Training Program in Graduate Education.' Paper presented to the American Psychological Association Annual Convention, September 1969.

Gottschalk, L. A. and E. M. Pattison (1969) 'Psychiatric perspectives on T-groups and the laboratory movement: an overview.' *American Journal of Psychiatry*, **126** (6), 823–839.

Keutzer, C., F. R. Fosmire, R. Diller and M. D. Smith (1969) 'Laboratory training in the new social system: evaluation of a two-week program for high school personnel.' Unpublished manuscript, University of Oregon.

Kohn, V. (1969) 'A selected bibliography of evaluation of management training and development programs.' Unpublished manuscript, American Foundation for Management Research.

Koile, E. A. and C. Draeger (1969) 'T-group member ratings of leader and self in a human relations laboratory.' *Journal of Psychology*, **72**, 11–20.

Kuehn, J. L. and F. M. Crinella (1969) 'Sensitivity training: interpersonal "overkill" and other problems.' *American Journal of Psychiatry*, **126** (6), 840–845.

Mangham, I. L. (1970) 'Interpersonal Styles and Group Development.' Ph.D. Thesis, University of Leeds.

Myers, G. E., M. T. Myers, A. Goldberg and C. E. Welch (1969) 'Effects of feedback on interpersonal sensitivity in laboratory training groups.' *Journal of Applied Behavioral Science*, **5** (2), 175–185.

Pollack, D. (1969) 'A sensitivity training approach to group therapy with children.' Unpublished manuscript, San Diego State College.

Powers, J. R. and S. L. Fink (1969) 'The effects of trainer orientation and group composition on the perception of the trainer.' Unpublished manuscript, Case Institute of Technology.

Rawls, J. R., D. J. Rawls and R. L. Frye (1969) 'Membership satisfaction as it is related to certain dimensions of interaction in a T-group.' *Journal of Social Psychology*, **78**, 243–248.

Index

Page numbers followed by the letter 'n' refer to footnotes. Numbers in parenthesis are reference numbers to the author's work quoted in full at the end of the chapter.